More Praise for *The Minds of Boys*

"*The Minds of Boys* is a wonderfully practical and enjoyable book to read and a great companion to *The Wonder of Boys*. The strategies presented help to empower parents to demand social justice for their boys in school. I highly recommend!"

> —Stephen J. Bavolek, Ph.D., author, *Nurturing Parenting Programs*

"*The Minds of Boys* provides a valuable service not only to parents and teachers but also to policymakers. Boys today are languishing academically. Gurian and Stevens provide important analysis and practical solutions."

> —Christina Hoff Sommers, Ph.D., author, *The War Against Boys*

"Reading this book may be the greatest act of love you can do for your son."

> —Scott Haltzman, M.D., author, *The Secrets of Happily Married Men*
> and founder of www.secretsofmarriedmen.com

"*The Minds of Boys* is a gift to parents, teachers, and anyone else involved in raising or nurturing boys. It is filled with cutting-edge neuroscience, yet has the warmth of a wise professional."

> —Daniel Amen, M.D., author, *Making a Good Brain Great*

"Gender plays a significant role in how children think, develop, behave, and consequently learn. *The Minds of Boys* is a timely, practical approach to helping boys succeed in educational environments, extracurricular activities, and daily life. A must-read for parents trying to provide the best for their sons!"

> —Amy James, author, the Knowledge Essentials series,
> including *First Grade Success* and *Second Grade Success*

"This book provides invaluable information for parents and educators to help them improve boys' academic and social success."

> —Michael Merrifield, Colorado House of Representatives,
> Chairman, House Education Committee

"As the mother of three sons, I'm grateful to Michael Gurian and Kathy Stevens for their breakthrough contribution to helping us understand how a boy's mind really works. We've always known that boys and girls learn differently, but Michael and Kathy have really shown us for the first time how we specifically can help our sons fulfill their potential. I highly recommend *The Minds of Boys* to all parents, teachers, and anyone who really cares about the future of our society. It is a must-read that is destined to become a classic."

—Michele Borba, Ed.D., author, *Building Moral Intelligence: The Seven Essential Virtues That Teach Kids to Do the Right Thing*

"Michael Gurian had the courage to talk about boys before it was popular. This book takes his work further and articulates the issues from a brain-based approach with supporting research. He and Kathy Stevens then give very practical examples for interventions. I highly recommend this book to anyone who works with boys professionally or personally. I found the book to be extraordinarily helpful."

—Ruby Payne, author, *A Framework for Understanding Poverty*

"In *The Minds of Boys*, Michael Gurian and Kathy Stevens provide a very readable description of the current academic dilemma affecting a large number of boys."

—Sandra F. Witelson, Ph.D., Albert Einstein/ Irving Zucker Chair in Neuroscience, McMaster University

"The crisis facing boys today is as damaging and dangerous as that which faced young women twenty years ago. With practical strategies, research-based suggestions, and a family-oriented support team, *The Minds of Boys* offers real help to restore boys' confidence, culture, and capability."

—Dr. Linda Karges-Bone, author, *More Than Pink or Blue: How Gender Shapes Your Curriculum*

The Minds of Boys

The Minds of Boys

SAVING OUR SONS FROM FALLING BEHIND
IN SCHOOL AND LIFE

Michael Gurian

and

Kathy Stevens

JB JOSSEY-BASS
A Wiley Imprint
www.josseybass.com

Published by Jossey-Bass
A Wiley Imprint
989 Market Street, San Francisco, CA 94103-1741   www.josseybass.com

Jossey-Bass books and products are available through most bookstores. To contact Jossey-Bass directly, call our Customer Care Department within the U.S. at 800-956-7739, outside the U.S. at 317-572-3986, or fax 317-572-4002.

Jossey-Bass also publishes its books in a variety of electronic formats. Some content that appears in print may not be available in electronic books.

Library of Congress Cataloging-in-Publication Data

Gurian, Michael.
 The minds of boys : saving our sons from falling behind in school and life / Michael Gurian and Kathy Stevens.— 1st ed.
   p. cm.
 Includes bibliographical references and index.
 ISBN-13 978-0-7879-7761-0 (alk. paper)
 ISBN-10 0-7879-7761-6 (alk. paper)
 1. Boys—Education. 2. Boys—Psychology. 3. Sex differences in education. 4. Academic achievement. I. Stevens, Kathy, date. II. Title.
   LC1390.G87 2005
   371.823—dc22   2005000229

Printed in the United States of America
FIRST EDITION

HB Printing   10 9 8 7 6 5 4 3

CONTENTS

To the special women in my life:
Gail, Gabrielle, and Davita

To the special men in my life:
Don, Kevin, Mike, Matthew, and Rodney,
And to Aspen, a most glorious child.

To all the children and students
we have met over the years.
They are the greatest inspiration.

ACKNOWLEDGMENTS

Every book is an ensemble effort. We gratefully acknowledge the ensemble that made this book possible. Alan Rinzler, our editor, has shepherded this project from its inception to its final form. He is one of the finest editors in the business, and we thank him for his care, acumen, skill, and passion. At Jossey-Bass and John Wiley, Alan is surrounded by some of the finest publishing staff around. Our thanks to Jennifer Wenzel, Lesley Iura, Michele Jones, Sarah Miller, Nancy Rothschild, Carol Hartland, and all others who were involved in this project. Many thanks also to publishers Paul Foster and Debra Hunter, who believed from the beginning.

Our profound thanks also to Candice Fuhrman, our advocate and agent.

Many thanks also to Daniel Amen, M.D.; Howard Schubiner, M.D.; Scott Haltzman, M.D.; Catherine Craddock; Lori Seyde-Mehrtens; James Zull, M.D.; and Lauren E. Valdes, who read the manuscript for accuracy.

In our writing process, Don Stevens was of great assistance with research and support. Our thanks to him and also to Phil Gurian, whose Web and research talents provided us with magic from the Internet that every book ought to have.

It is with great appreciation that we also thank the teachers, administrators, and parents who have shared their stories with the Gurian Institute so that we could share them with you. Our training institute (www.gurianinstitute.com) has had the honor of working both in the

United States and abroad because individuals, professionals, and communities have helped us do so. Special thanks to Helene Paroff.

Our special thanks to the Gurian Institute certified trainers, whose individual efforts can be viewed on the Institute Web site. These trainers are working with us to educate schools and parents, and we could not do what we do if it were not for their support. Special thanks to Marilyn Altman.

Our profound thanks also to the universities that support professional development in brain sciences, so that teachers can enter classrooms armed with learning strategies that give all children—boys and girls—the best chance for success. Among these universities is the University of Colorado-Colorado Springs, home of our Summer Institute.

Finally, as always, our thanks to our families, who listen to the music created by our ensemble, and tirelessly support it with their ears, their comments, and their love.

May this book read as it is meant to read: as an act of profound affection for all the families and communities who support the healthy growth of children.

INTRODUCTION

> You can pull me all you want, and I'll stretch, but I won't break.
>
> —FANTASTIC FOUR COMICS, CIRCA 1968

WHEN I WAS A BOY, I LIKED SUPERMAN, BATMAN, AND SPIDERMAN. MY SCHOOL friends and I traded our comic books on the playground, in our backyards, our homes. In fourth grade, I discovered the Fantastic Four. The special power of one of the Four mesmerized me: he could stretch his arms and legs elastically. Even when his enemies tried to kill him, he would not be torn apart, he could not be broken.

A lot was going on in our culture in 1968, the year I discovered the Fantastic Four. Martin Luther King and Bobby Kennedy were shot and killed. Every night my family watched TV, seeing soldiers with their faces mired in dirt and blood, the helicopters roiling great blasts of wind against the jungle grass. In 1968, I lived in Aina Haina, a neighborhood built at the leeward base of Oahu's mountains. My father, a junior professor at the University of Hawaii, came home very sad more than once because one of his former students had just been killed across the ocean. When I saw wheelchair-bound soldiers near Hickam Air Force Base rolling down the sidewalk, I felt my heart wince in fear and confusion.

I know now that I wanted to be a superhero, unbreakable and bold; I carried this longing, partly because I am human, but also because of those soldiers and the war that raged. I also know there were other reasons. At ten years old, I had problems at home and in school.

At home, my family struggled near poverty. My parents fought. Their discipline of their children was physical and brutal. Their marriage struggled, and I began running away from home at nine years old. In school I was called "incorrigible," summoned many times to the principal's office, a discipline problem. By fifth grade I had seen a psychiatrist and been put on Ritalin. Within a few months, my teacher, Mrs. Kono, suggested I be taken off the Ritalin. The drug had made me into something of a "zombie," in her words. She told my parents she missed my "spark." I was taken off Ritalin, but my troubles in school continued.

I didn't focus well on what teachers wanted me to do.

I had trouble sitting still for as long as was needed.

I wanted to learn one thing well rather than constantly move between tasks.

I didn't want to read textbook after textbook.

I got bored easily.

I wanted to *do* my learning, not hear about it.

I was never sure I understood the directions I was given, nor did I succeed at accomplishing all of what my teachers demanded.

I often didn't see why I had to be in school anyway.

By the time I was in seventh grade—we lived in Laramie, Wyoming, now, my father teaching at the University of Wyoming—I started skipping classes. By tenth grade, in Durango, Colorado, I worked twenty hours a week at a restaurant, paying rent back to my family in order to help financially. By the time I matriculated from twelfth grade (now back in Honolulu, at Kaiser High School), I got better grades and succeeded on the debate team.

But still my troubles in school continued. My behavior had improved, but I left high school a poor writer. My freshman year in college, my history professor gave me an F on my first paper. He wrote, "You have good ideas, but you can't write. Did you sleep all the way through high school?"

The year was 1976. I remember discussing my ongoing educational failures with a counselor at the University of Hawaii. I told her how I'd been sent to a psychiatrist at ten years old and given Ritalin. I told her that our family was suffering internal distress. A middle-aged woman with three sons of her own, she asked for more information about my schools. After she heard more about my difficult and painful years in school, she said, "Isn't it possible that something was wrong with the schools, too, that caused problems for you? I've had some problems in school with two of my own boys."

This was a revelation to me, a first hint that the problem wasn't entirely my fault—that something might be wrong with the way our learning institutions educate our sons. I asked the counselor what she meant, what might be wrong with my schools, but she said no more about it, and in the end I had to look back at myself. I saw a boy who tried to be elastic, tried to stretch himself constantly toward educational goals and methods that often did not help him. I remembered how it hurt, and how I acted out against that system.

In graduate school, three years later, I made friends with a house full of roommates, all guys, all of whom had been, in their individual ways, "a disappointment in school," "a kid who didn't work to his potential," "unmotivated." This was eye opening. There were so many of us. One graduate school friend shared with me a comment his father had made: "You're not supposed to like school or care a lot about it. You gotta just survive it and get to college. If a kid can do that, he'll be okay."

That comment stopped me short. I had heard it before, from inside myself somewhere, during boyhood. Now an adult, I didn't like it. Something was wrong here. The "something" wasn't just something wrong with me or with my "dysfunctional family." The "something" was, perhaps, intrinsic to the way I was educated in school and in life.

Pursuing that "something" became a large part of my professional work.

Now, a quarter century later, I recall my school years with a lot more information, greater perspective, and I hope a little wisdom. I've devoted the last twenty years to studying the arc of boyhood, from birth through adulthood, both in and out of school. As a therapist, educator, philosopher, and author, I've focused on helping our culture revise its parenting and schooling practices to bring out the best in our sons. Books I've written, such as *The Wonder of Boys, A Fine Young Man,* and *The Good Son,* asked parents, educators, and policymakers to take a very close look at just how much our boys today are struggling, emotionally, spiritually, and morally, at home and in society. *Boys and Girls Learn Differently!* began to discuss what new research in brain science, biochemistry, and child development was showing us about gender and education. *What Could He Be Thinking?* asked our culture to notice who men are, what they are striving for, and especially how they and their wives and partners can succeed in relationship and marriage. In *The Minds of Boys* I will plead, with my coauthor's help, that all parents, teachers, policymakers, and other concerned citizens look very closely at what is happening to boys in our educational institutions.

A system is in place today with which boys (and girls) are educated—but is it the system we all want? I have written this book with Kathy Stevens, a parent, an educator, and the training director of the Gurian Institute, in the hope that you can answer this question for yourself and, more important, so you can learn how to help your son and your students do their best in school. Kathy and I believe that we are losing too many boys today in our schools. More and more boys are doing poorly, dropping out, and beginning their lives handicapped without the education and skills they need to succeed in a world that is increasingly demanding and competitive. We believe this trend need not continue. Now is the time to change things for the better.

The Minds of Boys is our practical guide to helping boys learn, do better in school, and succeed in life. This book provides you with a kind of "operating system" that you can immediately "load into" your own life and your son's schooling.

Kathy Stevens

Kathy Stevens, like myself, is an advocate for both boys and girls. For thirty years, she worked in female development programming, most recently as executive director of the Women's Resource Agency in Colorado Springs. She ran the award-winning Intercept Mentoring program for teen girls.

After reading a book I wrote called *The Wonder of Girls,* Kathy contacted me, and we discovered a mutual interest in cross-cultural approaches to the lives of children. My work over the last two decades has combined neurobiology, anthropology, and psychology to understand how boys and girls develop along parallel but also different paths. Kathy had noticed in her work with girls that the struggles of girls and of boys were intersecting.

"To better care for our girls," she told me, "we have to get real about what's happening to our boys, too." Kathy is one of those wise thinkers who see the whole picture. Coincidentally, Kathy and I met at the very time when the institute I had founded to study this field was looking for a new training director. Kathy not only took over its direction but also has now helped develop Gurian Institute programs throughout the United States and in Canada and Australia. Much of the practical material in this book has been created and developed by Kathy Stevens.

My coauthor is not only a professional but also a mother of two sons. When she told me the story of her son Karl's education, I thought of how my own mother had struggled with me to get through school; I thought of all the parents and teachers who are struggling to help their sons do their best. Kathy's story is both chilling and inspiring. It represents so well both the power of human perseverance against institutional failure and the will we all have to protect the minds of boys.

Kathy's Story

Karl Michael was a risk taker from the day he was born. He pulled and prodded about in my arms. He was ready and eager to take on the world. With beautiful blue eyes and a smile that lights up a room, he grew into a bubbly toddler—outgoing and curious. He explored, burned up energy, slept soundly. And he enjoyed school early on. His teachers in kindergarten and first, second, and third grade helped him care for himself so he could stay on task and grow. He talked a lot and wiggled around a lot, but he learned well.

Then Karl went to fourth grade. This experience changed his attitude about school forever. His teacher didn't understand his energy, his way of learning, his boyishness, his difficulty sitting still. I saw these as "who he was," but she saw them as significant problems. She was very hard on Karl; she made him believe she didn't like him and that he was "bad."

Karl's attitude toward school began to change. Many days at a time, he didn't want to go. I talked with his teacher but couldn't get through. She said Karl had "behavior issues."

Watching this playful, energetic, and intelligent boy come to hate school tore at my heart. When I listen today to other moms and dads talk about losing their own sons to the same kind of crisis at their school, I remember my family's nightmare. Within the year, Karl was diagnosed with ADHD, even though his intelligence tests showed him above average for academic potential. Within another year, his sixth-grade teacher asked that he be placed in a special education class. At the advice of the school principal, we consulted a psychologist, who recommended Ritalin, which Karl started taking regularly. Karl was labeled a problem in school and was now being treated by a doctor. Karl hated school, and we, his parents, were deeply confused. We didn't know where to turn. The professionals around us seemed to be doing their best, but we saw Karl slipping away from happiness and success.

Sixth, seventh, and eighth grades were some of the most painful years of Karl's and our lives. Karl became increasingly negative about school. His special ed class was a mixture of children with very mild to extremely serious problems. Karl cried and begged to stay home. He was entering puberty, and in trying to navigate the complicated new social world of his peer group, he felt like an outsider. Teased by peers for being stupid and a retard, he felt that he was, in his own words, "a complete loser."

Outside of school, Karl played basketball, climbed, rode his skateboard, enjoyed family camping trips where we lived in a tent for a week during the summer, and fished and canoed on lakes and rivers. During the summers he mowed and raked lawns around our neighborhood, cleaned gutters, and earned money, which he spent going to movies and buying his coveted Michael Jordan athletic shoes.

But back at school, he turned into a depressed adolescent boy. During ninth grade, he started skipping school, completing little of his work, and finally he failed that grade. His big brother, six years older, was away at college by now, and an opportunity arose for us to relocate from Virginia to Colorado. Karl voted to move—right now. We packed the car and headed west.

The first day of our three-day drive, we talked about what we wanted life to look like in Colorado. Karl said he wanted to change everything, including his name. He didn't want to be his "old school self." In his new school, he wanted to be known by his middle name, Mike. He begged me not to let his new school put him in special education. I told him I would try. Because I had felt so impotent for so many years now, I had no confidence that I could satisfy his wish.

Things did get better in Colorado. We found some help there. From that day on he's been Mike. We chose a home in Colorado based on what school district could best serve Mike. We sat down with a wonderful counselor at Holmes Junior High School, and Mike told her his story. She asked a lot of questions and listened a lot. In the end, she counseled my son that he was going to have a tough time academically, as he had allowed himself to get behind, but she agreed to let him try regular classes.

The counselor was right: Mike did struggle. But he never took another pill, and he did not go into special education classes. Many of his teachers were patient and supportive, and he started playing football, which helped immensely. In football, he found a reason to go to school—he got motivation and mentoring. Very quickly he became more popular with his peers. Many of his teachers liked him, even the ones who were frustrated by his suspicion of school and academics. He became active in the church youth group, finding new friends there.

Karl Michael is now a young man of twenty-eight, a veteran of five years in the army. He is taking college courses so that he can be a teacher someday. He says, "I know what went wrong and what went right when I was in school, and I want to help other boys who are struggling like I did."

Mike again has a smile that can light up a room. He is again outgoing and curious. He is a risk taker. He constantly fights the demons of self-doubt that were planted so long ago, but every time he takes a step forward he is closer to achieving his dreams—and the dreams that I, his mother, have always had for him: to succeed in life as a man. In his case, to become a man who teaches children.

When Kathy told me her story, tears came to my eyes. The similarities to my own boyhood pulled at me. I was not as athletic as Mike, but still . . . so many of our issues resonated.

When I met Mike in 2002, I was impressed by a young man of intelligence and zeal. Though twenty years older than he, I could see how he too had survived what we have come to call "the institutional education of our boys." Our learning style often didn't fit the way we were taught. Our high energy was a minus, not a plus. Our need for movement, for less talk and more "doing," for innovative ways of keeping us focused, and for male-friendly emotional support and direction did not generally fit the schools we went to. We were not the boys many of our teachers wanted in their classrooms.

If meeting Kathy for the first time created in me a vision of a book she and I could write together for boys, meeting her son clarified that vision completely. Kathy and I came to agree that it was time to write a book that helped parents and teachers understand not only boys and families who were struggling in the current educational culture but all boys who want to move through their school years doing the best they can.

Our Method of Research

Every book that is needed by a culture grows first from some part of an individual heart that is stretched to its breaking point. Both Kathy and I had our hearts nearly broken by the institutional system of education that has been provided to boys in these last two generations. Our passion comes from our own life stories.

At the same time, a book that is needed can't be based on two stories alone; it must be based on the finest research available. So we committed ourselves to research in service of this project. That research often points to boys in trouble in school, but often does not. We don't believe every boy and every parent suffers, nor do we blame any teacher or particular school. Many boys are doing quite well in school. Most teachers care deeply for the hearts and minds of boys. We have not completed our research and written this book in order to complain.

Instead, we have a theory to share with you, as well as a great deal of practical information you can use immediately. Both our theory and the practical information are offered in alliance with teachers, parents, and school staff who feel that although the educational system today is very fine in many ways, it is also breaking at the ribs just enough to leave the heart of education unprotected. That "heart" is *success for all children.*

Our Theory

After studying, evaluating, synthesizing, and promulgating research in this field for twenty years, we believe that boys are being educated today in a system—comprising schools, homes, and communities—that is not well enough briefed on these four crucial elements of education:

- The male learning style
- The potential mismatch of that male learning style with many current educational practices
- The complete role parents and communities need to take, in any generation and in any culture, to ensure the education of sons
- New methods, strategies, and teaching techniques that have been proven to work in schools and classrooms that educate boys

Our Book

As we explore this theory with you, we'll begin in Chapter One by fleshing out the crisis that many boys experience in our educational culture today: the kinds of crisis situations that Kathy's son Mike and I faced.

You may well be shocked by how many of us are out there. If you are living through the crisis right now, you'll find immediate support as you hear other voices like yours. If you are not living through the crisis, you'll be moved, we hope, to notice a boy around your home, school, or community whose distress resembles the crisis we describe and fits the theory that institutionalized educational systems today are often a mismatch with the way boys naturally learn.

In Chapter Two we'll guide you on a journey inside boys' minds—their actual brain structure and how it works—so that you can see how boys in general learn, whether they are high or low performing. We'll bring you the results from scientific scans of male and female brains. You'll notice both similarities and key differences in the ways boys and girls learn math, science, reading, writing, and other subjects.

As we explore this with you, we'll look at how gender-different learning styles were nurtured in the past and how they must be nurtured in new ways in the future. Chapters One and Two represent the first two steps that you need to take before leaping into the practical strategies we offer.

Our theory and research—these two steps—grow in and from four combined disciplines: neurobiology, anthropology, sociology, and educational psychology. Both Kathy and I have had experience working in other countries; thus the information we use from these disciplines has been well researched both in the United States and on other continents.

It is our hope that because of the confluence of disciplines and sources in this book, you can gain a new vision of what works best for boys' minds wherever you find them, whether in a rural town or a big city, and whatever their educational status at this moment. The male learning style we'll explore with you is immensely diverse—nature does not stereotype, but instead thrives on diversity—yet as you explore male education, you will recognize how "boyish" a boy is. Understanding male energy from the inside out is very empowering to parents, teachers, and all of us who care for boys' minds. We believe that inside every boy there is an educational hero who is trying to flourish. We believe every boy can learn if his education is well cared for.

How to Care for a Boy's Education

Recently I went with my wife, Gail, and my children and some of their friends to watch the movie *Spiderman 2*. I enjoyed it, and I know the kids did. We all walked out in a "heroic" frame of mind, aware of our own self-doubts and of the innate courage that waits inside each of us to be activated toward the good. Spiderman is comic book wisdom at its best—simple, primal, powerful.

My older daughter, Gabrielle, who knew that Kathy and I were writing a book on boys and education, pointed out to me, "Dad, did you notice? Peter Parker is doing badly in school." This led to a discussion about how many contemporary films depict male heroes as "not good students." Even in the highly popular Harry Potter series, the best student is a girl, whereas the boys struggle in classes. These fictional sons of our culture, like Peter Parker, have given up somewhat on gaining the academic education their institutions and communities can give them; they feel isolated, and they turn inward, toward magical powers. How lucky for them if they, like Peter Parker, find superhuman powers within them but what about all the boys who have no comic book magic? School has afforded them too little success, and within these boys as well, there is not much hidden power.

I felt a little sad about this that evening. But I also felt a stirring of comfort. During the days of our Spiderman venture, I was working on a section of this book that involved very practical information on how to teach language arts to boys. It struck me, very gently, that even at forty-seven, I did not need to give up on the sense of magic. The problems of the world are not actually solved by magical mutations, but they can be solved by practical application of science and a great deal of hard work. That, for me, is the magic I turn to. That is what allows me to bend without breaking. That "practical magic" can be available to any boy who is having trouble in school.

I hope that for you the sciences of neurobiology, anthropology, sociology, and psychology can be "magical." I hope they can be heroic. I believe they have the power to help boys do well in school—even more, to help our boys love school. I hope in this book you'll feel the sense of magic in science and in research.

Kathy's son Mike has told me, "Throughout the whole nightmare of my school years, it was weird—I really wanted to like school. I just really wanted to."

Bravo to him. So did I. Don't all of our sons, at some level, really want to like the way they spend six to eight hours of every weekday? Don't they wish the magic were there in those schools, in their homework, in their learning adventures?

Your sons and your students want to live the magic, *do* the magic with their minds and hands. They, like you, are practical people, looking for practical ways to spin their webs or stretch their limbs or fly.

Following the first two chapters, we'll move on with you to practical information: direct and immediate steps you can take to care for your sons' and your students' educational success. Much of the research, ideas, and specific techniques we'll present come from the work of the Gurian Institute.

The Gurian Institute has become, especially under Kathy Stevens's direction, a resource for *practical* information on how to educate boys and girls. The Institute has developed a method by which parents, teachers, school systems, and communities can care for the minds of boys, in practical measure. This method has been used successfully in classrooms and homes in most of the states of the United States, including Alabama, California, Colorado, Florida, Georgia, Kentucky, Minnesota, Missouri, New York, Texas, and Washington, as well as in England, Canada, and Australia (for success data, please visit www.gurianinsti tute.com).

The practical measures you can take immediately in your home and school make up the bulk of the final ten chapters of *The Minds of Boys*. We've organized this practical information for you after listening to questions like these:

- What part does nutrition play in my son's education?
- What specific role does the nuclear family play in making school successful for him?
- Can parents be teachers too?

- At what age do I stop helping him with his homework?
- Are there certain classroom environments that work best for boys?
- How much television is good for learning? How much is bad?
- What role should computers play in a boy's development as a learner?
- Are there ways to fight the peer pressure some boys exert on others to stop them from liking school?
- What do teachers need in order to feel appropriately supported in teaching boys?
- How can single-gender education work for boys without hurting girls?
- What are boys themselves saying about the kinds of educational processes they need?

In Parts Two and Three of this book, you'll be coached on how to adapt home, school, and classroom environments to fit boys' learning styles and needs. These adaptations include changes to home and school schedules and policies, teacher-student ratios, classroom space and physical layout, and classroom procedures. Each innovation is tried and true—we have culled through twenty years' worth of successful strategies in order to present you with what works *best*.

As you read and apply the practical innovations in this book, you'll notice many stories and anecdotes from people like you. You'll meet teachers, parents, grandparents, and concerned citizens who are giving great care to boys' everyday education in homes, in schools, in parks, on streets. Their wisdom can guide us just as well as expert research can. You'll find testimonials from school principals, heads of schools, teachers, parents, and others who have instituted successful programs and experienced improved grades and test scores, as well as lowered numbers of discipline referrals.

There are some key academic areas of concern that many teachers and parents have reported. In Part Three, we specifically focus on the best home and classroom strategies for teaching the core curricula of reading, writing, language arts, math, and science. This focus includes information on the importance of arts and athletics in boys' learning. We'll also look closely at how single-gender education is working in certain communities, and why. Kathy and I believe strongly in coeducation, but we also believe that for both boys and girls, single-gender classrooms need to be part of the educational palette. We'll show you why we believe this.

Part Four looks at boys who are struggling with emotional issues, underachievement, bullying, academic distress, and learning disabilities. We'll focus on practical help for these boys, so that truly, no child is left behind. As we provide practical information to you, you'll notice some chapters divided into two major sections: What Parents Can Do and What Teachers Can Do. We'll explore with you the kind of parent-led *team*—mother, father, grandparents, neighbors, mentors—a boy needs in order to achieve the best learning at home. We'll look at how parents and teachers can do their separate and different jobs, but in concert with each other. For teachers, our chapters will include information for your classroom that you can put to work immediately.

In different parts of many chapters, we've include two kinds of material in boxes. These are highlighted lists of data, titled "Did You Know?" and highlighted innovations called "Try This." Kathy and I hope you'll pass the information from the highlighted boxes to friends and family members, put them in school mailboxes, and share them in teacher-staff meetings. We hope they'll help you and the others around you who care about boys to open communication about the needs of boys in your cities, towns, and schools.

The Minds of Boys

For Kathy and me, helping boys has become an essential purpose of our professional and personal work. It is at the core of our personal mission. We have experienced an unprotected male life in these last two generations. We have lived, from the viewpoints of son and mother, the pain and the passion of caring for boys.

The Minds of Boys is a joint venture, growing from our two visions and the combined efforts of the Gurian Institute's staff. We also know that it grows from all of your efforts. You care deeply about children's success, and we could not have written this book without the many stories and innovations that have come to us in person or via email from people like you—sons, daughters, mothers, fathers, grandparents, teachers, coaches, and school staff.

Our profound thanks go out to everyone who has entrusted their story to us. We feel, in a way, as if we have met your sons, the boys in your schools, even the young men who at this point are wandering away from you, searching for any help or magic they can find. You, like us, know just what is at stake as, together, we help our civilization awaken to the duty we have, as adult women and men, to better protect the minds of boys.

Together now, let us study and serve this male population. These boys cannot bend, stretch, spin, or fly forever. We can't afford to lose or nearly lose any more of our young men. We cannot abide watching these boys go away from school unhappy and inwardly empty for another generation. We must do something complete, passionate, and well informed. Let's begin right here, right now.

Protecting the Minds of Boys

The Current Crisis

> Because of the risks boys naturally take, a mom is ready to face a lot of little daily crises. But the crisis in my son's education—that took me completely by surprise.
>
> —KATHY STEVENS

THE SIGN OUTSIDE THE PRESCHOOL READS, "ALL CHILDREN WELCOME." A mother, father, and three-year-old son drive into the small parking lot. The parents have chosen this preschool among many others available in their neighborhood. Now their hearts are pounding, for this is their son's first day of school. They step out of the car, unbuckle their son from the car seat, lift him out, and walk with him to the front door.

A young woman comes to them and greets her new student and his parents. For a second the boy trembles, realizing that his parents are going to leave him here. He hugs them, cries a little, but then goes off with his new teacher, a kind young woman who holds his hand and introduces him to other kids. The boy turns, waves to Mommy and Daddy. They wave back, and leave silently.

This little boy can't fully understand his parents' hopes and dreams. He can't know how much they want not only this school but also the other schools their son will attend to inspire him and enrich his mind. These parents trust their educational system to be filled with teachers and staff who are trained to teach boys. As they turn away from the preschool, this mother and father already imagine the way their boy's mind will grow, the good grades their son will get, the teachers he'll have, and the knowledge, love of life, and wisdom he'll gain in twelve or more years of education. These parents have given their son to an educational system that they believe has shown, historically, great promise.

And for their son, it may fulfill that promise.

But it's just as likely that it will not. This may be the beginning of an educational crisis in this family. And this family will not be the only one experiencing such a crisis.

Is There Really a Crisis?

Because the word *crisis* gets thrown around a great deal these days, it deserves to be treated with suspicion. In fact, Kathy and I have tried not to use it, thinking, "But so many boys are getting by just fine. Can we really call the situation a crisis?" We've said, "Yes, the Gurian and Stevens families endured, struggled, and overcame their problems, but is it really a national or international crisis?" We've looked back on the months after Columbine, during which the Gurian Institute staff, along with many professionals, were asked by the media to comment and to offer our analysis of what happened and why. We learned then how using the word *crisis* can generate unwarranted fear about children's lives, a sensationalism that can wound schools and families, that can spread hopelessness and *hinder* necessary changes and healing.

Yet after all this we have ended up using the term. Yes, we're sorry to say, there really is a crisis. And in this chapter we hope to convince you to use the word not just as a negative alarm, but rather as an inspiration for positive change. Here are some of the things parents and educators are saying about the situation boys face in education today.

Laurie Hoff, a mother of three from Neenah, Wisconsin, wrote us: "I have a 13 year old boy. The middle school he attends is what I can only call 'anti-boy.' The assignments, the discipline, the structure of the day make him flounder in a system that works against him."

Netty Cruscan, a professional from Marion, Kentucky, wrote, "I'm a Developmental Interventionist, assessing and working on developmental delays. I'm noticing that the majority of the children on my client list are boys."

Linda Sullivan, a mother of two from Virginia, wrote, "I am becoming increasingly alarmed at the amount of boys being told they have processing problems, ADHD, LD, adjustment disorder, anxiety, and focus problems. By chance I happened to uncover today a new parochial school in our area in which 8 out of 20 in a third grade class are on Ritalin."

The Awful Truth

These parents and professionals are frightened. They have reason to be. Their communities are living out some painful statistics, as shown in the Did You Know? box.[1]

The issues boys face in school cross economic and ethnic groups. Although it might be politically tempting to say that upper-income white males must be doing well, that is in fact not a given. The Gurian Institute was just asked to assist a prestigious private boys' high school, populated by a majority of white males of high economic status, in which 50 percent of the boys in the school, across all grade levels, are receiving a D or an F in at least one subject. Even among white males there is a problem.

African American males are another group in which crisis is distinguishable. African American boys are more likely than other males (1) to be identified as learning-disabled and to end up in special education classes, (2) not to participate in advanced placement courses, (3) not to perform as well as other boys in math and science, and (4) to perform below grade level on standardized tests.

Pedro Noguera, professor in the Graduate School of Education at Harvard, has studied the academic performance of African American males and has reported that whereas 90 percent of black males surveyed "strongly agree" that they would like to succeed in school, only 22 percent responded that they "work hard to achieve good grades," and 42

??? **Did You Know?** ???

- Boys get the majority of the D's and F's in most schools—in some, as high as 70 percent.
- Boys make up 80 percent of our discipline problems.
- Of children diagnosed with learning disabilities, 70 percent are boys.
- Of children diagnosed with behavioral disorders, 80 percent are boys.
- Over 80 percent of schoolchildren on Ritalin or similar drugs are boys. As of 2004, the number of boys on Ritalin approached five million. (The United States consumes 80 percent of the world's supply of Ritalin.)
- According to the U.S. Department of Education, our sons are an average of a year to a year and a half behind girls in reading and writing skills. (Girls are behind boys in math and science but to a lesser degree.)
- Of high school dropouts, 80 percent are young males.
- Young men now make up less than 44 percent of our college population.

percent "strongly disagreed that their teachers supported them or cared about their success in school."[2]

The crisis in male education is not unique to the United States. The Organisation for Economic Co-operation and Development (OECD) implemented a three-year study of the knowledge and skills of fifteen-year-olds around the world using an assessment test called the Program for International Student Assessment (PISA).[3] The assessment measured reading, mathematical, and scientific literacy. In the United States, England, Canada, Australia, Germany, France, and Japan—indeed, in thirty-five developed countries—girls outperformed boys in overall educational markers, the male test results skewing the overall statistics most dramatically in the basic areas of reading and writing.

Canada's cyclical School Achievement Indicator Program was implemented in 1993; it assesses math, reading, writing, and science competency. In the 2002 cycle, there were significant differences between males and females in writing achievement.[4] Consistent with PISA results, girls outperformed boys at almost all levels.

In October 2002 the Commonwealth of Australia published a report titled *Boys: Getting It Right.* This report, focusing on the education of boys in Australia, was the result of a large national effort by the House of Representatives to identify the factors behind the declining educational performance by boys in their country. Hearings were held around the country, and more than two hundred witnesses presented research findings and information, leading to a series of conclusions and recommendations. In general, this study found that the existing gender equity framework was not adequately addressing the social and educational needs of Australia's boys.[5]

Likewise, England has been studying its data, which show that boys are being outperformed by girls in "most subjects and at most ages." The gender gap documented among English students was identified across all ethnic minority groups, and researchers argued that "it is not boys who are the problem but schools."[6] Interestingly, most of the significant findings in Canada, Australia, and England were not reported by the U.S. press.

Many of our sons can indeed learn in nearly any environment: they are gifted; they win spelling bees and debate contests; they read the newest Harry Potter book in a week. Nevertheless, the vast majority of children who are not succeeding, in class after class, are boys. The struggling, dysfunctional, and failing students for whom parents and teachers request extra academic help are mainly boys.

The children who bring down the state and federal test scores are mainly boys. The children who lash out against the educational system are mainly boys. The children with whom our teachers feel the least trained to deal are our sons.

What the Experts Have Found

Kathy and I are not the only ones who are deeply disturbed about the crisis in educating and developing the minds of boys. About elementary education, Harvard researcher Dan Kindlon and school psychologist Michael Thompson have written in *Raising Cain:* "From kindergarten through sixth grade, a boy spends more than a thousand hours a year in school. . . . there the average boy faces a special struggle to meet the developmental and academic expectations of an elementary school curriculum. . . . Some boys are ahead of the others on that developmental curve, and some girls lag behind, but when we compare the average boy with the average girl, the average boy is developmentally disadvantaged in the early school environment."[7]

Harvard psychologist William Pollack, author of *Real Boys,* studied the learning self-esteem of middle and high school boys, and he reports, "Recent studies show that not only is boys' self esteem more fragile than that of girls and that boys' confidence as learners is impaired but also that boys are substantially more likely to endure disciplinary problems, be suspended from classes or actually drop out of school."[8]

In her book *The War Against Boys,* Christina Hoff Sommers notes a recent MetLife study, one of the largest of its kind, which found that in our educational system today girls are more likely than boys to want a good education, and more boys than girls (31 percent versus 19 percent) feel teachers do not listen to what they have to say.[9]

Sommers also points to studies conducted by the U.S. Department of Education. When eighth- and twelfth-grade students were subjects of professional research on expectations, the girls in both grades held higher professional expectations than the boys—more schoolgirls than schoolboys envisioned themselves completing high school, college, then graduate or professional training.

Government researcher Diane Ravitch has summed up the situation in our educational system this way: "In the view of elementary and high school students, the young people who sit in the classroom year after year and observe what is going on, both boys and girls agree: Schools favor girls."[10]

Gurian Institute Research

Gurian Institute research corroborates the findings of these other researchers: after twenty years of study and countless pilot programs in school districts in nearly all the United States, as well as in Canada and Australia, we have concluded that whether the boy in your life is high performing or low performing, he is at risk of being taught, managed, and guided in a system that may find him defective and may not know how to fix either him or itself.

This pattern of difficulty creates a problem for boys that will afflict our civilization with increasing discomfort over many decades to come, unless we confront it immediately. Parents bringing their sons to their first days of preschool will increasingly find that at least one of these sons could eventually face an educational crisis.

Terry Culpepper, a mother in Arizona wrote us: "My son and three of his friends have been skipping school a lot since they got to middle school. I'm doing my best, but I don't know what to do."

Isaiah Olson, a father in Detroit wrote, "I see a big problem with our African American boys in school. They don't fit. It's not just about race. It's something else. The drop out rate for black males is now twice what it is for black females. It's about gender in our community, too."

Trace, a high school freshman in Oregon, told his school counselor, "I'm a failure as a student. I know it, my parents know it, and my teachers know it. There's nothing I can do."

These people are definitely in crisis. At some level, their trust in education is being destroyed. And these emails and letters are just a few of the thousands of messages that we and other researchers are receiving constantly.

The Boys You Know

Statistics, personal stories, a sense of a crisis—these are still far away unless you know boys, schools, and families who are suffering needlessly. What is the situation in your school, home, and community?

As a parent:

- Do you know boys who are bright but underperforming in school?
- Do you know boys quite capable of task success in the home or elsewhere, but unmotivated at school?
- Do you know boys who are getting weak or low grades, are falling behind, are unable or unwilling to fulfill the assignments given to them?
- Are there sons who are good at one thing, perhaps math, but disproportionately behind in another, perhaps reading?
- How many of the boys in your child's school are on Ritalin or Adderal? Have these boys been scientifically tested for ADD/ADHD, or is the medication a response to a general problem the boys are having in the school?
- Do you know boys and families for whom educational distress is going on year after year?
- Do you know adolescent boys who are not being prepared adequately to get a good job or—even more painful—to flourish in a healthy, happy life?

As a teacher or educational professional:

- Do more boys than girls in your classes chronically underperform?
- Are boys in your school receiving a disproportionate number of lower grades, especially in reading, writing, and language arts?
- Is medication becoming a first or second resort for far more boys than actually need it?
- Are boys in your classrooms giving up on learning, becoming labeled, getting in more trouble than they should be?
- Have you noticed how many bright boys are deciding not to go to college?

Our educational system does many things very well, yet nearly every classroom has one or more young Michael Gurians or Karl Michaels in it. They act out against other boys, against adults, and against girls. When they withdraw, they may take another boy or girl with them. When they fail, they "turn off" their minds, seeing nothing of interest in school and thus, quite often, in society. Some of these boys turn anger at school and life into violence that is played out with guns or fists in school cafeterias or classrooms. More often, these boys just fall behind and "check out." They end up in special education or diagnosed with a learning disability or put on medication. Some of them drop out of school. Many do not succeed in life. They become the boys, and the men, we try so hard to make sure our sons don't become.

Our Young Men and College

For the first time in history, males make up less than 44 percent of our college students in many of our nation's institutions.[11] Females were underrepresented for centuries, but now the pendulum has swung in the opposite direction. Since the mid-1990s, the number of boys entering and graduating from college has dropped to less than the 50 percent one would wish for gender parity. This would not be a problem if college were "not worth very much," but in fact, a new study has confirmed what many of us intuit, not only that college is often essential for adult success but also that a disproportionate number of our males are not finding a home in college.

A new longitudinal study by the Center for Labor Market Studies at Northeastern University in Boston reveals the long-term effects of disenfranchising large groups of young males from educational success.[12] According to the study, if present educational trends continue, our young males will be graduating from high school and attending college in ever declining numbers, with those numbers going down to a 30 percent college attendance rate.

Must a boy go to college to succeed? Not always. Bill Gates didn't finish college, and he is known to be a good father, a business success, and an effective public servant. Calling attention to the college problem for males is not to decry an individual's particular qualities, nor to

??? Did You Know? ???

According to the study by the Center for Labor Market Studies, even at the present 44 percent college attendance rate, this generation of young men will

- Be increasingly unemployed or underemployed
- Earn significantly lower lifetime earnings than their peers
- Pay less Social Security, state, and federal income taxes over their lifetime, with the size of these tax revenue streams steadily decreasing commensurate with lower levels of education
- Depend more on in-kind benefits (food stamps, Medicaid, rental housing subsidies) than their better-educated counterparts
- Be more likely to father children out of wedlock and not live with or support their offspring
- Be less likely to accomplish personal and social goals for success in a competitive society

lament women's successes in increasing their college attendance, wages, and financial independence from males. Rather, it is to say that college is still the best average indicator of personal and social success for adults in the industrial and postindustrial world, and it is becoming less and less available to our sons.

Understanding and Fixing the Crisis

Something has gone wrong in the way we educate our boys. Studies are noting it in early education, elementary school, middle school, high school, and even college. What is that something? Can we define the problem? Can we root it out? Can it then be fixed?

As you'll see throughout this book, our Gurian Institute research indicates that the crisis is systemic, with no single person or group to blame: not teachers, not parents, not girls, not boys. Blame is like ice—it freezes an issue without changing it. The problem goes deeper than blame.

At the same time, we can identify the "something," we can define the problem, we can root it out, and we can fix it. The first step in this process is an act of collective memory: let's go back for a moment to where all this began, to the way we once brought up our young men, so that we can see how the roles of parents, children, and schools in educating the minds of boys have changed.

How Did This Happen?

If you think back to how your ancestors were educated, you'll notice that until about a hundred years ago, in all parts of the world, our sons' primary teachers were not lone individuals in schoolrooms but families, tribes, and natural environments. Whether your people came from Europe, Africa, Asia, or anywhere else, the boys and men in your ancestry mainly hunted, protected their families, farmed, worked intertribally, and mentored adolescent males into manhood. When the first schools opened in urban centers a few thousand years ago, the broad backs of males were needed for work within ever larger economic hierarchies, work for which they needed better intellectual and logistical training. They got some of that in newly built schools, but most boys did not spend much time inside a schoolhouse. After a few years of "schooling," they moved in late childhood into fields or workplaces.

Right up into the nineteenth century, most boys still learned what they needed to know mainly from their mothers, fathers, mentors, and hands-on work. They imitated their elders, they practiced, they learned by doing. Not until about two hundred years ago did printing and the written word become a major part of a boy's educational life. It was at that point that the Industrial Revolution was upon us.

Margaret Gayle, executive director of the American Association for Gifted Children at Duke University, and Hugh Osborn, an educational consultant, wrote a starkly titled article for the *Los Angeles Times:* "Let's

Get Rid of Learning Factories." In tracking the roots of many of the issues we now face in our schools, they described the rationale for the development of the "industrial schooling" we have today. "Economic foundations set up by industrialists helped design our schools to prepare children for factory lives. Kids were to live by the bell, move through schools as if on conveyor belts and, especially, learn to follow instructions so they could work in the rapidly proliferating factories."[13]

The industrial model of educating children had a certain logic to it. Population growth and nation building required all children to go to school.

The industrialization of the classroom and the school occurred within a few rapid decades. Parents, grandparents, and tribal mentors became somewhat obsolete in the institutional education process. Children were educated far less frequently in environments that relied on family leadership and tribal apprenticeship. Learning became less hands-on, less physical, less experiential. The trend of educating kids through reading, writing, and sitting in one's seat became the "acceptable standard" for huge numbers of children who entered school year after year.

Over these decades, our boys by the millions tried (and often succeeded) to adapt. Often, however, they did not. The boys who learned what they needed to know by hunting with their relatives, managing a farm, fixing machinery, or devising a new invention for everyone in their tribe to use—these boys now found themselves in boxlike rooms. For most boys in public schools, gone were the classical academic models of verbal debate between young thinkers on issues of vital importance to the polis.

Gone too were many of the family members who understood the minds of their own sons and protégés: the parents, extended families, and tribes who had led the child's education by providing his early learning experiences in the family or larger community, then by managing his later apprenticeships. Now there were a lot of kids—peers—and one teacher per classroom, who was supposed to be the parent, mentor, grandparent, instructor, and everything else to all these young minds. The juggernaut of industrialization in schools moved so quickly toward this model of teaching and learning that not until now have we begun to realize its possible flaws—beginning with what it lacks in human terms.

Who Is Responsible for a Boy's Education?

A former professor of mine, referring to the words of the philosopher Bertrand Russell, said to me, "No life experience compares to family love. There is nothing I have done that rewards me as much as being a parent." Each of us who has children has probably expressed a similar idea to someone during our child's upbringing. These words touch our hearts. My professor, who was very involved in his kids' lives, went on to say, "Especially rewarding was my attention to my children's education. I considered it my responsibility." This sentiment might also ring true for the rest of us—but most of us are not trained teachers so it runs counter to how we educate our children today.

Are parents today ultimately responsible for their children's education? Is it even realistic to answer yes, when we are not "teachers"? In fact, isn't it more accurate to say that yes, we sense how important we are to our children's education, but also that we must trust—through paying taxes or tuition and holding high expectations of our schools, whether public or private—that our contemporary systems of education will prepare our children for the technologies and skills of modern adulthood?

Most of us do indeed send our children away from their homes and families into square rooms with desks and books, where they learn reading, writing, math, science, computer programming, and many other subjects they need for success. At the end of the school day, they return to our homes, to our parenting. Perhaps we've been working away from home all day just as our kids have. As parents, as family members, as grandparents, as neighbors, as family friends, we've spent little time in our work or retirement day thinking about our responsibilities for our boys' education. Neither we nor our schools have conspired to do harm in all this—it is simply "the way things are."

But must it be this way? Is it possible that the family's general abdication of a son's (or daughter's) education to an industrialized system may constitute, without our realizing it, a major reason for the current crisis? Is it possible that through this abdication we have broken a promise to our children, a promise made in the commitment to loving and caring for offspring?

The Lost Role of the Family in Education

If you look back at your family's distant past, you'll notice that whether your ancient ancestry derives from Viking, Teutonic, African, Roman, East Indian, Japanese, or Chinese roots—on all continents, no matter the race, your human ancestors relied on *extended family teams* who were *intimate with the child* to educate offspring in the technologies and values of life and work.

No matter where they lived, your biological ancestors relied on teams of educators, led by parents, matriarchs, and patriarchs in tribes, who considered themselves as ultimately responsible for the boy's learning. There were very few strangers in a boy's schooling. Because the child was considered an extension of parents, grandparents, and tribe, his education was an extension of his blood relationships. When someone outside his tribe was given control of his education, it was not done at three, four, or five years old, but only much later, during late childhood and adolescence, if he was apprenticed to a faraway mentor in a trade.

Konrad Lorenz, the noted biologist and anthropologist of the last century, explored the protection that families of all species offer their offspring. His work later joined others in anthropological studies of human dependency. This biological approach to the human family served ultimately to show how crucial the human family is in the education of children, and to warn of the crisis that can result when the family drifts from its attachments and responsibilities.

What is intuitive to most parents was clarified by biological research: *families matter.* In the last two decades, scientists in the area of attachment research have shown just how dependent children are on the parents and close extended family for life success. In their book, *The Dependency Tendency,* Dr. Jay P. and Julia Gurian (my own parents, a sociologist and anthropologist, respectively) brought the work of Lorenz and other biologists together with anthropological evidence. They note that in a biology-based view of family, "The human family is more than a collection of interlocking emotional needs. . . . families are interlocking life-units in which the well being of one is inherent in the well being of another. From a dependency point of view (and contrary to popular myth), parents do not make themselves dispensable, and the children never fully outgrow being the children of the previous generation. Nor do grandparents or others of their generation ever 'disengage' from their responsibilities or privileges within the family circle."[14]

This is a bioanthropological model of family, rather than an industrial one. It is the model with which Kathy and I begin this book because it is the model that seems to work very well in communities and schools around the country. This model does not diminish the importance of the school—the school is responsible for the education of the child—but the child's family is *equally* responsible: the child's mind is connected always to the family's mind, and family is responsible for its care. In this model, the family considers itself less than adequate if it gives up leadership of the care of that mind to a massive structure of society, an institution, which does not really know the child. Families and schools are coteachers of the child's mind.

This ancient and universal model of family was set aside during the Industrial Revolution. In our sons' case, we have systematically relinquished the responsibility for their education to institutional systems that are not malicious—that are, in fact, filled with some of the finest people our children will ever meet—but are not biosocially responsible for each individual child's success and often are not set up to care intimately about that individual success.

Is part of the crisis we face with boys and school rooted in human parents' giving away too much when we gave our children's minds to institutions? Is it possible to begin fixing the crisis in male education by taking back some of the responsibility we once had for our sons?

Kathy and I believe the answer is a resounding yes. The first practical step toward dealing with the crisis in boys' education is to understand our lost role as parents and families.

Reviving the Role of Family in Education

In asking you, as parents and teachers, to begin our journey out of low grades, discipline problems, and male malaise by rethinking the role of the family in our educational history, we are not asking parents and extended family to deny the role of schools and teachers in helping our boys develop. We are as supportive of teachers as we are of parents. Our hope is that the family's role will be revived to become *the leadership team* that takes a profound rather than distant responsibility for a boy's educational success.

The remaining chapters in this book provide equal amounts of advice to parents and teachers in hopes of helping revive the important partnership between the child's first and second schools, the home and the formal classroom.

Because fathers and mothers are now working away from families; because industrial mobility has moved many families away from grandparents, tribe, and family groups; because divorce and changing family values have created additional stress on family cohesion, our children do indeed need the best of the industrial model—they do indeed require increased supervision away from mom, dad, grandparents, aunts, uncles, mentors—they are "school reliant" in ways they were not a thousand years ago. We clearly can't go back to the small tribes in which our ancestors were brought up and educated.

And yet, in the shadow of educational distress and malaise, we can revise and update what we call the *parent-led team* that once helped educate a boy (and also a girl). Let's define this team more carefully. A child's parents will generally lead this effort, and the team may consist of

- Parents
- Grandparents
- Other relatives, such as aunts and uncles, cousins, in-laws
- Tutors
- Coaches
- Neighbors
- Friends
- Service agencies

- Clergy and mentors in faith communities
- Siblings
- Other peer mentors

In this parent-led team, each person and organization is asked to join an educational team, built by parents with children at its center, whose job it is to educate the child. If this team moves into place, no matter what crisis the boy now faces (and even if he faces none), his chances of being lost to educational crisis diminish significantly. He now has ten or so trusted individuals to help him outside the school system.

Building Your Parent-Led Team: The First Step Against Crisis

This parent-led team, this first step against crisis, can be put together out of what is available around you. It is enhanced by your blood relatives, but not dependent on them.

Here are some ways it can work organically in your home or neighborhood.

- Grandpa George is a retired engineer, who lives in Florida. Your son, who lives in California, is having trouble in math or science. You can contact Grandpa George and set up a weekly tutorial for your son via phone and the Internet.
- Grandma Estelle, who lives a few hours away, is an avid reader. Your son is having trouble with his language arts curriculum. Once a week, Grandma Estelle can come over to help your son with his reading and writing.
- Your son has a best friend, Max, who lives a few neighborhoods away. Max's father is a computer designer. Once or twice a week, your son and Max can spend time with this father at the computer, learning what they need to know.
- You are a single mother, perhaps raising two or three sons, one of whom is having trouble in school. Perhaps you have another son or daughter, already grown, who is away at college. You can arrange for the boy having trouble to connect with his older sibling on the Internet at least once a week, so the older sibling can check out his

homework, keep him focused on papers that are due, and give him tutoring on tough subjects.

Healing the crisis that faces our boys today begins with a parent-led team. As this book progresses, you'll get help in making sure that your family learning team is ultimately responsible for making sure that boys are provided what they have always needed in order to learn: close, intimate mentors and advocates throughout the journey of institutional education.

Sandra, a mother in Deer Park, Washington, is developing a parent-led team. She wrote:

> I have five sons. I realized after my fifth was born that I had to take time off work in order to help them get the best upbringing and education they could. Their schools were doing their best, but the boys needed me to shepherd them, too.
>
> Now, a lot of my time is spent tutoring them. A lot is also spent driving them here and there. A lot of it is spent listening to them, trying to help them. And when I don't know an answer, a lot of it is spent finding someone who does.

This last sentence is especially compelling—Sandra has constructed a parent-led *team* that can help her sons through the difficulties (and the successes) of institutional education.

Whether you as a parent take time off work or simply make the child's education a primary focus, the effective use of a parent-led team will probably require you or your spouse to focus, at least for a time, on creating it, networking it, and mastering its design. The rewards are well worth the extra effort.

Once you have established your team, it's important not to wait until there's a problem to call on members. You might find it fun and rewarding to have periodic gatherings to celebrate milestones in your son's life.

Parent-led teams can work wonderfully for girls. There is actually nothing that makes teams inherently better for boys than girls. We are calling attention to the parent-led team in the context of male learning because while our nation's girls gained much educational equity in the last two decades, now statistics show that our sons are failing to learn.

Try This
Assessing Team Members' Suitability

The following are questions to think about as you evaluate the appropriateness of individuals you are considering for your team:

- Does this person seem to really like kids? (Just because a person is related doesn't mean he or she enjoys spending time with youngsters.)
- Does this person have some basic understanding of developmentally appropriate ways to deal with my child?
- Does my child seem to enjoy being around this person?
- Does this person seem likely to make participation on my child's team a priority when necessary?

Kathy and I have taught families and communities how to develop this team for their sons' learning. We've been honored to become a part of families' sense of reward, responsibility, and joy as boys' learning improves and their life success becomes more ensured. A parent group in Georgia shared these results with us:

We are a group of five families, all of which have boys. In three of the families, our boys were having trouble. In one of them, one of the girls was having trouble in school. In the fifth family, the kids are already grown. We all became friends ten years ago when our kids became friends in the same elementary school.

When we decided to work with this "parent-team" concept, we had a meeting of parents and kids, we talked about what the team was (we called it our "learning tribe"), and we divided up labor based on people's abilities. Luckily, within the five families, there was always some adult who knew something that could help one of the kids.

Our children are now moving through high school. This parent-team has made all the difference. We even created a rite of passage for our graduating seniors. Other friends from our church have noticed how much better our kids are doing in school and we've sat down with them and talked about how it has worked. I think the word about this is definitely spreading.

These five families, like Sandra, have refreshed the role of learning teams for the youth in their lives. They have done this none too soon, answering the call of a crisis in male education with a first practical step forward.

Facing the challenge of working and advocating for change within a large, often bureaucratic institutional system like a school can be a daunting task for a parent. Sometimes parents (and even educators themselves) feel powerless, overwhelmed, stressed out. Often they feel frustrated by an institution's inability to change. In Chapter Six we'll be talking more about how parents can advocate and work collectively to change their schools.

Meanwhile, though, Sandra and others like her who have built these parent-led teams are already dealing with institutional difficulties in two powerful ways: they are making sure each family has allies who can help ease the intimidation of sometimes feeling like a very small fish in a very large pond. And they are providing their children with learning buddies who can help them persevere even when the institutions in their district or neighborhood just won't change. The educational loneliness that one parent or child can feel is alleviated as now the family becomes more than one fish—indeed, becomes a "minischool" of fish that can cohesively make some serious waves when necessary.

No matter what situation you face in your school district or neighborhood, creating a parent-led learning team for your son constitutes a crucial first step in protecting the education of your child.

The Next Step

In our next chapter, we'll take a next step: we'll take a close and multifaceted look at how boys actually learn—what's happening inside the minds of boys—in order to discover our boys' *natural* learning style. This discovery helps both parents and teachers alter teaching and mentoring methods to meet boys' specific needs.

As we move to this next step, it seems clear that avoiding the word *crisis* regarding our boys does no good. Research in the 1990s clarified ways in which our schools fail our girls, especially in areas of math and science, the dynamics of self-esteem in the classrooms, and computer design instruction. Because our culture recognized a girls' crisis, it has addressed those problems and to a great extent has changed things for the better as far as teaching girls is concerned.

Now we are called by a crisis in education to take care of our sons in our schools. If we don't, the future success of our young men, our community, and our society is at stake. Our boys simply can no longer get the vast majority of our D's and F's without our doing something about it.

When the mother, father, and three-year-old boy walked up to that preschool door, they had the highest of hopes and aspirations. Certainly, one thing they assumed was that the teachers in that preschool—and in all schools thereafter through college—would know how their son's mind works, so that they could teach directly and effectively not just to "kids," but to boys.

Do teachers know how boys actually learn? Do parents know? What if everyone did know? Would this knowledge make things better for our sons?

Let's find out.

2

How Boys Learn

To respect that fury or those giddy high spirits or a body that seems perpetually mobile is to respect nature, much as one respects the strength of a hurricane, the rush of a waterfall.

—SARA RUDDICK, AUTHOR AND MOTHER

HAVE YOU EVER GONE TO A PLAYGROUND WITH YOUR CHILDREN AND JUST watched the children play and interact? As a father, I had numerous chances to do this when my children were young. I enjoyed watching them climb, jump, explore. Sometimes I would read a book on a bench; other times I would get involved with them in their game.

"Be the monster, Dad!" they'd cry.

Like so many fathers, I learned quickly that this was one of my expected roles, so I chased them with arms wide until they found their safe hiding places.

I have two girls—thus my journeys to playgrounds were a little different than the journeys I remember as a boy. Both my daughters carry in their personalities a strong piece of Huckleberry Finn, Tom Sawyer, Harry Potter. Yet I have been well aware throughout my daughters' upbringing that I did not have sons. Kathy and I have often compared notes about playgrounds. As a mom raising two sons, she too participated in their play when they were young, then found herself watching her sons at play from a bench. They didn't play quite the same way girls did.

Have you sensed in your own life the differences between boys and girls? Have you stood at a playground or watched kids on the street, and noticed "girl energy" and "boy energy"? Have you wondered, "Am I seeing things correctly? Is there really a difference?" Have you known instinctually that there is and asked, "But why does the difference exist? Is it part of nature, is it socialized? Is it both?"

For many decades, our culture's scientists and social thinkers have studied how our boys and girls learn by observing their social interactions and personal motivations—their psychological development, socialization, and gender roles. These studies have been pedagogical, sociological, and psychological; they have documented how our various Western cultures "nurture" boys and girls differently.

In the last two decades, however, a new method of understanding how children develop and learn, one we might call a "hard science" approach, has become possible. It explores what's inside our children's minds and bodies as they develop—physiologically, biochemically, neurologically.

In the last decade especially, scientists, social thinkers, and parents and teachers have begun to apply these "brain sciences" to understanding how boys and girls learn—specifically, how boys and girls learn differently. The new brain research shows that boys and girls are intrinsically not the same.[1] Our parental instinct at the playground is now validated by scientific findings regarding fundamental differences in male and female hardwiring, biochemistry, neurological development, and anatomy of boys' and girls' brains.

In this chapter, we want to guide you into the actual minds—the brains—of boys. We're doing this not only because it is interesting but also with a second motive: to inspire you to use these intriguing new brain sciences to rethink and revise how our schools, homes, neighborhoods, and playgrounds care for boys' minds. Understanding the actual nature of our boys' minds is essential for parents, parent-led teams, teachers, and concerned citizens who want to give boys the best education and care possible.

A New Science

A new science is emerging in our culture—*gender science.* Some who work in this field hold a strongly sociological view of how gender happens to boys and girls. Others take a strongly biological view. Kathy and I are in the middle, with a leaning toward the biological. We are in the middle because we never rely merely on biological sciences—we always check brain research with anthropological, psychological, and sociological studies. You could call us *nature-based theorists.* When we ask questions about how human beings learn, we start by seeking answers in "nature"—biological research. We feel that the most helpful dialogue regarding children should begin with the actual nature of the child, rather than with external social assumptions about the child. After we have a foundation in how the biology and brains of children—both boys and girls—actually work, we then move to social sciences for assistance. We are nature based, but not nature confined.

Nature-based theory was less possible a thousand years ago, even a decade ago, than it is today. It's important to remember that most educational theory on which our school system and our classroom pedagogy is based actually grows out of social thinking four to six decades old. The social thinkers of the 1950s, 1960s, and 1970s did not have PET scans, MRIs, SPECT scans, and other biological research tools available to them. They had to make assumptions about how children learn without any real scientific evidence. Because they could not look inside the heads of human beings to see the differences in the brains of males and females, they had to lean away from nature-based theory toward social trends theory. They had to overemphasize the power of nurture in gender studies because they didn't have a way to study the actual nature of male and female.

Some of the assumptions they made have turned out to be good ones. Our school systems are quite good, actually, in a number of ways. However, new gender sciences show that some of the assumptions about gender in the last century of education were not accurate at all. One prevalent assumption of thirty years ago was that boys and girls learn the same way—that each child was an "individual," not a boy or a girl, when it came to learning. The human brain was considered the "human" brain—there was little "male" or "female" about it. It was assumed to be a blank slate on which male and female came later, through the work of culture.

The new gender science—which includes the brain sciences *and* the social sciences—sees children not as blank slates, nor as determined by genetics alone, but as creatures of three formative powers: nature, nurture, and culture. In this chapter and in this book, you'll find that we've based our work on making sure that we, and the communities we work with, are briefed in the interplay of a boy's nature with his nurture and culture. And although we know that there is still much to be learned about the human brain—both male and female—we believe that our current knowledge base provides significant opportunities for families, schools, and communities to design educational environments that will support success for our sons and daughters.

The new nature-based gender science can arm teachers and parents with successful methodologies for teaching boys (and girls) language arts, reading, writing, math, science, athletics, and the arts. This new science makes it possible to care for boys (and girls) who are highly sensitive, who are undermotivated, and who have learning difficulties. New science makes it possible to understand the challenges of parenting a boy or girl.

In many cases, the pedagogy and the strategies that emerge from gender science show boys and girls thinking, feeling, and learning differently. Boys, the subject of this book, have a certain kind of learning energy, their own "male" path to successful education, and it begins in them before they are born. When we fully understand this "boy energy," we discover new ways of teaching the minds of boys.

Boy Energy

Up to No Good: The Rascally Things Boys Do is a collection of anecdotes written by men in their forties and fifties about their boyhood learning experiences. One of the contributions to the collection is from Charlie, born in New York in 1960, who tells this story:

When we were thirteen or so my friends and I had this game. We'd go down to the basement where it was completely dark, and each of us would find a hiding place. Then someone would start the game by turning out the lights, and we'd try to hit each other with darts. You'd think you heard someone make a noise, and you'd come out of your hiding place throwing darts—but cringing because you were fair game, too. There would be complete silence, and then you'd hear someone yell, "Ow!" One time we turned on the light and a guy had a dart dangling from his cheek, just below his eye.

After that, we wore goggles.[2]

When I present this anecdote in the first hour of a parent or teacher gender training, I often joke, "Isn't this a typical boy innovation?" A participant inevitably responds with something like: "Innovation? Are you kidding? When the first boy got a dart stuck in his face, the game should have been called off!"

This is a logical thing to say, but as the seminar continues, even this participant ends up agreeing: if we look closely at boys' innovations, we see something we can call boy energy, something definable—physical, in motion, kinesthetic. Even when they are reading a book, boys are so often tapping their feet or peeling the skin off their nails, or their eyes are darting about in exploratory, impulsive passions. The boy, fueled by his boy energy, tends to learn by innovating in risk-taking ways, wearing goggles so the dangerous game can go on. This energy involves a lot of physical movement and manipulation of physical objects. It can be quite competitive energy—though not always. It sometimes demands few words, preferring stealth and silence. It often favors spatial challenges and the use of tools. It often looks for a learning experience that thrives in its forceful containment of chaos—a game in the dark, throwing darts—with a low threshold for failure, executed in large or small spaces, such as a field or, in Charlie's case, a basement. It is often singularly task focused.

If we can agree for a moment to call this kind of energy "boy energy," we can probably also agree that it is one of the greatest assets of a civilization. Our homes and buildings are built by it. Our roads are laid down in its vision. Our rocket ships fly because of it. Video games that involve on-screen physical and spatial movement are played predominantly by boys, some of whom become the race car drivers who entertain us, the mach 1 pilots who challenge the known boundaries of time and space, the soldiers who protect us, the teachers, construction workers, shopkeepers, and writers. Boys learn through impulsive trial and error, then become the men who, as lawyers or doctors or athletes or corporate managers, force innovation into the human theater.

Boys' bodies are out there in the wind waiting to be buffeted by life. Boys gain their toughness and tenderness by pushing through the seams and edges others may not yet see, or may fear. In all this, the minds of boys are carried as much in their bodies as in their heads.

Can we say the same of girls? Girls do live the life of the mind through the life of the body. Girls are great athletes. Girls become women who fly planes, invent, and innovate. Girls become women who protect their values and their country. Girls become lawyers, doctors, and engineers. All this is very true. A focus on boy energy is not meant to indicate a limit to the life of girls and women. The view is more like looking into a concave mirror. For most of us, even when we work for gender equality, our gaze into the minds of girls reveals not only the girl but also the boy who is not quite like her. When, at the playground, I played with my daughters, I sensed difference—as Kathy sensed she was not male when she played with her sons. The difference does not limit a parent's love or a teacher's will to teach, but it is there.

Most boys, even the most verbal—the reader, writer, or public speaker—carry in them boy energy, and there are few girls who don't know it. There are few mothers who don't notice that their sons are gifted with a way of learning and relating and seeing the world in game groups and learning teams that involves climbing the walls, being wild and noisy, trying desperately not to take things personally. Boys swallow their pride and try again, grinning when a true piece of praise comes their way for an innovation well executed. Boys yearn as if from inchoate nature to move around as freely as we'll let them and, often, to learn in the dark. Boys internalize, without knowing it, a wonderful image from the poet Mark Strand: Boys don't necessarily move around in order to break things but instead to keep things whole.[3]

We all sense this energy, but now we can do more than sense it. We can identify this boy energy with *science*. Charlie and his buddies didn't know they would become part of a new science, but indeed they have. They provide a humorous base for a brief course in how boy energy plays out in the brains of your sons and the boys in your classrooms. (In the Bibliography at the end of this book, you'll find a number of books and other sources of information from which you can gain even deeper knowledge into the results of PET scans and other technologies that help us look into the minds of boys.)

The Male Brain

PET scans and MRIs allow all of us to observe the structural and functional differences between the brains of boys and girls. When you look at a scan of male and female brains doing any kind of task, you see different parts of the brain light up, with differing levels of brain activity in these cortical sections. This is a primary way we've been able to discern the nature of boys and the nature of how boys learn.

Nancy Forger, of the University of Massachusetts at Amherst, reported recently that "at least 100 differences in male and female brains have been described so far."[4] She is joined by other researchers—many of whom you'll meet in this book—such as Jill Goldstein, a professor of psychiatry at Harvard Medical School, who studies male and female brain differences in order to help cure diseases in males and females. Kathy and I specifically apply such gender science research in order to help develop educational and parenting strategies that work for boys and for girls.

The Did You Know? box lists some biological tendencies that we have observed from studying what is hardwired into male nature. We have provided illustrations of the human brain so that you can see the different parts of the brain. We've also included scans that show differences between the male and the female brain.

The issue of brain difference becomes increasingly important the more words a teacher uses to teach a lesson (that is, the less diagrammatic a teacher is). The male brain, on average, relies more heavily than does the female on spatial-mechanical stimulation and thus is inherently more stimulated by diagrams, pictures, and objects moving

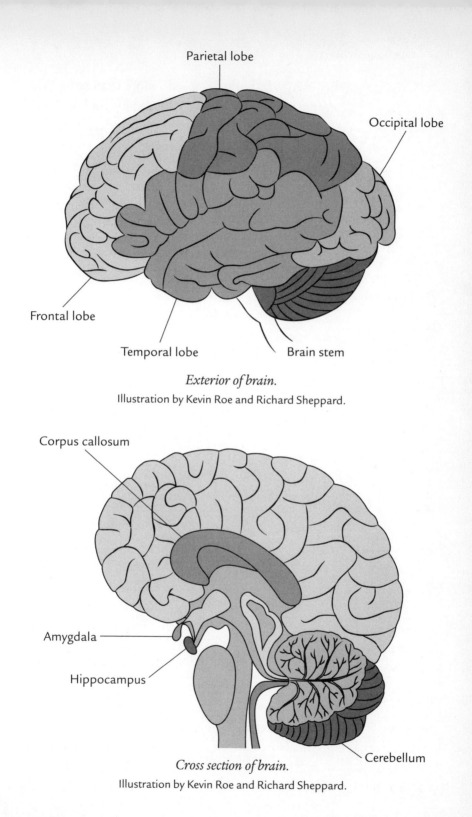

Exterior of brain.
Illustration by Kevin Roe and Richard Sheppard.

Cross section of brain.
Illustration by Kevin Roe and Richard Sheppard.

?⁇? Did You Know? ?⁇?

- Boys tend to have more dopamine in their bloodstream—
  which can increase impulsive risk behavior—and they
  process more blood flow in the cerebellum (the part of
  the brain that controls "doing" and "physical action").[5]
  (Although dopamine can't cross the "blood-brain barrier," L-dopa, an amino acid in the brain, is converted to
  dopamine.)[6] These factors are believed to contribute to
  boys' tendency to learn less well than girls (on average)
  when sitting still or being sedentary. Boys are more likely
  than girls to attach their learning to physical movement.[7]
  This movement is in fact often crucial to male brain
  learning (and to the learning style of females with higher
  dopamine-cerebellum functioning as well).

- A boy's corpus callosum (the connecting bundle of tis-
  sues between hemispheres) is a different size than a girl's
  (some studies show up to a 25 percent difference in size).[8]
  Researchers have shown that the female corpus callosum
  (as well as other related nerve fibers) allows more cross-
  talk between hemispheres than does that of the male.
  One of the obvious behavioral differences that grow
  from higher levels of cross-talk between hemispheres is
  the greater ability to do more than one task at once with
  equal success (multitasking). On average, girls test out
  better at multitasking.

- Girls have, in general, stronger neural connectors in their
  temporal lobes than boys do; these stronger connectors
  appear to facilitate more sensorially detailed memory
  storage and better listening, especially for tones of voice.
  Boys in general pick up less of what is aurally going on
  around them, *especially when it is said in words,* and need
  more sensory-tactile experience than girls in order for
  their brains to light up with learning.[9]

- The hippocampus (another memory storage area in the brain) works differently in boys than in girls.[10] Boys will tend to need even more time to memorize classroom items—especially written items—than girls. However, because the male hippocampus favors list making, boys tend to succeed well in memorization when greater amounts of information come in list organization and in listed substrata of categorization (point, subpoint, sub-subpoint).
- Girls' frontal lobes are generally more active than boys, and grow at earlier ages.[11] For this reason, girls tend to make less impulsive executive decisions than boys. Impulsivity used to be much more useful and desirable in learning, especially when children did more of their learning outdoors and independently.
- Girls tend to get earlier and more advanced development of the Broca's and Wernicke's areas in the frontal and temporal lobes—these are the main language centers of the brain.[12] In general, the female brain utilizes more neural pathways and brain centers for word production and expression of experience, emotion, and cognition through words.
- Girls have more estrogen and oxytocin than boys. (These chemicals have a direct impact on the use of words.) Boys have higher levels of testosterone (a hormone closely associated with aggression and sex) and vasopressin (which relates to territoriality and hierarchy). Oxytocin rises when girls communicate verbally with a friend or family member. Boys, with less oxytocin in the bloodstream and less verbal emphasis in the brain, don't learn as much through sitting and talking, nor gravitate toward it as naturally. Their formation of learning bonds often develops through action-response, hierarchical

competition,[13] and aggression nurturance (a topic we will cover in Chapter Four).

- Boys compartmentalize brain activity (that is, they use less of the brain), their brains overall operate with 15 percent less blood flow than do girls',[14] and they are structured to learn with less multitasking. Boys therefore tend to do better when focusing for long periods on one task in which depth of learning takes place; they do less well when required to move from task to task very quickly. One primary brain response to the overstimulation of doing many things at once is frustration (a swelling of the amygdala, which is an anger and aggression center in the brain and has a significantly higher volume of tissue in males[15]). Gradually, increasing frustration levels lead to heightened levels of stress hormone (cortisol), which also link to heightened adrenalin—thus, it ought not surprise us that males create more discipline problems in classrooms.

- Research continues to explore the implications of gender on the functioning of many brain areas, including the occipital lobe (involved primarily in visual processing), the parietal lobe (involved mainly in movement, orientation, calculation, and some types of recognition), and the brain stem (often referred to as the reptilian brain because of its similarity to the entire brain of a reptile—responsible for much involuntary movement and vital bodily functioning, such as heartbeat, breathing, and temperature).

- The male brain is set to renew, recharge, and reorient itself between tasks by moving to what neurologist Ruben Gur has called a "rest state."[16] The boy in the back of the classroom whose eyes are drooping, his mind ready to doze off, may have entered a neural rest state. The man zoning out in front of the television after a long day at work is recharging his brain by entering a neural rest state; so too the grandfather sitting in his fishing boat for hours, content but unstimulated. The rest state, which MRIs have now discovered to be essential to male brain activity, can create big problems in a classroom. Boys make up the vast majority of students who drift off without completing assignments, who stop taking notes or fall asleep during a lecture, and even who begin to tap pencils or fidget in order to self-stimulate (and thus keep themselves awake and learning).

With greater blood flow in the brain, girls and women tend to recharge and reorient neural focus without pronounced rest states; thus a girl can be bored with a lesson but nonetheless keep her eyes open and take notes. As Ruben Gur has observed, "In the resting female brain, we find just as much neural activity as in the male brain that is solving problems." The female brain, in other words, doesn't really go to a rest state in the way the male does. Female blood flow even during brain rest is very active. Male blood flow during a rest state is not.

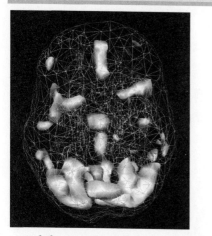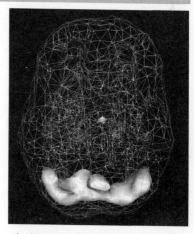

At left, scan of a girl's brain. At right, scan of a boy's brain. Both are at rest. Note significantly greater activity in the female brain.
Brain scans courtesy of Dr. Daniel Amen. Used by permission.

through space than by the monotony of words. If a teacher uses a lot of words, the male brain is more likely than the female to get bored, drift, sleep, fidget. This is just one difference.

Boys and the Reading and Writing Gap

These biological tendencies are just the tip of the iceberg, yet can immediately help teachers and parents understand a number of things they've observed in homes and classrooms. First and foremost, we can understand why girls are an average of a year to a year and a half ahead of boys in reading and writing, with the gap extending from early childhood throughout school life, according to the U.S. Department of Education, the Ministry of Education in Canada, and the OECD study of thirty-five other industrialized countries (as noted in Chapter One). Because boys' brains are not as naturally well suited, on average, for classrooms that emphasize reading, writing, and complex word making, any culture that relies greatly on those techniques is set up for problems with a number of boys and young men. With more areas of the female brain devoted to verbal functioning, sensory memory, sitting still, listening, tonality, and neural cross-talk, the complexities of reading and writing come easier, on average, to the female brain than to the male.

The Mismatch Between Boys and Conventional Education

We've hinted at it already, but now, with the actual nature of the male brain in mind, parents and educators can confront a crucial mismatch between how our boys learn naturally and how many of our schools are set up.

If you think about how many boys are getting bad grades, failing tests, not performing in class, becoming discipline problems—and if you look beyond the reading and writing gap, which itself is instructive—you might notice other key elements of male nature that are now a mismatch with conventional schooling.

- Boys who were once schooled in various bonding and instructional methods—apprenticeships, tutoring, action, and practice through works of the hand—are now learning through one primary method—verbal learning groups—and without physical movement (sitting in chairs).

- Daily learning on farms, in marketplaces, on journeys has nearly disappeared; increasingly, books fill little hands.
- Fidgeting and physical movement, once a show of energy, vitality, and willingness to move to wherever learning needed to take place, have become liabilities.

The image of a schoolchild as someone sitting and reading has become the poster image for education, especially in the last fifty years. This is not a bad image, but it is an incomplete match with the way the minds of many of our boys work. Perhaps you have seen the mismatch in your own homes and schools: boys struggling to learn in the ways provided for them, teachers and families becoming frustrated, boys being labeled "difficult" or "failures" and becoming morose with self-doubt.

In a recent Gurian Institute training, material on boy energy and the male brain led to a spirited discussion about the issues our sons face. A teacher raised a key question—a question that is raised in nearly every setting in which the nature-based material is presented: "Should we keep trying to change the boys and their energy, or should we change the educational system they find themselves in?" Another teacher said, "Is this just a pedagogical issue, or are we now facing a moral one?"

These are questions each of us must now answer, armed as we are with scientific information about the nature of our sons.

If you agree with the material in Chapter One—that though many boys are doing quite well, the male gender today is nonetheless facing a crisis in education—and if you agree that the new sciences can show us how our boys really learn—a way that is mismatched with many of the tenets of contemporary conventional education—then you may already be inspired to make a personal, and therefore civil, decision about whether the boys dropping out, the boys getting failing grades, the boys in line at the nurse's office for their daily dose of Ritalin, the boys who feel they are defective as learners now represent a moral issue our civilization must face.

Kathy and I believe that every time a teacher wonders why the boys are "trouble in the classroom," he or she is asking a moral question. Every time the faculty lounge becomes a place of conversation about why boys are bringing down standardized test scores, the teachers are asking the same question. When a mother and father agonize over whether to put their son on medication, they are asking the question. Among our children themselves, the question is silently resounding, as the kids who are having trouble learning their lessons look at others who learn so very well.

"Should we keep trying to change our boys, or should we change the educational system in which they are now taught?"

In your home, school, and community, your answer to this question will require you, your parent-led team, and your school to decide what parts of nature, nurture, and culture can and should be changed, and what parts can't and shouldn't. You'll be tacitly—or directly—asking these questions:

- To what extent is male nature—the male brain—plastic enough to be changed to fit the industrial classroom?
- To the extent it is, how do we better effect change than we are now doing, so that boys no longer get most of the failing grades?
- To the extent it is not, how can our educational system change to accommodate the male brain so that we can gain the positive results we all want for our sons?

I hope you'll be intrigued and moved to action by the answers to these questions that follow in the next few pages. The science-based logic in our answers constitutes a step two in solving the crisis we face today.

Confronting an Educational Myth

Janice Conway, a mother of three sons, wrote us as follows:

> I was an English teacher and a school counselor before I retired. I raised all my boys the same way, reading to them from day one, talk-

ing to them, hugging and nurturing them. It was a big priority for me to make sure I raised sensitive sons, boys who would love reading, boys who could cry and not worry about masculine stereotypes, boys who would become talkative, gentle husbands.

My sons have turned out great, but not exactly how I planned. One of them is indeed the "nurturing" type. He's a journalist, actually, so he followed a little bit in my footsteps, in regards to his love of reading. When he was a little boy he was always a good reader. My other two sons, however, did only what they had to do to get by in English. At first, this shocked me. No matter what I did, they seemed to resist their "English teacher Mom." Neither of them ended up being much of a talker, either, at least where feelings are concerned.

I've thought about my boys a lot, especially as I keep up with the research on the brain. I know a parent and a school can have a lot of influence on a child, but I wonder what *kind* of influence. The human brain is plastic, I know, but that doesn't necessarily mean it's going to mold into what the school or I may think we want at any given time. My boys' schools and I did our best to make these boys turn out how we wanted them to turn out, but something inside them resisted us. Maybe we don't have the influence on a child's mind we think we have—maybe our influence is something else. My sons have definitely made me rethink the role of schools and parents in making boys learn a certain way.

Janice's point of view is crucial as we take a next step in confronting how our educational system, indeed our cultural imagery as a whole, conceptualizes the minds of our sons. Her intuition that certain aspects of the brain might be "resistant" or impermeable to cultural influence is worth thinking about. It is the same intuition the teachers at the workshop had when they asked, "Can we change our boys?" and "Should we?"

Can We Change Our Boys?

Janice, like the rest of us, was trained by our culture to believe in the *gender plasticity* of a child's brain—the idea that a child's brain is a tabula rasa, or blank slate, which gains its gender only through socialization influences. From this idea came the idea that because gender is social-ized, not inborn, a boy's (or girl's) brain could be taught successfully in whatever way was theoretically determined to fit the teaching needs of industry-based educational institutions.

When Janice considered how her sons turned out, she was called to reassess her views. She realized that there were important things about them that she hadn't been able to mold or shape, things the schools were also unable to alter in the boys.

Janice ultimately came to her conclusions about the male brain through maternal and professional intuition, and also through the brain research we are sharing with you in this book. Having the PET, MRI, and SPECT scans of the brain is a great boon for those of us who explore the moral aspects of male educational distress today and want to provide the best learning modalities for the nature of boys.

What's exciting about this is that Janice no longer has to wonder if her intuition is correct. The scans of the brain now show just how nat-ural boy energy is. Armed with these scans, Janice and all of us can press our educational culture to change not the boys, but rather the *myth of gender plasticity* under which we labor against our sons' natural energy and learning style.

Our civilization can now see plainly and understand fully how gender—maleness and femaleness—happens in the brain, and can put to rest the idea that humans can, should, or need to reengineer the brain into what-ever our recent educational institutions or ideologies want it to be.

How Gender *Really* Happens in the Brain

In reality, human nature hardwires gender into our brains in three biolog-ical stages. The first stage has been clarified by genetics research, the sec-ond by endocrinological research, and the third by psychosocial research.[17]

Stage 1. Chromosome markers for gender are included in the genomes of girls and boys at the time of conception. Researchers at UCLA have identified chromosome markers—built into the fetal brain—for the development of a male and female.

Stage 2. These chromosome markers compel surges of male and female hormones in the womb that format XX brains to be female and XY brains to be male. In-utero bombardment of hormones into the brain occurs with intense frequency between the second and fifth month of gestation. Researchers at various universities around the world, including the University of London, McMaster University in Canada, UCLA, and the University of Pennsylvania, can now trace the development of gender in the fetal brain via bombardments of testosterone and other hormones.

Stage 3. The child is born a boy or girl, sending nonverbal and then verbal cues to parents, the nurturing community, and the larger culture. These cues are biological cues—based in the child's genetics and hardwiring. Mom, dad, and extended family, then teachers, schools, and community members like you, like us, like Janice, read the male and female signals, cues, and characteristics. These signals and readings are now being visually traced through SPECT and PET scan research in attachment theory, conducted in many parts of the world, including the University of Denver and Harvard University.

It's important to remember that none of these researchers is involved in a nature *versus* nurture framework. All of this research recognizes the *vast interplay* between genetic, hormonal, neural, and social forces.

All of the researchers also recognize that maleness and femaleness are things we start out with—we are born with them. Although it was popular thirty years ago to believe otherwise, scientific research in our era has put to rest the idea that gender is completely a matter of nurture. Gender is inborn and then it becomes socialized by cultures.

Why is the human genome, brain, and bonding system set up to be male and female by nature? No researcher can be completely sure. People with a religious base for understanding human nature say, "This is how God created us." The more science-based work in evolutionary biology suggests that the most probable cause for our male-female brain difference lies in the millions of years of human evolution, during which humans primarily hunted and gathered.

Because males mainly hunted, they needed to develop a more spatial-mechanical brain. They needed to see well, but did not need fine-detail sensory awareness as much as females, who cared for offspring. The male brain was wired, therefore, for more physical movement—with more blood flow in the brain stem than the female brain has—but for less verbal input and output. (Words weren't needed much during the hunt.)

Whether you choose a religious or scientific explanation, the new brain technologies allow us to see the differences for ourselves between male and female in the brain. And even if you don't have PET scan equipment in your living room—none of us do!—you can still see what the geneticists, biologists, and sociologists are getting at.

The Nature of Boys and Girls in Your Home

To bring the chromosomal and hormonal hardwiring out of technical science and into your own life experience, think for a moment about your own sons. Did you notice something hardwired in them from early on? Although there is, of course, immense variety in all children—there is no single "boy" or "girl" stereotype—did you notice any of the points listed in the next Did You Know? box?

Ending the Myth of Gender Plasticity and Supporting the Way Boys *Actually* Learn

Given the biological and social evidence of male-female brain difference, can a nurturing community, a school, a family, a culture make a boy change the gender of his brain? Can a mom like Janice, by just talking to or reading to an average little boy, force his verbal centers to be like an average girl's? Should a school compel a boy to become the kind of learner it has decided will be "easiest to teach"?

Where do you stand on these questions? The new sciences now challenge all of us—moms, dads, grandparents, teachers, policymakers—to come to an informed conclusion about the relationship between a boy's nature, his nurtured life, and his cultural experience. We spend only a

??? Did You Know? ???

- As of four days of age, girls tend to spend twice as much time as boys maintaining eye contact with adults. Bonding chemistry and the visual cortex of boys and girls already differ at four days old.
- By four months of age, boys are less likely than girls to distinguish between who is a known individual and who is a stranger. Memory centers as well as spatial-mechanical pathways already work differently in boys and girls. Male babies are in general more inclined than female babies to spend more time during a day looking at objects moving in space—for instance, mobiles hung from a ceiling. Girls, in contrast, are more likely to turn their gaze immediately to their caregivers.
- Infant girls also pay closer attention to the words of caregivers. Verbal centers are developing in the female brain more quickly than in the male.
- Little boys, when given dolls to play with, more often than girls pull the heads off, hit them against a table, throw them in the air, or generally engage in some kind of physical, kinesthetic, or spatial play with the dolls. Girls, in contrast, from very early in life, begin to use words with the doll. Given how much earlier the female centers for verbal communication develop in the brain, this comes as no surprise. Because of higher levels of oxytocin, girls form bonds with objects that boys merely use as physical learning tools.[18]

few years in a close, day-to-day supervisory relationship with our children; how do we want to spend those years? What kind of care do we want to give to their very human nature, their wonderful minds?

Here's our position: the new scientific research merits concluding that although all children are unique and individual, and although everyone is constantly learning new skills and developing new modes of communication, we believe that *the gender of the human brain is not plastic, not a new skill to be learned, not a new mode of communication.* It is as hard-wired into the brain as a person's genetic personality. In the same way that you cannot change an introvert into an extrovert, you cannot change the brain of a boy into the brain of a girl.

The idea that not all elements of the brain are plastic—especially not gender—is very important to our dialogue about the state of boyhood in education. Our educational system has bought into the idea of "over-all neural plasticity." Because of this mythical concept of the brain as a magical, changing device, very few academic institutions train teachers in the neural sciences of gender. This aspect of human development is ignored, and young teachers, like young parents, are taught that being a "boy" or a "girl" is culturally insignificant in education, that basically all kids learn the same way and can be educated in a way that ensures gender-exclusive, predictable results.

Research from the new gender and brain sciences begs us to move beyond this myth. This move constitutes a second major step toward solving the crisis of male education. As this step two finds its way into schools of education, young teachers will be shown PET scans, SPECT scans, and MRIs of the male and female brain and be trained to under-stand the gender reality we all experience.

You as an individual—and your school as a collective—can become a leader in making this happen. Because our biological sciences are now able to use PET scans, MRIs, and other tests, we can now discern how gender is marked into our genomes from millions of years of human development and still lights up the individual brains of boys and girls. You can bring this information to your home, schools, social policies, and universities and colleges. You can help your community notice how tough the myth of gender plasticity is making life for our sons. When you notice males in educational distress, you can point out that we are creating for our sons an educational system not well suited to certain aspects of their brain; a system that claims they are defective, disordered, or incorrigible because they can't learn; a system that insists that they should be able to change—even further, that their inability to change is yet another flaw in their character as males, one that supposedly requires medication.

If our civilization continues to buy in to the myth of gender plasticity, larger numbers of our sons will continue to do poorly in school. They will emerge from years of waste and failure without the normal development and skills we've all assumed for years that they would acquire, and, during this entire struggle and conflict, they will continue to frustrate us by "not changing."

A Boy-Friendly Model for Protecting the Minds of Boys

If you agree with our argument that the current educational system often fails to accommodate the hardwiring of boys' brains and does not provide them with an appropriate system of learning; and if you agree that our homes and schools should do less to try to change our boys and more to help them learn naturally, then you can become an ambassador for boys, a protector of their minds. As an ambassador you'll join us, not in trying to alter the nature of boys or girls, but instead in working toward these two goals:

1. *Expression and development of the natural self of the child.* The child's genetic self is most important to his or her learning, and those who aid the child are charged with helping that self become fully expressive and developed within the frameworks of a humane society.
2. *Compensation for areas of inherent disadvantage or fragility.* These areas of disadvantage emerge for any child because of particular genetic or environmentally caused weaknesses in his or her learning brain or because the child as an individual carries learning characteristics that don't fit the mass.

Part Two of this book begins a journey of expression and compensation that delineates specifically how to accomplish these two goals. As we present this information to you, we'll avoid joining with any ideologies that measure success of the child's education by *measuring significant alteration* of the child's mind, whatever part of the gender-brain continuum the child is on. We believe that to base a child's education on the hope of altering a brain's inherent method of self-development is an affront to freedom and ultimately leads to suppression or disengagement of the child's true self and potential for success.

A child who expresses himself and learns to compensate for weaknesses is following one of the most natural instincts of our species: to *adapt*. We as adults protect the minds of children when we help the children adapt, using their own natural skills and talents, to the needs of a society. We don't protect their minds by putting a generation of school-boys on drugs or watching them gradually fail.

Breaking down the myth of gender plasticity will not be easy, just as step one—the building of a parent-led team—is not necessarily a simple thing to accomplish. But adapting the home and the school to fit our sons' needs is the best future for human education. What we've done to help our girls is proof of this.

Very inspiring in our work with boys is our society's success with girls. Our culture has, in a few decades, successfully confronted a great deal of the patriarchal, sexist, and industrial system that was hurting girls, and improved the lives of girls and women. There's still a ways to go, but there has been substantial change. And in this process, our culture did not force girls' brains or nature to change in order for them to succeed in our educational system. All of us came together to change the system in order to fit girls.

Specifically, we brought more verbal functioning to our math and science classes, trained teachers to use more writing and group conversation in teaching those subjects, changed our testing of those subjects to include more explanative and discursive essay answers, and developed new ways to encourage our girls at home that fit their natural need for verbal encouragement.

The proof of our success with girls is measurable today: the industrialized world has closed the female-to-male math and science gap in our schools. Girls now receive grades as good as and better than boys in these classes. In California, girls are now actually outperforming boys in math and science. As we noted earlier, girls are no longer short-changed in many schools—they are high performers. The changes we made to our educational system worked!

Changing our educational system to help boys will admittedly be harder, because the changes that have been made to help our daughters will actually make boys' education more problematic. Furthermore, in our consideration of girls' needs, we never had to fight the myth of gender plasticity—we never said, "Our girls are defective." We always said, "The system is defective." Changing the system for our boys can be done (without hurting our girls), and it must be.

Becoming Practical

This chapter—indeed this whole book—could not have been written in its present form in the 1980s. Only after completing twenty years of brain research, and noticing significant differences in the way the brains and bodies of girls and boys learn differently, could we show how our educational system is set up to handle boy energy so incompletely. Only after twenty years of tracking statistics and studies on the distresses our males are experiencing in school can we finally awaken to what is happening to our sons in the educational system, both the positives and the negatives—and develop theories and programs that protect boys.

If the 1990s were the decade of the girl, perhaps this present decade will be the decade of the boy. We can accomplish this without disenfranchising girls, as you'll see in the remaining chapters of this book. These chapters constitute a practical blueprint for social change—a new way of supporting, nurturing, protecting, and educating boys. Each of these remaining chapters discusses new research about the male brain, as well as techniques for helping boys' minds grow and learn. The chapters provide strategies and methodologies for setting up homes and school environments to handle boy energy and teach boys successfully. They take on specific curricular challenges, such as reading and writing. They also look at the wide variety of boys—from the nonathletic to the athletic, the great readers to the weak readers, the math geniuses to the math-challenged.

Boys and girls are different from each other, but each boy is an individual, too. Kathy and I hope you'll find every boy cared for in some practical way in the remaining pages of this book. We hope you'll join us in beginning a journey of practical forward steps right inside your home, where a boy's education begins.

Starting Boys Out in Boy-Friendly Learning Environments

Helping Boys Learn Before
They Begin School

Parents are our children's first teachers. In the heart of every parent
is the desire to prepare children for school. In the heart of every
teacher is the hope that parents will follow that desire.

—MARIA MONTESSORI

MARSHA AND STEPHEN LIVE IN COLORADO SPRINGS, WHERE THEY ARE BOTH PRO-
fessionals in the computer industry. They have three adolescent sons—
Robert, eighteen, Adam seventeen, and Josh fifteen—each of whom was
part of a family experiment years ago. From the time of Robert's birth,
Marsha and Stephen committed to preparing all their children to love
learning by instituting a family tradition of family reading time. It lasted
one half hour, every evening (growing to one hour as the boys became
school age). Whether lying as infants against mom or dad's chest, or sitting as toddlers against their sides, the boys enjoyed the sounds of language and the sight of pictures in *Good Night, Moon* or *Hope for the
Flowers*.

As Marsha likes to say, "We sat together on the couch very happily.
But my Lord did those boys fidget!"

Marsha and Stephen noticed that Robert was the first to stop sitting still. "When he was maybe a year-and-a-half or so," Marsha observed,
"he seemed to be getting bored with reading."

"We really wanted the quality time as a family tradition," Stephen remembers. "But it got difficult, especially when Adam started copying Robert."

There were pillow throwing, balls bouncing off walls, lots of restlessness. Then the complaining began. Robert and Adam became defiant and resistant to settling down and focusing on the book and the family time. They were now six and four, Josh now three. What had happened to the earlier happiness? Thinking that this family tradition would need to die out—frustrated by the tension of getting the boys to sit still and listen (or, in Robert's case, read more than a short picture book before wanting to watch television), Marsha and Stephen nearly gave up.

But during this time, Stephen's father, Hank, came for a visit. Hank said, "You know, Stephen was the same way when his mom used to read to him. I remember one time he was trying so hard to keep his hands folded in front of him like he was at a school desk, but they kept squirming loose like they had a life of their own, so he tried sitting on them. Finally, Claire decided to just let him move around. After that, he could listen well enough."

Stephen did not remember this experience, of course, but for both Marsha and Stephen, the idea rang true.

"Dad was right. When we looked at what was happening, we could see that at one time or another, one of those little guys just couldn't stop moving around. Once Dad said it, we kind of went 'Duh!'"

Marsha and Stephen immediately modified their valuable family tradition. They told their sons that they could do other things while they were being read to—play with Legos, draw pictures, squeeze a ball, or fidget with a toy while they sat in a chair or lay on the floor. The family reading time got back on track after this adaptation.

Marsha and Stephen are quite proud of this family learning ritual, even now that their sons have nearly grown. Marsha said:

Whether my boys were just listening when they were little or doing the actual reading aloud when they got older, these years of stories affected their lives. They modeled after the stories in their play, even conversation. When we talked the next day about what was happening in the story line, they contributed. As we graduated to longer and longer books, they remembered the ideas and images. We're talking about complex stories here, books like *The Fellowship of the Ring*. When the Lord of the Rings movies came out, we went together as a family. It was great! Stephen and I are really glad we made this happen in our kids' lives. We're especially glad we got over the tough time, and found the right way to make it work for them as little boys.

As both Stephen and Marsha describe it, their sons turned out to be "themselves, not something we tried to make them." They developed their own selves, and live as young men in the world. All the boys still like to move around; they fidget; they like video games. The evening ritual didn't change the natural personality or brain structure of these male children. But it was a primary activity within a parent-led team that prepared the boys to learn before they entered the school system. It is the kind of activity that we will call attention to in this chapter as we detail what a boy needs before he enters school in order to be prepared for its rigors.

Protecting the Learning Potential of a Young Brain

As the leaders of a learning team, Marsha and Stephen discovered what studies of the neurology of the learning brain have now proven around the world: young children learn best *within an attachment system that emphasizes learning.*[1] All children have brains that are made for learning—which is the neural action of changing sensory experience into perception and expression. All human brains can learn no matter how much they suffer abuse, neglect, starvation, malnutrition, or alienation. The human brain is the only part of nature that constantly thinks about itself. It is amazing, indeed, and like the Energizer Bunny, it keeps on going.

At the same time, the brain, like any other organ, has a range of success and failure in its operation. Certain stimulations enhance its perception and expression toward the high end of the success spectrum; a lack of those stimulations can move its learning toward the lower end. Marsha and Stephen ensured that their children would be in the middle of the success spectrum just by being loving, caring parents. At the same time, they moved their sons' learning capacities toward the high end of the learning success spectrum because of the learning ritual that grew from that love.

If we could have been a proverbial fly on the wall in this family's home (this fly would, of course, need X-ray vision!), we'd have noticed that throughout the regular reading ritual each evening, the sounds of a broad variety of words helped grow neural pathways for language connections in the frontal lobes of the three boys. These pathways would have grown anyway—but they likely grew more quickly and efficiently because of the learning ritual. The pictures in the books linked visual images in the right hemisphere of their brains with words in the left, building pathways in the visual cortex and the memory-storing hippocampus—even better than fast-moving TV images ever could.

As X-ray-vision flies on the wall, we can look into the minds of any boys—indeed, any children—who spend their time in homes and schools that emphasize attachment, bonding, and appropriate learning stimulation. We will see that these homes and schools are affecting the development of the corpus callosum, hippocampus, frontal lobe, and all the other parts of the brain that are crucial for enhanced learning success.

So let's consider how we can enhance a boy's educational experience through bonding, attachment, and the rituals of love in a home and family.

Building Bonding and Attachment

"When they are infants, toddlers, and preschoolers," writes Betsy Flagler, a preschool teacher in Davison, North Carolina, "each child is reaching out toward learning, and all of us who care for these children hold the child's future in our hands." Every parent has certainly sensed this—how profound is our adult responsibility for the child's future; how little time we actually have, just a few years, to set the right foundation for the love of learning.

Betsy notes, "In our Davison preschool, most of our problem areas occur with the boys. We're trying to address this with parents' help because parents are these kids' first teachers. They are the first teachers with whom the little guy bonds and learns."

Betsy's preschool emphasizes parental bonds in the learning process because new research shows how crucial it is for children to gain a secure base for learning by having a secure base of bonding and attachment in the home. Many people consider secure bonds and attachments as being important for physical and emotional development, but don't realize how important they are for building a *learning brain,* too.

Bonding is the powerful emotional connection between parent and child that begins from the first moment they see each other, touch each other, become close and intimate. *Attachment* is the actual ongoing process of affectionate caregiving that nurtures the instinctual bond throughout a lifetime.

With few exceptions, parents have a powerful yearning to enjoy bonding and attachment. They want to feel the wonderful intimacy between parent and child, and they want to create relationships, safety, and homes that motivate and encourage the emotional, cognitive, and physical health of the child. In feeling this bond, they usually—instinctually—set up a future of optimal learning for their children by trying to create a well-organized and secure *attachment system.* This attachment system involves not just one person and one bond but a number of individuals—what we've called a parent-led team—that cares for the developing child.

Over the last thirty years, attachment studies at the University of Minnesota, Harvard University, Oxford University, and elsewhere agree that well-attached children, raised in secure attachment systems, are most likely to have positive self-esteem, enjoy good relationships with others, develop a conscience, be curious and confident, and, most important for our purposes in this book, learn more successfully.[2] Children with secure attachments are more likely to make learning gains for a biological reason: *the organic mechanisms in the brain by which the brain learns require secure attachment in order to grow fully.*

Bonding and attachment affect the very organization of the child's nervous system, promoting or diminishing healthy emotional, social, and intellectual development. When a child experiences inadequate bonding and attachment, impairment has been shown in the corpus callosum. This can cause children trouble in regulating their emotions, developing cause-and-effect thinking processes, and enjoying a good sense of self during later school years.

Developing an Attachment Plan

Given this brain research, we encourage parents and members of parent-led teams to develop an *attachment plan* for a child's first years of life. It is a conscious way of focusing families on what attachment system they can best develop—through their individual talents, proclivities, and personalities—to nurture the learning brain of the child.

The development of an attachment plan begins, of course, in a parent enjoying (and being supported in) his or her bond with the child. But in addition to that primary attachment is the importance of attachments with parent-led team members from the extended family, childcare community, and networks of friends. Often, busy parents today find that they must consciously guide their family members, friends, and other professionals in bonding with their child. This is especially important for single-parent families. In our long ago past, it wasn't as necessary for professionals to coach family members in how to take conscious steps toward long-term bonding between the child and the parent-led family team. Attachment systems were inherently tribal, and most often there were already enough people around young children (even when the mother died in childbirth) with whom the child could bond and attach. Times have changed. Today we still must ensure the physical survival of our children; we still have to keep our children safe and loved; *and* we've got to pay special attention to building the attachment systems that help grow the brains of our children so that they can become strong, successful learners. Our schools and social technologies are so stressful today that we need to make sure our kids have not just one parent around them to help their brains grow to full potential, but a number of "first teachers."

This is the first major use of the parent-led learning team we'll explore together in this book. If you are a birth parent or adoptive parent of an upcoming baby, we hope you're able to meet with your parent-led team members even before the child is born in order to determine how each team member will contribute to the child's healthy attachments and consequent brain development. In our ancestors' lives, this kind of meeting occurred normally—godparents were decided on among the ancient Christians and even, in many cases, among the ancient Jews. These days many of us still arrange for godparents before or just after the birth of our children, and we can also make an attachment plan for the first five years of a child's life by talking with the three or four other key people who will give him love and attention. If you are in the process of having a baby, you can make a list right away of three to five people you will call this week in order to "sign them up" for the duty (and privilege) of attaching their brains, bodies, and souls to the brain, body, and soul of your new child. And if you already have children, such a team can be formed at any time.

Avoiding an Attachment Drop

Part of making an attachment plan is deciding how time spent with the child will be allocated and fulfilled. If both parents are planning on working eight- to ten-hour days, for instance, there is risk of an "attachment drop" for the child.

If both parents in your home are out of the house working all day, it's dangerous not to add two parallel members to the parent-led team, whether nannies, godmothers, grandparents who live close, or other professionals, who can fill the space and time of attachment with the child when you know you're not going to be around. If the boy is going to be placed in day care within the first few months of infancy, it's also crucial that your parent-led team find day-care providers who share your desire to create the best environment for bonding, attachment, and, ultimately, learning.

We'll go into day-care standards in a lot more detail in Chapter Four, but let us say here that as you begin to look at the best place for your infant son, you might hold the day-care facility to the "touch standard." This is a science-based attachment standard. It asks you to make sure that the professionals at the day-care facility know that a two-month-old infant must be touched, must be physically held against the body for two to four hours per day—not only to feel warm and secure but in order for natural brain development to come to full fruition.

So when you visit the day-care facility, glance around to see if its staffing pattern is set up for this amount of physical touch of infants. Are infants crying unattended in cribs throughout your visit, or are they being picked up and held?

The Positive Legacy of Good Touch

When you make your attachment plan, you might find yourself wanting to get a little "obsessed" with good touch. Obviously, the phrase *good touch* is meant here as the counterpart to the kind of bad touch from which we are vigilant to protect our children. Kathy and I specifically coach parents and teachers about the attachment and brain benefits of good touch because in our cultural vigilance against bad touch, we are losing some of the importance of good touch.

A teacher recently told me, "Our principal is getting so worried about this issue that she told us to avoid touching the opposite-sex child at all, even with pats on the back." Human touch has become problematic in our culture, yet good human touch is a great deal of what helps the brain love, grow, and learn in its early years.

Allan N. Schore, a researcher-professor at UCLA, is one of the first attachment specialists to use PET and SPECT scans to notice what happens to infants who don't get enough touch.[3] He has noticed that the human brain, even from within the womb, is already learning a lot. While in the womb and in its infancy, however, a child isn't learning as much by sight (eyes haven't opened yet or don't see yet as well as they will) as he or she is by touch vibration. If you think about it, this makes a lot of sense: even the sounds of a parent's individual words are auditory vibrations— not yet understandable language. They "touch" the child's ear as vibrations; the child doesn't yet hear them as meaningful words.

Dr. Schore has pointed out that in infancy, a child's greatest initial brain growth occurs in response to touch. The boy's skin and touch receptors are incredibly sensitive, sending direct signals to the brain, and the child longs to be held, stroked, hugged. Thus pediatric neurologists like Dr. Schore want all of us to hold our babies even more than many of us do.

If you again think about our ancestors, ensuring good touch and good brain development was less difficult in the past. Like the development of attachment systems, touch attachment came more naturally to many human societies before the Industrial Revolution. Moms and grandmas and aunties who provided child care did so by holding their babies on their hips or carrying them on their backs, chests, or sides while they worked in fields or markets all day. In our busy world today, moms, dads, and other caregivers love their kids just as much as our ancestors did, but we often work away from children, so we can't hold them as much.

This can become difficult or even dangerous for our kids. When we look at the emotional difficulties many of our children have today, and we match those to their learning difficulties, we are being cautioned by attachment neurologists to remember where some of this alienation and discomfort begins for a child: in his brain, which might not have enjoyed the value of enough touch in those first few years of life. Attachment specialists, such as Robin Carr-Morse in her book *Ghosts from the Nursery,* have pointed out a new area of research that now has begun to link birth-to-three attachment issues with criminality and lower performance in learning.[4] Like so much of the new brain research, these links between attachment and learning have a gender component.

Boys' Special Attachment Issues

Although lack of touch and lack of secure attachment are bad for all kids, there's a difference in how boys' and girls' brains react to a lack of attachment. For girls, incidents of anorexia, bulimia, and depression are higher among children who experienced the lack of attachment during childhood. For boys, incidents of violence and learning disorders are higher in the same circumstances. For infant boys, there is an additional learning disadvantage. Boys, on average, not only use fewer words as infants and toddlers than do girls, but infant pediatric specialist T. Barry Brazelton has also pointed out this interesting fact: boys don't hold eye contact with caregivers as long as girls. They are thus more "set up" for lack of touch, holding, and physical attachment.

If you think about it, his point makes sense. Boys tend to fidget and pull away more than girls, anxious to explore the world of things. This may make caregivers of boys inherently less likely to hold and touch boys for as long as they do girls. This creates a subtle male disadvantage in the area of bonding, attachment, and touch that can later affect learning. An infant boy may pull away, fidget, and break eye contact—but he still needs lots of touch and embrace.

Nancy Bayley's research at UCLA showed that for boys more than girls there is indeed a direct link to learning difficulties when this early childhood touch and attachment don't occur.[5] In her study, boys who experienced insecure attachment as infants tested out lower in adolescent intellectual skills than girls who did not receive secure attachment. Although girls can end up with severe problems or diseases, the effect of lack of early attachment is harsher on the "learning brains" of boys. This is another example of a male-female brain difference that does not negate female vulnerability but can now bring to light male vulnerability.

Ten Strategies to Promote Attachment

In all this, the bottom line lies in you and your parent-led team becoming involved in bonding, attachment, and good touch with your infant. Here are ten practical strategies you can apply immediately with young boys, beginning in their earliest days of life. They are like a circle of embrace for a child's growing brain. The Gurian Institute has developed this model in conjunction with Pat Crum, the director of the Family Nurturing Center of Michigan.[6]

1. *Bursts of attention.* Offer your son five long bursts—many minutes at a time—and many shorter, intermittent periods of undivided attention throughout every day.
2. *Lots of affirmation.* Notice and support your son's efforts and accomplishments verbally and, when appropriate, with other rewards, including physical hugs.

3. *Verbal mirroring.* Describe in words back to your son what he is doing. "I like how you just put that book on the shelf." Listen carefully to your toddler son's words as he produces them and then repeat back to him what he says. "You're right, that is a big car."

4. *Physical play.* Because playtime is organic learning time for body and brain, engage in play with your son a number of times per day.

5. *Leadership.* In work and play relationships, let your boy take the lead as much as you lead him. Imitate him, playing follow the leader. Let him imitate you.

6. *Enthusiasm.* Infuse your interaction with joy, enthusiasm, and the pleasure of being together. Find things to do that inspire your son's enthusiasm and joy. The feeling of joy is often directed through the temporal lobe of the brain, and development of that lobe helps a great deal with later enthusiasm for learning.

7. *Predictability.* Provide consistent, predictable structure and clear limits (more on this later). For infants and toddlers, predictability and consistency promote secure attachment.

8. *Self-management.* Implement behavior management strategies that are based on your son's developmental stage rather than a later or earlier stage. Expecting your son at three to "use his words" when he's angry will, almost every time, be developmentally inappropriate. He may just need to throw a tantrum (in a safe place), hitting the floor with his fists until he releases his energy.

9. *Choice making.* Teach your son to make acceptable choices. Making the right choices builds that crucial learning center in the brain—the frontal lobe. Do as little "for" the boy as you can, making him do as much for himself as he can.

10. *Appropriate discipline.* Avoid behavior management strategies designed to frighten your little son. For infants, yelling, name-calling, and spanking are hurtful and rarely helpful to brain development. Until eighteen months old, your son's brain is not developed enough to understand what an

authoritarian parent is really getting at. All he learns from inappropriate discipline is that he's a failure.

The Importance of Emotions in a Boy's Early Education

In exploring the importance of bonding and attachment systems in a boy's life up to this point, we've looked at the people and the plan of action a boy needs in order to protect his early brain development. We've noted the scientific link between human love and human education. We've noticed how crucial it is today that parents and their teams remain vigilant about human touch. We've gotten down to some nitty-gritty ways to accomplish daily attachment. We've put all this in the context of setting a good foundation for a boy's later learning in school and the world. What we haven't overtly mentioned is the word *emotions*. Yet—it's emotions that we're talking about, so let's look at your son's early emotions for just a moment.

Boys are very emotional creatures, in their own way. Even though, by nature, they may not experience their emotions the same way girls do, often more indirect or delayed in processing them, boys are indeed very sensitive in their reactions and feelings to everything around them.

Throughout the chapters of this book, we'll look at boys' emotional lives from different angles—especially concentrating on how their emotions and their learning blend together. We'll note how what a boy is feeling at a given moment during his learning experience will affect his ability to learn. We'll look at how to develop emotional literacy in boys.

In this chapter, we'll begin this exploration by looking at the "good stress" and "bad stress" experiences our little boys are having as they are emotionally affected by their exploration of life and the world.

The Pitfalls of a "Bad Stress" Home

Susan, a mother of two, shared this story with Kathy during a workshop in Florida. When her son Jake was just over a year old and starting to walk, she put some of his toys on the coffee table in the living room so he could play with them while she worked in the kitchen nearby. There were other items on the coffee table (and on nearby end tables) that Susan didn't want him to touch—they were collectibles, lamps, and other breakables. Susan told Jake that he couldn't touch the breakable items but could touch his own toys.

Unfortunately, this whole affair became an emotional roller coaster for Susan and Jake. Quite often Jake would "fail" at his task—he would try to touch and hold the wrong items, the valuable and fragile stuff. Susan would have to tell him *No!* Then Jake would become frustrated or intimidated. Susan would calm him, talk to him, even let him throw a tantrum. Sometimes she put him in time-out.

Clearly it was not working to tell Jake not to touch certain items but to go ahead and touch certain other items—he had not reached the developmental stage to understand the difference. After speaking with another slightly more experienced mom, Susan decided to change tacks. Now, to make sure that her son couldn't fail at this learning exercise, Susan made sure that no breakable or irreplaceable items sat within Jake's reach, only things she didn't worry about, which she left on the coffee table for him to bang together however he wanted. As a young parent—like so many of us were at one time or another!—Susan had to adapt to the way her child was trying to learn. She was compelled to make the adaptation because she, as a well-attached parent, could see that her son was getting into too many "bad stress" situations under the present circumstances.

The Rewards of a "Good Stress" Home

Making successful, developmentally appropriate choices creates good stress in the child's learning brain. Setting up this kind of successful choice compels tissue in the cerebral cortex, especially the frontal lobe, to grow. When children's brains are under bad stress—when children feel like failures or are traumatized physically—they may learn a coping or survival skill, such as how to escape, how to stop touching objects in the living room, or how to appease, but they must also shut down complex functions in parts of the brain that promote learning—the cerebral cortex, the frontal lobe, and the temporal lobe—to deal with the emotions that take over their brains and compel learning to be truncated or stopped altogether.

This emotional takeover is a shutting down that occurs because a child's cortisol levels rise high enough during the bad-stress experiences to stimulate increases in survival mechanisms, such as adrenal functions. In turn there is a decrease in higher brain functions.[7] Given that most of a child's cognitive learning requires higher-brain, cerebral functions, not brain stem or lower limbic functions, good stress is better for education of the child than bad stress.

Initially, Susan created bad stress for her child; his one-year-old brain couldn't internalize her verbal cues as she wanted it to. But Susan's instinct to set up win-win choices on the coffee table was solid. Around the age of one, her son was able to begin making a choice between items, rather than just grabbing at whatever is near. When Susan adapted her strategy—removing dangerous and breakable items so that he could pick among his own toys—she allowed him to experience success without setting up a situation of "emotional takeover"—bad stress.

Because so much of a child's early learning world is a microcosm of the big real future world, providing reasonable choices between appropriate toys, as Susan ended up doing, allowed Jake's brain to learn about the future world of education inside his own home. In the future world of social and intellectual education, choice making is one of the most crucial things a child can learn.

The Core Philosophy of Choice Making

If you recall your own years at school, you'll probably recall how many choices you had to make every day. Things you studied were "either this or that." Doing homework with a friend, you might have asked, "Is it 23 or 24?" In English class you might have debated the meaning of certain images in the work of Charles Dickens. In studying history, you might have debated the most intriguing elements of the human past, the choices our leaders made.

In all this, *choice making* is a primary element of being human. It is a skill crucial to learning. Focusing on choice making—and therefore focusing on the frontal lobe—is important especially for boys, who do not develop their frontal lobe as quickly as girls. Helping boys choose among elements, facts, objects, ideas, and feelings is good for enhancing frontal lobe development, especially when the choice is developmentally appropriate. A choice like "Do you want to eat today?" is not appropriate for a four-year-old. Sometimes it's better that the child not be given a choice—for example, if spaghetti is what's being served, then that's what he eats tonight, no exceptions. When developmentally appropriate, however, choice making is a good stressor for the brain.

As soon as the boy is old enough to understand basic language, his parents and the parent-led team ought to consider *verbally* offering him "good stress" choices at every turn:

Shall we make carrots or peas for dinner?
Do you want your sandwich cut into two halves or four quarters?
Would you like strawberry preserves or peanut butter on your
    toast?

Making these choices for him doesn't help grow his frontal lobe as well as getting him to move through the good stress of focusing on choosing developmentally appropriate items for himself.[8] If you practice this appropriate choice making, not only will you challenge your son's attention centers and focus centers at an early age in healthy ways but you will also be able to enhance the choices with questions and experiences that build other sensory, scientific, and mathematical parts of his learning brain.

For example, you might ask your son, "What *color* are the carrots? What *color* are the peas?" Boys often don't differentiate colors as well as girls, but color detail will be important in later language arts essays. Starting the boy's mind to work toward thinking about colors in his early years can help him with sensory details later in life.

You might ask him, "How many pieces of the sandwich are there now?" The male brain tends to make an internal visual diagram of its sensory experience. Boys also tend to make internal lists and rely on counting. Asking a question about the number of pieces in the sandwich immediately stimulates that young brain to attach words to these neural experiences. Development of the ability to attach words to personal experience is crucial to later success in school, especially among boys, who tend to use fewer words than girls.

You might ask him, "What happens to the bread in the toaster?" Curious about mechanics, many boys (indeed, many girls too) will enjoy developing their minds through questions of function, giving parents a wonderful opportunity for a series of questions and answers about toasting, burning, and what role oxygen plays in heat. Building word use in a boy's brain is aided when a young brain can involve itself in a series of word responses associated with natural curiosity.

There is a golden rule to this choice-making philosophy and to the development of the frontal lobe: avoid offering a small child a choice whose potential answer you are unwilling to accept.

For example, if your goal is for your son to drink milk with his lunch, don't ask, "Would you like milk with your lunch?" He could too easily say no, which is not the outcome you want. A needless argument—and family frustration—could ensue. Better is to ask, "Would you like a half glass or a whole glass of milk with your lunch?" Your son still has a choice, and you are more likely to achieve the outcome you want. He gets his upper brain learning experience without having to engage his limbic system in emotional defiance of parents or in unnecessary "bad stress."

Promoting your son's early brain development even before he enters the school system—a system that will build from that firm foundation of early learning—is an important part of being an attached parent. As your son grows, you can encourage ongoing brain growth and development by continuing his choice making with healthy parent-child "debates" and "dialogues" that not only compel choice making but also increase word production in your son's brain.

The following section describes some other things you can do when your son is young to prepare him to "use his words" when he enters school.

Promoting Verbal Development in a Young Boy

Research shows that boys start school, on average, up to a year and a half behind girls in verbal skills (reading, writing, complex speech).[9] Although some boys are natural readers, writers, and speakers, the male brain often has fewer areas of the brain wired for language, reading, and writing.

Because the elementary years of school will rely heavily on development of verbal skills, boys are often at an inherent disadvantage. Anything you can do to promote his verbal development—as Marsha and Stephen did—will help your son do better in school and increase his social success. Given what a "bad stressor" reading and writing have become for so many boys in our educational system, let's go into ways we can alleviate this problem right from the start, in our own homes.

The following techniques are especially good for developing Broca's and Wernicke's areas of the brain—the human reading and writing centers:

- When answering his questions and posing new ones to him in response, listen to his answers and then *answer him by using some of his own key phrases and sentence stems.* This kind of paraphrasing helps him build language skills. It is good to train at least one other caregiver in the parent-team in this technique.

  parent: What happens to the toast in the toaster?
  son: It gets hot.
  parent: Yes, it gets hot. And what else?
  son: Sometimes it burns.
  parent: Yes, sometimes it burns. And why does it burn sometimes?

  The repeating back of sentence stems and key phrases helps the boy's brain "re-hear" them and thus inculcates them into brain centers.

- *Ask your son questions about his daily experiences.* The "peas and carrots" question mentioned earlier could become this dialogue:

  parent: Son, do you want peas or carrots?
  son: Carrots.
  parent: So you like carrots better than peas?

son: Not really. I just want carrots.

parent: Why?

son: I don't know. I just like carrots.

All these "little" conversations promote development in Broca's and Wernicke's language areas in the brain. These little conversations in your son's early years become larger conversations later on.

• *Make eye contact when your son is talking to you, and encourage him to do the same.* Boys, in general, are less comfortable making eye contact than girls. A boy may need to practice in order to increase his comfort level with eye contact during his preschool years. Eye contact helps all children engage in verbal interchanges later in life. A warning note: forcing eye contact can backfire in behavioral rebellion, so you must achieve a delicate balance of your social intention versus his internal wiring and comfort level.

• *Turn the use of words into a game.* Many boys are inherently competitive, and they love games of all kinds. Boys often use pictures (spatials) when they learn, so combine the two for an entertaining and productive promotion of language skills.

The emphasis in the next Try This exercise is to attach words and language to spatial-kinesthetic experience. Because the male brain is often occupied with more cortical areas for spatial-mechanical and kinesthetic experience, your little boy will tend to experience life through physical interaction with his environment and internal pictures that form from that interaction. In managing his brain's experience through the techniques described here, you are helping him build connectors between these spatial-mechanical and kinesthetic centers of natural experience to verbal centers that might naturally develop more slowly in him but that need to be more utilized if he is to succeed in his formal education.

You aren't trying to change him from being a boy who experiences the world "his way." Instead you are helping him experience his way, while connecting it just a little more each day to the verbal-emotive way that he'll later be required to engage in more heavily.

Try This

Cut some card stock or poster board into rectangles, approximately four by six inches. Cut pictures out of magazines and newspaper sale flyers of common items around your house—a refrigerator, bed, bookcase, trashcan, couch, chair. (If you have a digital camera and a printer, you can actually take pictures of the items in your house.) Glue the pictures onto the cards. Give your son one card at a time and help him find something in your house that looks like the picture. If you are working on potty training and personal care, include a toilet and a bathtub.

When he finds the item that matches his card, help him say the name of the item. Encourage him, with questions, to talk about the item. "What's this for?" you can ask as he matches his card to the bed or the couch. "What do we do in here?" you can ask when he labels the bathtub. If a conversation starts about refrigerators, open the door and look at the items in the refrigerator. Name a few. Close the door and ask, "What did you see in the refrigerator?" And don't stop there.

Balancing a Boy's Fine and Gross Motor Development

"Why do so many boys have worse handwriting than girls?" a father wrote us. "Is there something going on in their brains? I still have bad handwriting, and so does my son. It seems to be naturally male."

Many boys have very legible handwriting. However, this father is noticing a male-female difference in brain development. It's an important difference to notice, as your son's later schooling will require him to develop his *fine motor skills,* which he'll use for many tasks, most especially printing and writing. Many boys, and a lot of girls, are able to develop fine motor skills without much encouragement. However, because of the female brain's greater involvement in fine motor centers—and the male brain's greater reliance on gross motor centers (such as the brainstem, which can independently organize gross motor control[10])—more girls tend to be better at holding a pencil or writing cursive at an earlier age. This advantage is enhanced by the fact that the female brain tends to link fine motor activity to verbal activity better than does the male.

While parents and other attachment figures work to promote language and verbal development in our infants, toddlers, and preschoolers, we can also protect children's developing brains by giving them a little extra help and encouragement in developing the fine motor skills they'll need in the future. You and your team can do this by providing your son with opportunities to work with his hands on fine motor tasks and small muscle development, including the following:

- Stringing beads (make sure sizes are age appropriate)
- Building with interlocking building toys, such as Lego and Tinkertoy
- Putting together puzzles, increasing the number of pieces gradually with developmental age
- Making a collage out of various sizes and colors of dried beans, peas, alphabet macaroni, and other tiny objects and letters (again making sure sizes are age appropriate)
- Knitting

In asking parents of boys to be vigilant about fine motor development, we don't want to encourage parents to neglect gross motor activity. Gross motor activity is the running, jumping, climbing, kicking a ball, riding a tricycle, swinging—the large muscle exercise the body and brain need. Many boys are actually more likely to talk, read, and write better after they've gained the brain stimulation of gross motor movement. (In other words, their verbal centers "wake up" because their body movement has stimulated the whole brain.) This wonderful boy energy that your parent-led team is stewarding in the world needs to move through the spaces it finds. Yet if you emphasize only gross motor skills and don't focus also on fine motor skills, you may not be taking full advantage of the early childhood years as training years for future learning success.

One way to measure how your family is doing at balancing gross and fine motor development is to keep a one-week diary. See how many times your son engages in something fine motor, how many times in gross motor. Then create a plan for balancing fine and gross motor activities. If the child is two-and-a-half or older, we suggest you create a home life for him in which he engages in fine motor activities at least 20 percent of his play and learning time. This will help him with many later tasks, including two of the most important ones in today's world: reading and writing.

Calming the Hidden Stressors in a Boy's Life

When Marsha and Stephen set up a nighttime reading ritual in their home, they gave their boys a quiet time in which the boys would not only develop their brains but also calm themselves against any hidden stressors they were going through, at home and in the world. Their nightly session became like what the poet T. S. Eliot called "the still point in the turning wheel." A child's day has many spokes on it, many stimulants moving quickly around him. He needs the steady axle in the center of that turning wheel to be still and calm. The family reading ritual was that still center.

Kathy and I hope that the suggestions in this chapter have helped you manage one of the busy and important spokes in the child's daily wheel. We also hope you'll create a few rituals, as Marsha and Stephen did—reading time, family dinners, nature walks, "hanging out" at a lake or river, extended family picnics, even prayer time (should you be raising your children in a faith). Any of these can become still points in the turning wheel.

There are hundreds of choices and options for parents today. It is hard for any of us to keep up with all the "expert" advice. In recommending the specific techniques and guidelines in this chapter, we hope you're inspired to pick out some new ideas in setting up your home as your child's first school, and yourself as his first teacher.

We've especially emphasized techniques for developing the frontal lobe. In a sense, we've treated the frontal lobe as the still point of early childhood development, and attached a lot of spokes to it—verbal development techniques, choice making, good stress, emotional development, attachment and bonding, increased sensory perception of color and texture, and fine and gross motor development choices. Each of these is "managed," in part, by the frontal lobe—that very crucial learning center in the brain.

No matter where your son goes in his life, the way you organize and run your home will set the foundation for the success of his learning brain. In the next chapter, we'll begin to track your son more closely as he leaves home and enters preschool and other early learning environments. We'll specifically detail what preschool environments best help the male brain learn at its highest potential—and help the child find, when he needs it, the still point, the sense of calm that every boy yearns for.

Effective Preschool and Early Learning Environments for Boys

The primary aim of education is to enable youngsters to learn how to invent themselves—to learn how to create their own minds.

—ELLIOT W. EISNER, PROFESSOR OF EDUCATION,
STANFORD UNIVERSITY

NANCY SHERIDAN HAS BEEN THE DIRECTOR OF AN EARLY CHILDHOOD CARE AND education center in Wisconsin for four years. There are seventy-two children in the center, divided into groups of two-, three-, and four-year-olds. Many of the boys and girls arrive as early as 6:30 A.M., dropped off by parents on their way to work, and some stay as late as 5:45 P.M. Each classroom has a group leader who arrives at 7:30 A.M. and works with the children until 4:00 P.M., every day, Monday through Friday. Along with an aide, the teacher spends an average of forty-five hours weekly with these children, overseeing their meals, their play, their learning, and their rest. Nancy's school takes teacher-student ratios very seriously, making sure there are enough adults present to handle all the kids. Her school is also one that has become concerned about the boys.

I became a preschool teacher because I love kids. But I wasn't well enough prepared to work effectively with many of these boys. They are so much more active than the girls, less willing to sit still and listen at story time, or complete worksheets when we're working on letters and numbers. They want to play, and *everything they play is loud.* The girls will spend time in housekeeping or dress-up centers, playing calmly a lot of the time while the boys are running around the room, building block towers and knocking them down. While some of our group leaders seem to be more successful getting the boys under control than others, I don't think any of us are really doing the best job we can. We've just begun to realize we need help figuring out how to give the boys what they need.

It's possible to read Nancy's comments and wonder, "Is hers a second-rate child development program?" Indeed, it is not! It is an accredited program with educated and dedicated staff. Unfortunately, however, few of the staff received teacher training in college or graduate school on the differences that gender makes in how children learn.

Betsy Flagler, a preschool teacher in Davidson, North Carolina, noticed a problem, too. "At this age," she wrote, "we consider every preschooler to be too young to fail. Not to know how the boys think was just too much like setting them up for failure."

Preschools and preschool teachers are parents' allies in these early learning years. The purpose of this chapter is to provide day-care, preschool, and kindergarten teachers with specific answers to this often asked question: What preschool and other early childhood educational environments best allow boys to develop social, emotive, and cognitive skills that will help them be successful in school? Nearly everything mentioned in this chapter will be of interest to parents who are selecting preschools and are interested in early childhood education. Nearly everything in this chapter also has structural and functional application to grades 1 through 12. However, because Parts Three and Four will get into specific advice for parents and teachers of boys in elementary, middle, and high school, this chapter is directed to those of you who are specifically involved in raising and educating our youngest boys.

Kathy and I have heard for many years now from day-care and pre-school teachers who feel frustrated and saddened by difficulties they are seeing among our youngest males. There is a hidden, unspoken burden on preschool teachers: because preschool teachers are usually a boy's first professional educators, parents and society are often especially watchful of their actions.

In working with preschools like Nancy's and Betsy's, we have found that knowledge of the male brain often leads to the "aha's" that make work fun. And at the deepest levels of human adult-child relationships, this knowledge allows parents of our youngest children to trust the teacher. In turn, teachers who become trained and proficient in creating male-friendly learning environments can offer parents a depth of advice about boys that parents and other concerned citizens are hungry for.

Providing a Boy-Friendly Learning Environment

What constitutes a boy-friendly learning environment? What makes a preschool particularly boy-friendly? In what environments can a boy best "create his own mind"?

Perhaps the most important characteristic of a boy-friendly learning environment is the physical space.

The Work Space

Most of a boy's early life is spent in the play and the small tasks with which he'll grow his brain and learn what he needs to know. His play is his brainwork, and like anyone who works, he needs to do it in an appropriate work space.

For a lot of boys, that work space is going to need to be roomier than you might have initially imagined. The young male brain tends toward spatial-mechanical play and learning, so it tends to "use more space" than girls often will. When confined in smaller spaces, boys often get antsy and frustrated and "bounce off the walls." In turn, discipline problems ensue. When you engage the world more through verbal centers of the brain, your body tends to need less physical space in which to move. It takes more space to engage the world through the spatial centers of the brain, and males tend to cry out for that space—even in undisciplined behavior.

To judge how different girls and boys are in the way they use space, you might stand and observe for twenty minutes how it works out in your child's school. Watch who moves around in that space and how much space each child uses. Do this a number of times a day, for at least three days, perhaps keeping a journal. After a few days, you'll have a pretty good "anecdotal study" of the preschool. Many of the boys will use more floor space, more wall space, and more table space than many of the girls.

Noticing this can be a real revelation. Many preschools like Nancy's and Betsy's with which we've consulted have expanded their physical floor plan once they saw this. Not surprisingly, discipline problems decreased when the amount of physical space increased.

There are other important things to notice about space. For example, within the children's work space there are often tables, and even in the use of tables boys and girls differ. Boys tend to need more room on a table than girls do. That spatial male brain likes, quite often, to spread things out. This is one of the ways that the male brain often learns. It spreads things out or takes things apart, then organizes or rebuilds them.

We suggest that preschools also pay attention to their use of bulletin boards. Bulletin boards are good for all kids. If you provide boys with a large bulletin board where they can proudly display their creations, you'll give them an opportunity for a lot of joy. It's useful to place the boy's bulletin board within reach of the boy's arms so that he can arrange and rearrange his treasures.

Books, Blocks, and Karate Kicks

All children need books, and boys especially need to see books in their environment—books with lots of pictures; books about things they can take apart, things they can put together, things they can measure and figure out; books that talk about how things work, how things grow; books about heroes; books that promote creativity and questioning.

Boys also need blocks of all sizes—large blocks, small blocks, interlocking blocks that will give them a chance to exercise their spatial-mechanical brain by creating structures, tearing them down, and building them again.

Although most or all preschools agree on books and blocks, we have found most preschool staff to be a little suspicious of "karate kicks."

Kathy and I began using the two alliterative words in 2001 in response to an in-home day-care provider who told us about her policy of disallowing all "karate kicks" in her day-care space—both inside her house and outside in her backyard.

"I don't want to promote violence," she said, "so I have a no-hitting, no karate kick policy." When we spoke in depth with this provider and walked through her day care, we noticed a wonderful array of books and blocks, but we also noticed an intense vigilance against any physical displays of aggression.

This kind of vigilance is common throughout the early childhood education community. There is a general need to maintain discipline and curtail injury, as well as a tacitly accepted logic that physical shows of aggression will inherently lead to increased violence among males.

Yet—have you noticed how often boys want to communicate with each other through physical aggression? They kick each other, push each other, knock up against each other, throw a ball at each other. They grin, they wince, they cower, they glower. They are entranced by the aggressions, made sullen at times, often made joyful with the intimacy of physical contact.

In 1996, I coined the term *aggression nurturance* for this male-male communication, arguing that boys, who often lack the "use your words" methodology for intimacy, nurture themselves and others through aggressive gestures and activities. Given the hormonal and neural makeup of males, it's often the case for boys (and men) that aggressive gestures (which we've called "karate kicks") are as nurturing as words, as bonding as hugs. These karate kicks build trust and loyalty by exploring weakness and strength in a playful, teasing way. This kind of physical aggression is a safe form of intimacy and bonding between males (and, of course, can be as well for aggressive females). There is as much love transferred by two boys pushing each other and laughing as by two girls sitting and talking.

Where do you stand on this idea? Have you seen it at work in your school? Day-care centers and preschools are wonderful testing grounds of both this new theory of the nurturing elements in male aggression and of the best ways to manage karate kicks so they don't cause injury or break down discipline in a preschool or day-care center.

If you do indeed notice more male desire to be involved in karate kicks and other physical aggressions, you might also observe in your study journal how much aggression nurturance is going on among these boys—how much of this aggression leads to attachment, bonding, and lasting friendships. Keep a record of the ways in which boys are communicating and nurturing others and themselves through these karate kicks. Some of the physical aggressiveness is too violent, of course. Some of it is not appropriate to the small space the children are in. Some of it is hurtful. You'll note this kind. A lot of the aggression, however, is also nonverbal communication of nurturance.

Whether in your role as teacher or in your role as concerned parent, you have the power to help nurture male love or leave a great deal of it undernurtured—"shut down"—depending on your school's attitude toward karate kicks. If your day-care center or preschool has a lot of books and blocks in it but does not allow karate kicks, perhaps it's time for a schoolwide—even community-wide—meeting to explain to parents of girls and boys the wonderful secrets locked in the male mind, and the possibility of setting good limits, supervising a preschool appropriately, and even having parent volunteers come in during playtime, so that your preschool can embrace a broader form of male nurturance.

Lighting

The male and female brains don't experience light in the same way.[1] Although all children benefit from lots of light, boys see better in bright light and thus especially benefit from lots of light in which to work, read, play, and learn. Light can really make a difference in how boys perform—

both academically and emotionally. Low light can affect serotonin levels in the brain and also makes learning difficult. Boys are more often likely to "act out" under these circumstances, becoming discipline problems.

Ruben Gur, at the University of Pennsylvania's Neural Imaging Unit, has looked at some fascinating science of "light" in the male and female brain. Because the male brain has more white matter than the female, and because that white matter moves material from the eyes and optical nerves more quickly to the visual cortex in the male brain than in the female, males are quite vision and light dependent; in fact, vision is the male's best-developed mode of sensing and acquiring information.[2] Girls and the female brain tend to rely more heavily on the other senses. Given the male's dependence on vision, lighting is even more necessary for boys, who are trying to learn through the visual cortex. Perhaps you can do a walk-through of your day-care center or preschool right now and make sure it is well lit. Perhaps you can do this again in the winter to make sure that during the long winter afternoons, when the kids will be indoors so much of the time, the lighting is especially good.

Personal Responsibility

In preschool, as in the boy's home, choice making is good for the brain. Mealtime is a perfect time for developing personal responsibility. As soon as it's age appropriate (earlier than we usually think!), you can show the boys how to set the table for lunch, then expect them to set it themselves. Janet Ridgeway, an in-home day-care provider and parent of two boys, ages three and seven, uses mealtimes as a way to help her sons and the other children learn mathematical and number concepts and also to break down what she perceives to be certain already established gender roles. She told us:

> Over the course of a few weeks, I noticed that sometimes the girls jumped more quickly to set the table than the boys. I decided to change that. I now make sure to encourage the boys to set the table as soon as they can reach it, and I attach the work to math. In one instance, I had the oldest boy, Chad, count out the silverware

aloud—"three spoons, three forks, three plates, three cups, three nap-kins, three placemats." The other kids joined in. Chad especially likes to give a littler boy, Tucker, instructions. Just as soon as the younger boys became old enough to reach the table, Chad taught them his silverware counting.

What a boy-friendly environment! Janet is not only making sure these boys learn the kind of personal responsibility that can only enhance later learning but also breaking down needless gender stereotypes about kitchen and cleanup work, and linking personal responsibility to math lessons.

Janet gained her early childhood training in the methods of Maria Montessori, an early childhood innovator who believed in linking learning to responsibility and self-motivation. If you ever have a chance to visit a Montessori preschool, you might really enjoy it. You'll notice how intensely those classrooms teach self-motivation through techniques like Janet's.

Boys and Sensory Issues

Even more than the home, a preschool might be a place of either sensory overload or sensory deprivation for some boys. This can be especially true for the boys who are having a problem in preschool. Preschool teacher and parenting columnist Betsy Flagler told us this story:

Charlie was three when he came to us. The year started off with "No, Charlie, no!" all the time. He was very aggressive at times, but at other times he withdrew. He was sensitive to noise, didn't want to wear shoes, wasn't aware of his own space, wanted to wear only certain clothes, and seemed to have a need for pressured touch. He ran into furniture a lot, bumped into classmates. When he was in a really aggressive or active phase, it was hard to stay positive with him.

Then we got trained in how the brain and its senses worked, and we realized he was having trouble with sensory integration. This was an important insight for us. Now we work closely with his parents, who got him into occupational therapy in Mooresville. For us as teachers and for Charlie's parents, learning about how his brain worked was a goldmine for problem solving. Since then, we have adjusted Charlie's participation in our classroom to include our understanding of his senses, his brain, and his behavior. Things are going much better.

Betsy's story of Charlie is a tip-of-the-iceberg tale. In any preschool classroom of twenty-five, there will be a number of boys who need your immediate understanding of brain, gender, senses, and behavior. Whereas our adult brains are developed enough to spend lots of time preoccupied in memories, the preschooler's brain has far fewer memories. The young boy therefore lives almost completely in the immediate senses, the present.

If you can try to put yourself inside the child and look through his eyes at your preschool classroom, you might immediately see an important list of solutions to areas of concern. Check out the next Try This box.

This period of observation will give you a sense of what areas of your classroom are creating sensory stimulation that is useful to learning and what areas are distractions from learning. We hope you'll enjoy how much of your classroom is just right for early childhood learning and for the boys and girls in your class; at the same time, perhaps you'll identify ways in which the room can become more boy-friendly and more protective of children whose senses are acutely alert.

Once you've reviewed your notes, you might make a number of adjustments to your classroom. Here are just a few that can have an impact on sensory issues faced by some of your boys.

- Because boys tend to hear less well than girls, you might adjust the tone and timbre of your voice to make sure the boys are hearing instructions. You might also ask boys to repeat the instructions back to you, just to make sure they are hearing.
- Because boys are often less responsive to soft tactile stimulation, a light touch on the arm might not be enough to get a boy's attention. You might need to join the touch with eye contact and spoken words. This three-pronged approach is

Try This

Sit on one of the children's chairs just inside the door to your classroom.

- What catches your attention first? How long does it seem to hold your attention?
- What items distract you from your first learning choice?
- How quickly does your adult brain have to "move on" and "move between" sensory items?
- Is there a predominant color that jumps out at you? What are the secondary and tertiary colors?
- How "busy" is the room? Measure this with all five senses: sight, sound, touch, smell, taste.
- Take time to identify each of the noises you hear in your classroom. Notice how many sounds you hear and then look at the children—their brains are generally even more auditory than yours!
- How are the various areas of the room seen from your position? Are they boy-friendly? Are there large tables, bulletin boards a small child can reach, plenty of space?

multisensory communication, which increases the certainty that the boy "gets" what you want him to do.

- Boys by nature tend to maintain less eye contact when verbally interacting, so expecting a boy to look you in the eye when you are talking to him might cause stress—resulting in increased cortisol levels in his brain and thus an inability to stay on task with learning. Your awareness of this preference might improve the boy's comfort in your care.
- Boys don't generally move between tasks as quickly as girls. It often takes male sensory centers longer to make a transition. A number of "discipline problems" emerge because teachers (and

parents) will ask or instruct a little boy to put away something and do something else, but he'll seem not to hear or won't do it in the time frame the adult wants. Allowing sixty seconds (or more) for transitions can help a great deal.

- Because many boys rely so greatly on the visual cortex, it's useful to make sure preschool classroom walls have visuals that reinforce the concepts teachers are trying to help boys learn. Studies have shown that although the brain's ability to remember words is limited, the brain's ability to remember pictures is almost unlimited. This is true for all kids, but it's especially useful to help boys learn through pictures, diagrams, and designs, because of the male brain link between visuals and memory.

- Verbal repetition is a good learning tool for all children, but one tool teachers of little boys have used with success is to teach the boy to repeat your verbal instruction (or other lesson) at least three times. He can do this repetition aloud (in a low voice) or do it internally. "Put my paper away in the cubbie. Put my paper away in the cubbie. Put my paper away in the cubbie." Teachers and parents must constantly repeat things to children and will always have to do so, but teaching the child to "self-repeat" can help him guide his own actions toward the goal. This can be even more useful with "auditory learners"—learners who are not as visually oriented, but in fact rely greatly on the words and sounds they hear.

Brain Breaks

Let's stop a second and talk about brain breaks, special activities that give a small child (and even an adult!) some relief from the pressures of the school day. One interesting result of studying the male brain is the knowledge we gain of how boys' brains can often try to work at either the overstimulated or understimulated end of the learning spectrum. Some boys' brains are going so fast that they can't organize their thoughts. Others are just not activated—the rest state is kicking in, and they are bored and listless. Girls, too, can find themselves in these binds.

Brain breaks are a good solution to both areas of difficulty. If you have too many brain breaks, you can increase distraction and focus problems. But if you use them appropriately, you can cut down on overstimulation, listlessness, and acting out.

The next Try This box describes a brain break activity you can use immediately in your class. You can use it in a ritualized way—perhaps every day at a certain time—or you can use it when you can see the fidgeting or groggy brain symptoms in the kids.

There is generally some laughter during this activity, and humor can decrease stress levels for children who are struggling. In a few short minutes, the children are less stressed, have reduced their fidgetiness, and are more easily able to get back on task. This is also an excellent way to help your nonverbal boys focus just before a reading, spelling, or other verbal activity. Brain breaks can help refocus their brains toward learning. In the early- to midafternoon slump (after lunch) you can use it, too. Quite often, school lunches load the body with excess carbohydrates, which make it hard for the brain to perform midafternoon learning tasks. A physical brain break can help "jump-start" the brain.

Music and the Brain

A boy-friendly environment is one with books, blocks, and appropriate karate kicks. It is well lighted. It has a lot of useful (nondistracting) visual stimulation. It is filled with opportunities for attachment, bonding, mentoring, and developing personal responsibility. It encourages and provides resources for gross motor activity and fine motor activity. It allows a lot of physical movement—desks are not nailed down! Children move freely in order to learn, although they are well supervised in their learning. It provides lots of opportunities for children to make choices. It is a place where we are vigilant about sensory difficulties in males. It is a place where we care for the natural rhythms of attention and neural recharge that every brain needs in order to perform effectively.

Try This
Using Brain Breaks

Have students stand behind their chairs with enough room between each child to move their arms and legs freely. Play some active music, and lead the students in movement: clap your hands straight out in front of you, then to the left, then to the right; bend over and clap your hands down by your feet. Straighten up and clap in front of you, then point to a new leader, a student who gets to lead the next few movements. Encourage creativity of movement within the boundaries of the space available. Instruct each student in turn to point to another student until two to four minutes have gone by. Because not every student will have a chance to be a leader every day, keep a record in your memory or on a note card of who needs to get a turn to lead tomorrow.

It is also a musical place. The link between musical sound and learning is wired into our brains, but we often don't realize it. Music is what neuroscientists call a whole-brain activity—it engages both the left and right hemispheres at the same time.[3] You can use this whole-brain stimulation in many ways. In later chapters, we'll provide you with "arts techniques"—ways to connect academic learning to areas of the arts, such as music. In preschools, music is like a child's second language.

Your preschool can have music playing during the opening of the school day. This whole-brain stimulant prepares the brains of the children for activity, promoting brain chemicals that soothe and stimulate. It is useful (and quite joyful!) for a preschool to maintain a diverse library with all kinds of music—classical, pop, jazz, folk, country—music that stimulates movement, music to accompany an art activity, music for relaxation. There are wonderful collections of culturally diverse music, appropriate for classroom applications.

In addition to playing recorded music, your preschool can provide opportunities for children to create their own music, with rhythm, melody, and words. Especially for male brains that by nature produce fewer words, the linking of words (lyrics) to music is very helpful. All of our ancestral religions knew this (and still practice it), fitting a number of religious "messages" into songs.

In the Jewish and Muslim traditions, for example, congregants remember thousands of words in complex liturgy (often in a second language—Hebrew or Arabic) because those words are linked to music and song. In Catholicism, some services still use the old Latin chants. In our secular schools, we can help all children memorize, learn, and perform verbally through links with rhythm, melody, and song.

Nature, of course, provides its own music. Children benefit from listening to rain, wind, leaves rustling along the sidewalk on the playground. This kind of intimate listening is helpful for the male brain in a number of ways. As "nature therapy," it can induce calm. Listening to water flow over rocks, for instance, releases chemicals in the brain that calm the brain. This calm can be especially important for the high-energy boys in your classroom. Fountains in classrooms can be helpful.

A very useful tradition for a preschool is to put a parent sign-up sheet near the front door so parents, grandparents, older siblings, and other trusted friends can sign up for "music time" with your class. These volunteers can play an instrument or sing songs aloud with the children. They can also do volunteer reading time accompanied by music—one parent reads the story while another plays mellow music in the background on the guitar, piano, or other instrument.

For students with behavioral or learning issues, music can make the difference between success and failure. A preschool teacher in Alabama told us about a boy of four-and-a-half who was so difficult to manage that the school administrator had nearly decided to tell the parents he could not continue at the preschool. After receiving training in how the male brain works, one of the school's teachers decided to use a combination of music and nature therapy with the boy. She helped him make a rain stick (a traditional Australian instrument that can be made from a hard cardboard tube with rice inside). The boy learned to pick up the rain stick and turn it over and over and over when he was having difficulty managing his impulses. His behavior improved, and he was allowed to stay in the school.

The Outdoor Classroom

Preschool teacher Betsy Flagler tells a wonderful story about a worm:

> We had a consultant come to our school one day. She was charged
> with seeing how our students and we fulfilled our stated mission and
> school objectives. The incident I'm remembering happened during
> outside time. While she spoke with the students, a bunch of the boys
> became distracted. This distracted her also. "Pay attention," she kept
> saying. "Listen!" Most of the girls did so, but now a number of the
> boys joined the initial group of "trouble-makers." I went over to find
> out what was going on here. Once I got to the boys' location, I discov-
> ered the culprit—a big juicy worm! The consultant kept trying to bring
> the students back to her attention, but they kept wanting to play with
> and study the worm.
>
> As I watched this tension build, I thought, "It's time to switch the
> lesson to the worm." Finally, we did do that, and everyone—boys,
> girls, and adults—enjoyed the learning. The consultant got relief from
> an uncomfortable situation. Later in the day, we gave the kids a re-
> search lesson in worms.

As Betsy has observed, something moving around in nature, even as
tiny as a worm, can lead to far more learning—and love of learning—than
a teacher's set curriculum. The human brain is wired to learn in natural
settings, so of course kids love learning outdoors; this is true for all children, boys and girls.[4] The beauty of Betsy's story in the context of understanding boys' minds is that boys often, by nature, gravitate toward
outdoor experiences because of the way the male mind is wired for hunting and natural wandering. The little boys' brains are designed to manip-
ulate objects moving through space as much as or more than they are to
listen to words. Although they certainly learn how to listen to voices that
provide them with necessary instructions, choices, and love, they are less
inclined than more naturally verbal girls to enjoy a speaking voice. If they
have access to a natural environment in which to learn, the boys will often
rush out into that place of physical "natural" experience.

A preschool can measure its success with boys in part by adjusting
itself to include nature—not only for play or for energy release but also

for hands-on learning. In the winter, only an hour a day might be spent in outdoor learning. But in the spring, summer, and fall, perhaps two or more hours can be spent in outdoor activities. Also, in all seasons, the outdoors can be brought indoors, through caring for pets; research on animals and plant life; picture books about outdoor life; volunteers, such as a grandpa who brings in a fish he's caught; and discussions of birds' nests, beehives, and anthills.

Do You Have to Use Your Words to Use Your Brain?

A teacher at the Princeton Montessori School shared this with us after her school participated in a daylong training on how boys learn:

"Our school motto, 'Use Your Words,' is on our brochures, our newsletters, even on our assembly podium. It's very 'female,' isn't it? It's not bad for the boys to use their words—and I still think it's a good motto—but given what we've learned today, what is the actual power of words, especially with young boys? When we say, 'Use your words,' are we leaving a lot of boys out?"

This teacher is asking a question we all face. We are word-oriented learners, workers, parents, teachers, and children. We are a civilization built on words. To make "Use Your Words" a school motto is to be in sync with humanity. Words are a great deal of what separates human beings—and the human brain—from other species.

And yet . . . can words be overemphasized in early childhood learning? Yes, they can. Twenty years of research into male-female brain difference lead to the conclusion that words cannot do all of what we want them to do, especially with boys. If your preschool heavily emphasizes the "use your words" strategy, we hope you'll have a team meeting that uses this chapter as a starting point for discussing options we've explored (and the many others you may have developed over the years of your professional and personal care for children).

If teachers and parents in your community are constantly saying to boys, "Use your words!" and if it has become frustrating and at times shrill, we hope you'll keep a one-week journal to track the other ways that the boys (and the girls) are instinctively and naturally trying to manage themselves.

After receiving training on how the male brain functions and then assessing her school's classrooms through her new point of view, Yvette Keel, an assistant principal in Georgia, shared her development in this area:

> With boys, there is of course a loud level of sound and activity. Until I got an understanding of what was really going on, I was sure the boys were not on task—they couldn't be working and be so active and animated! Now I see how absolutely on task these boys are. They are engaged with the lesson, and learning. It was a surprise, and a lesson to me. Now, I often find myself drawn into their excitement. I sit down at the table and ask a couple of questions, and before long I am working with them. Their enthusiasm is contagious!
>
> What a blessing young boys are! They may not have all the words we think they should with which to bless us with their wisdom, curiosity, and love, but they may also have other talents and skills that go unrecognized in contemporary education.

5

Removing Key Environmental
Stressors from Boys' Lives

Everything we do with and around our children has a potential positive or negative effect on how their brains will function. Everything our children eat, everything they drink, everything they watch on TV, everything they touch, everything they hear finds its way into their minds.

—DANIEL AMEN, AUTHOR OF *CHANGE YOUR BRAIN, CHANGE YOUR LIFE*

I REMEMBER THE FIRST TIME I READ A BOOK ABOUT THE HUMAN BRAIN IN 1981. A neurology textbook, it explained the functions of the brain stem, the limbic system, and the cerebral cortex. It talked about how the human brain had evolved over millions of years. It explained things that in those days were quite mysterious to me—how the human brain possessed as many neurons as there were stars in the Milky Way; how the brain is the only organ in the natural world to be able to reflect upon itself; how everything we do, feel, think is a reaching out from our brains into the universe and a reaching of the universe into our brains. A student of philosophy, literature, and psychology in my undergraduate and graduate school years, I found the human brain to be the most impressive part of human life I had ever studied. Over the next two decades, I judged what I learned in all disciplines by whether it fit with what I learned about the human brain.

That first neurology textbook—and the passion it created in me—came back to me when I sat recently with Daniel Amen, a neuropsychiatrist who bases his cutting-edge treatments of stressors in the lives of adults and children on brain scans of the physical health of the patient's brains. Over the last couple of years, he and I have struck up, via the phone and the Internet, a professional acquaintanceship. Now, in a restaurant in Spokane, we finally got to meet for lunch.

"Listen," he said. "At this point, I don't treat anyone with a complicated case involving brain disorders without, if possible, first doing a brain scan." This principle is crucial, I believe, as we move into the twenty-first century. The Amen Clinics use this principle to provide clear, correct diagnosis of brain disorders. (In Chapter Nine, we'll explore boys' brain disorders more fully.) During our conversation, Daniel told me about many of the positive results his Amen Clinics (there are four clinics, spread around the United States) have gained from brain-based health strategies. I shared with him similar results the Gurian Institute has gained in classroom and home environments through application of laboratory research like his and that of others whose work you find featured in this book.

Daniel and I both remembered the first neurology textbook we read—he in medical school, I in my professional research. These textbooks provided essential information, but both Daniel and I agreed that most textbooks in neurology or other fields spend very little time training readers on how to care for the "brain health" of children. Daniel pointed out that key environmental components of brain health—basic human attachment and the need to protect children from abuse—make up small sections of textbooks on the human brain. I pointed out that in the two major textbooks in educational psychology today, there is no significant analysis of how our educational environments affect the health of boys' and girls' brains differently.[1] We both agreed that what a person eats and what they watch on TV also make up a very small part of textbooks—yet are proven to significantly affect brain health.

"It's difficult to focus on the health of a child's brain—whether boy or girl," Daniel pointed out, "if our own textbooks neglect to deal with so many of the major brain stressors our children face." Parents and teachers, he noticed, are the primary individuals in our culture who have to make up for our lack of academic focus on brain stressors in our own homes and schools—parents and teachers like you. We hope that Daniel's book *Change Your Brain, Change Your Life,*[2] and this one can supplement basic academic knowledge of the brain with the newest cutting-edge research in children's brain health.

Promoting Brain Health

In the previous four chapters, we've been discussing brain health without using those specific words. We've been looking at environmental stimulants that protect the learning brain of a boy—how you can affect brain physiology through increased human attachment, protection against abuse, boy-appropriate learning environments, and increased knowledge of differences between the male and female brain. What we have not done until this chapter is focus on specific areas of physical stimulation that directly, negatively affect the learning health of a boy's brain. Now it is time to look at these things more carefully.

The Gurian Institute staff has trained schools and communities in two major *physiological* stressors on boy's brain development that directly affect daily learning tasks: nutrition and visual screen time (TV, video games, movies, computers). Dr. Daniel Amen has added a third to our list, and we thank him for bringing this third one to our attention.

Brain Injuries

The element Amen and the Amen Clinics added to our list of stressors on male brain development is the prevalence of brain injuries in our schoolboys. As Amen puts it: "In our clinics, we are scanning boys and seeing a lot of surprising brain injuries. Many of the learning disorders and behavioral problems families and schools face with children today relate to major and minor brain injuries." Daniel continues, "It makes sense that boys would acquire more physical brain injuries than girls.

When you think about it, boys are very physical and they are more prone to physical accidents, such as hitting their heads. The aggressiveness of certain male sports adds to the statistics for boys."

Amen explained to me how his clinics' process of diagnosing brain disorders has changed to accommodate information about brain injuries:

Ten years ago, my staff and I were seeing kids with anger problems or other issues, and we would, of course, look at family dynamics. Let's say a boy came in who had been acting out severely. We would bring the family in for structural family therapy. This was not a bad thing by any means. However, now that we use brain scans, we're discovering that in some cases these boys are suffering from some kind of brain damage. Because of the scans, we're not missing as much as we missed back then. We can see a brain injury in the first few hours of our interaction with the child. If we see that injury, we don't have to work with the family for a year or two trying to discover how the family and the boy are creating a bad family dynamic as the source of the boy's problems. Now when we bring the family in, we're armed with the scan. Our job becomes training the family in how to deal with the brain injury.

According to Amen, two million Americans suffer from brain injuries, and most don't know it. If your son, or a boy in your classroom, is evidencing behavior patterns that "don't seem like him," or "don't fit who he was when he was little," or "seem off the charts," this boy might have a brain injury. If the boy is having trouble learning (we will cover learning disabilities in detail in Chapter Nine), he may have a brain injury. If the boy is acting out constantly in class, he may have a brain injury. Such an injury can result from a major or minor blow to the head in incidents like these:

- He may have fallen from a swing or a tree, hitting his head or affecting his neck.
- Someone may have hit him on the head.
- He may have been in a motor vehicle accident.

In these and other similar circumstances, the health of the boy's brain has been affected by the physical impact of a fall or other injury, which is now impairing the boy's learning ability. One can make an initial assessment of the possibility of a brain injury by looking back on his early years, talking with parents and other caregivers about those years, and talking to the boy himself, should he be old enough to communicate verbally. If you are the boy's parent, discovering the possibility of a brain injury can lead to your approaching your insurance company about approving a brain scan—probably a SPECT scan—or, if you can, paying for that scan yourself.

In many cases, a brain injury is preventable, as in the case of child abuse. In many other cases, however, a brain injury may not be preventable. We can't stop children from playing, from running, from riding a bike. We can try to keep children safe, but we can't stop every car accident from happening. In many cases, we are powerless to keep our children safe from brain injuries. We can only get the right diagnosis and react appropriately.

There is, however, one source of our boys' (and girls') possible brain injuries that we can do something about. Amen told me, "The human brain is about the consistency of soft butter. It's very delicate. One of the largest new areas of brain injury—especially temporal lobe and frontal lobe damage—is 'soccer headers.' While some children—boys and girls—can head a soccer a ball many times without significant injury, many cannot." Amen reiterates, "In all athletics it's important to remember that both boys and girls are equally susceptible to injury, but because males are naturally more aggressive, we see in our clinics that boys tend to get more of these injuries."

When Amen and I discussed why the rate of learning disorders, ADD/ADHD, and other brain disorders has skyrocketed in the last two decades, we listed a number of reasons (all of which will be covered in various parts of this book), but one on his list that surprised me was this matter of "sports injuries, specifically soccer headers." He admits there is no statistical way at present to prove the link between sports-related head injuries and the increase in brain disorders, but it is his opinion, after thirty years in the field, that those brain injuries in general, and soccer headers in particular, play a part.

When it comes to any "expert advice," you are the final expert. In opening this chapter with Amen's work, and specifically with this warning about brain injuries, we hope you will include the following two ideas in your toolbox as a parent or teacher—especially when dealing with children who have learning or conduct disorders:

- That a brain scan might be helpful in ascertaining the exact part of the brain that is not working effectively, if and how it is injured, whether it's inactive or overactive, and how it got that way.
- That protecting our children's heads is a major and necessary priority, especially as our children play sports like soccer in increasing numbers.

As an avid soccer player myself—a fullback who plays twice a week in a men's soccer league—I can say that when I head a ball that has come at high velocity and with long hang time, my head hurts! Sometimes, in these circumstances—so pumped up with adrenalin that I just can't stop myself—it seems I can feel my brain splash around in my skull. If I, at forty-seven, feel the head pain of heading a ball coming at me at breakneck speed from very high, what's happening to the heads (and necks) of five- and ten-year-old kids?

Vigilance about all kinds of head accidents and injuries is crucial. Such vigilance might very well save a child from a great deal of learning distress. The following are two of several Web sites that address soccer heading issues: http://www.safety-council.org/info/sport/soccer.html and http://www.med.unc.edu/chms/ProjectsSH.htm.

Screen Time: TVs, Videos, Video Games, Computers

When I was young, I watched a black-and-white television. There were just four stations—NBC, ABC, CBS, and PBS. Quite often, the antennae worked badly. Sometimes I stared at "snow." For me, *Gilligan's Island, Mission Impossible,* and *Star Trek* were entertainment. They put me in the "TV trance" I sometimes see my own children experiencing. In my era, of course—as perhaps in yours—the blue glow inside houses when you walked in the neighborhood at night had just become a national phenomenon. You and I perhaps watched an hour or two of TV a day.

Things have changed. Consider the statistics in the next Did You Know? box.

Perhaps everyone today has read the media reports linking our enormous use of television, videos, and computers to increased physical health problems, including increased obesity. You might not have heard as much, however, about the causal link now established between screen time and emotional and learning issues among children, and specifically among boys.

The Relationship Between Screen Time and Brain Development

Dimitri Christakis, a brain researcher at Children's Hospital and Regional Medical Center in Seattle, has pointed out that the brain needs touch, hearing, seeing, smelling, tasting—the complex interaction of the five senses with the external environment—in order to grow its tissue fully.[3] Our brain relies mainly on direct and various sensory experiences for this brain tissue growth. This is especially true, Christakis points out, in the first three years, when our abstracting functions in the top of the brain have not developed yet, making screen time especially worrisome in the case of infants and toddlers. But he has found that it's also true throughout our brain growth, all the way into our twenties.

In studying the relationship between brain development and screen time, Christakis and other researchers have shown that "passive, hyper-mechanical stimulation" (watching images moving on a flat screen) can have lifelong negative consequences on the learning brain. In the April 2004 issue of *Pediatrics,* Dr. Christakis presented research that followed twenty-six hundred children from birth to age seven and discovered that "for every hour of television watched per day, the incidence of ADD and ADHD increased by 10 percent." This is a powerful finding!

Helping our boys succeed in school and in life requires each of us as teachers, parents, and members of parent-led teams to manage screen time with more vigilance than we may do currently. This was not something our ancestors had to worry about. Their children learned by moving around in nature, touching things, feeling things, smelling them, experiencing them using both fine motor or gross motor abilities.

??? Did You Know? ???

- The average American child now spends 900 hours a year in school, but 1,023 hours a year watching TV.
- In the average American home, the TV is on 6.7 hours per day.
- By the time your son reaches eighteen, he'll have spent 22,000 hours watching TV, more than he spends in any other activity besides sleeping.
- The number of videos and DVDs families rent every day is twice the number of books read.
- By the age of sixteen, your son will have seen 200,000 acts of violence on television, 33,000 of them acts of murder.
- One-fourth of children under two years old now have TVs in their bedrooms.
- Two-thirds of preschool boys sit in front of screens for two or more hours per day—more than three times the hours they spend looking at books or being read to.[4]

Human industrialization and mechanization—with all its advantages in areas of comfort, medical health, and personal entertainment—have cut down on our children's opportunities for natural brain development. Some of our children may be suffering attention and other difficulties because for too many hours each day their brains don't receive fine motor and gross motor development based in physical movement and whole-sensory experience.[5]

Brain scans like those done by the Amen Clinics show that when the growing human brain overemphasizes nonmotor brain stimulation, our brains develop what are called *brain bypasses* in key development areas, such as attention centers. Here's how this works.

The passive, nonmotor stimulants of TV, videos, and computers do the attention work for the brain; thus the brain doesn't have to learn how to do it organically. Because the young brain isn't "moving around"—physically interacting with its environment—it's not feeling the touch receptors from skin, hearing the natural complexity of sound, and, most important, attending in a focused way to a complex, whole-sensory brain development task. The mechanics of the TV provide neural hyperstimulation (constant auditory and visual bombardment of the brain) but complete physical passivity. Thus the TV is doing half the brain's work. Because the brain doesn't have to do that work, it doesn't fully develop (it bypasses) the neural elements it would naturally develop were it fully active, both physically and mentally, in the natural world.

This problem affects both boys and girls, but it has a special impact on boys, who generally need a lot of physical movement in order to grow their brains. Given what we know about the male brain, it should not surprise us that mainly boys suffer from attention and hyperactivity disorders[6]—their brains don't grow these centers as easily or naturally as girls, so they are especially prone to attention problems linked to passive entertainment, screen time, and passive hypermechanical stimulation.

Setting Limits

If you are parenting a boy, we hope you will consider the suggestions in the next Try This box.

One father at a workshop Kathy gave found our suggestions quite stringent. "I see you have a lot of physicians on your side," he said, "but I look at this a different way—if my kids get exposed to everything when they're young, they'll be more mature, more sophisticated later on. In adolescence they'll know everything that's out there. They'll be more independent and mature as adults."

This is an important philosophical question for parents and teachers to grapple with. Given the potential for learning difficulties linked to screen time, the issue of moderation becomes crucial. We strongly believe that the benefits in emotional and educational health far outweigh any independence or sophistication that might be gained from unlimited TV and computer time for kids, at an early age especially.

Another father said, "I don't mind your strictness about TV, but why computers? I want my son to be adept at computers as early as possible. He'll have an edge later in school, right? Computers are the future." This father didn't know what psychologist Jane Healy has shown in her seminal work on computer use, *Failure to Connect:* that even if a child starts using computers for the first time in adolescence, within months he gains computer skills equal to those of children who began as toddlers or young children.[7] In other words, being good with computers does not depend on starting young. In 2004, the Alliance for Children completed a major worldwide study that showed the same results as Healy.[8]

Given the potential disadvantages to male brain development from overuse of computers, TVs, movies, and other screen activities, we hope you'll position your parenting philosophy on the side of caution.

The "No-TV" Option

"I watched TV when I was a child, and I turned out okay." You've probably heard this said, or you've said it yourself. Personally I must say that I watched a moderate amount of TV as a child and turned out fine. If my parents had decided to get rid of the television in our house, I'd have been furious, like perhaps any boy would be.

Or would he? What in fact does happen in homes and schools when TVs are taken out of children's lives? Dr. Barbara Brock, a professor of recreation management at Eastern Washington University, decided to find out. She engaged fifty volunteers in fourth and sixth grade to go without television for thirty days (the average pretest viewing time for these children was two to four hours per day). Buy-in from parents and teachers was essential, and Brock got it. As she notes, "The teachers actually voted to have the children give up screens of all kinds." For thirty days, the children watched no TV, did not use computers, and did not play video games.

Brock reports:

> Surprisingly enough, over three fourths of the children actually made it for thirty days. The results in this three-fourths group were stunning. Our study saw:
>
> - Significant improvement in grades
> - Significant improvements in sleep habits

Try This

- Both the American Medical Association and the American Psychiatric Association recommend no TV for children until two years old.
- Never—not in his toddler years, his prepubescence, not even in his adolescence—allow your son to have a TV in his room.
- When you do allow your young son to play video games, have strict time limits on use—use a timer to enforce the limits, if necessary.
- Watch TV with your child, scheduling programs that are developmentally appropriate, and talk about what you've seen.
- Avoid the use of videos and DVDs as media baby-sitters for your son. Most parents use these baby-sitters now and then, but if doing so becomes a habit, your son may end up with educational problems.
- Avoid early attachment of the child to the computer. A few minutes a day for a three-year-old is part of the novelty of growing up. But an hour or two on the computer at that age can have the same effect as TV and videos do at that age: it can hurt the learning brain of the boy.

- Significant improvement in mood
- Significant increase in time spent reading
- Significant increase of physical activity
- Significant increase in family bonding

Brock notes that the three most popular "replacement activities" for the TV time were

- Playing outside
- Talking with friends and family
- Reading, drawing, and games

- Avoid taking two-, three-, and four-year-olds to movies that contain any content you consider difficult for the child. If you think the scenes on the screen are violent, they are probably too violent for your preschooler. It's useful to remember that the attention span of a toddler is never as long as most movies. His brain wants to learn in bursts of movement, and developmental learning will stop occurring for much of the last hour of the movie. He'll absorb the violence but not be able to learn anything from it except, potentially, to imitate it in his imagination or even in his physical world.

- When your child reaches an age when you believe using television, videos, or DVDs is appropriate, be sure that you have researched or previewed any videos you share with your son. Similarly, research or preview all television shows. Talk to others in the parent-led team—other moms and dads, neighbors, teachers—to make sure the content of a program is useful to your child. The parent-led team has the responsibility as well as the honor of being the arbiter of what a boy takes into his heart and soul during his most formative years.

In two of the three replacement activities, Brock noted something crucial to brain development. The children who gave up television spent more time in individual sensory and physical play activity—the very activity that helps the brain grow.[9]

Brock's study is not the only one of its kind, nor the only one to show such positive results. As Brock notes in her book, *No TV? No Big Deal,* Thomas Robinson, of Stanford University, completed a study in 2002 of nine hundred schoolchildren who reduced TV viewing to six hours per week. His study found a 25 percent decrease in verbal and physical aggression among these children after six weeks. In 2004, researchers reported positive results from a study in which sixteen preschools in Cooperstown, New York, cut TV viewing time during the preschool day.[10]

Brock concludes, "No one thinks everyone should turn off the TV all the time. We all value computers. Video games are not evil. The studies don't ask us to over-react. They ask us to pay closer attention. What our children spend their time doing is what defines them. This is true of what children watch on TV, what they do with their time, even what they eat and drink."

What a Boy Eats and Drinks

As we move into a new millennium of industrialization, it's crucial to remember that 16 percent of all American children are now officially obese.[11] Two primary contributors to this obesity are (1) screen time and (2) what children eat and drink.

What We Now Know: Asking the Right Questions

Terry, a father in Utah, wrote the Gurian Institute: "Whenever I drive through a fast food restaurant I wonder, 'Am I being a good parent?' I read *Fast Food Nation* [an exposé of how fast food affects our country and our children] and Schlosser makes it sound like we're poisoning our kids and our culture with that junk. Then I saw the movie *Supersize Me*. It scared me to death. What is the truth about the effects of diet on children?"

Twenty years ago, we didn't know the answer to this question. When I was a boy sitting in front of the TV and munching potato chips, my parents didn't have access to clear information and guidelines. When Kathy was helping her son Karl Michael deal with his educational issues, she did not know what part his diet played in his learning difficulties.

Fortunately, brain research has now clarified the way that bad nutrition leads directly to bad brain health and learning problems. The American Medical Association, as well as many other medical groups, have now linked what we eat and drink to how we think.

Here are four questions that the Gurian Institute staff always ask parents to focus on. Their answers can alter a child's educational experience.

QUESTION I: IS MY SON GETTING ENOUGH WATER?   The brain is 80 percent water. It needs fresh, clean water every day for optimal learning to take place. Although a number of beverages may seem to quench your son's thirst, only water will really quench his brain! Soft drinks, iced tea, and fruit juice are processed by the body as food, and if they contain caffeine (as do colas and many teas), they are diuretics and actually reduce water in the body.

Being thirsty causes problems for learning because it increases cortisol levels, creating a bad stress experience for the learner. The cortisol washes through the brain, making attention to learning tasks more difficult. Within five minutes of drinking plain water, cortisol levels can decrease.[12]

If you can help your preschool son decrease "bad" drinks and increase water, he'll learn better right now, as a youngster, in whatever tasks he undertakes. He'll also gain the kinds of nutritional habits that will better serve his brain, and his whole body, when he goes to school. At all ages of schooling, he'll also behave better, for when the brain is depleted of water, mood and behavior regulators in the limbic system and the frontal lobe don't work as well.

At home, you might put water within your son's reach as soon as he is able to handle a cup, allowing him to quench his thirst as needed. As he gets old enough, put a container in the refrigerator that will dispense cool water easily. When you take your son to preschool or day care, make sure the staff will allow him access to water on a regular basis. Ask them just how much water they serve in relation to other beverages, and advise them that you prefer that your son not be offered soft drinks. Also, request that only one apple juice or similar beverage be served per day. (These carton juices are basically sugar water, not water—more on sugar in a moment.) Increasingly, early childhood programs are implementing healthy nutritional policies and curtailing the use of soft drinks. This is going to help all our kids.

QUESTION 2: IS MY SON GETTING ENOUGH PROTEIN?   A typical breakfast of a Pop-Tart and boxed juice, though convenient, is doing little to help a boy's readiness to learn. Along with the lack of pure water, the high concentration of carbohydrates in such a breakfast makes his brain "groggy" and will make paying attention during the day much harder for him. Protein would be better for his learning brain.[13]

Judith Wurtman, a research scientist in MIT's Department of Brain and Cognitive Science, has researched the ways in which amino acids, found in protein, set the stage for learning in the brain.[14] An array of amino acids—such as tyrosine, which enhances thinking, and trypto-phan, which has a calming effect—not only help keep the brain in a state of alertness but also help counteract the negative effects of sugar, which children tend to consume regularly.

Japanese culture has highly emphasized protein consumption, especially the omega-3 fatty acids in fish. Studies have been coming out of Japan that show consistent positive results. A recent one found fewer neural learning difficulties in the Japanese than in Americans.[15] It looked specifically at how Japanese diet restricts calories (Japanese children consume one-third the calories that American children do) and how they emphasize proteins. Amazingly, not only are there fewer brain disorders among Japanese children, but also their life expectancy is 78.32 years for men and 85.23 years for women—the highest in the world. In cutting back on carbs and calories, and increasing proteins, especially in the morning, Japanese children avoid "learning grogginess" caused by the carbs and get the fatty acids that learning requires.

Although only you can know your son's preferences, allergies, and other special issues, the suggestions in the next Try This box are handy ways of approaching the brain's need for protein.

QUESTION 3: DOES MY SON EAT TOO MUCH SUGAR?   Sugar can give the brain a big surge of energy for a little while but then begins negatively affecting the learning potential of the brain. One sugar treat a day is "special." More than one can become a dangerous routine for the child's learning brain (and can increase the risk of obesity, too). Our ancestors didn't eat nearly as much sugar as we do. They ate food and

---

Try This

- Spread peanut butter on your son's toast (or let him do so), should toast be his common breakfast—the peanut butter will add protein.
- Keep shredded cheese in a container in the refrigerator; sprinkle it on toast and zap it in the microwave.
- Cook a bunch of hardboiled eggs on the weekend to have available for quick meals during the week.
- Keep yogurt and cottage cheese on hand. Encourage your son to eat them.
- Arrange your schedule so that some mornings you have time to cook a full breakfast and sit down at the table to share a meal.

---

drank beverages depending on the body's natural needs. Although we are not our ancestors, we can learn from them to respond to need rather than want. Sure, just about everyone *wants* the pleasant sweetness of sugar, but given its risks for learning, your son's *need* for it is the best developmental and educational standard to follow.

Especially difficult for your son's brain is the intake of sugar just before a learning task. Both from a cognitive and a behavioral standpoint, this is a setup for learning difficulty. Sugar not only makes it hard for the learning centers in the cerebral cortex to work but also can stimulate more adrenalin than is required for sitting down and doing a learning task; that adrenalin also increases the likelihood that the child will be a discipline problem. Sugar might be a good boost for a mountain climber, but not for a classroom student.

QUESTION 4: DO OUR FAMILY AND SCHOOL PRACTICE HEALTHY EATING RITUALS?   Helping your son develop a morning routine that includes eating a brain-healthy breakfast will help him throughout his school years and beyond. Providing a calm, stress-free environment within which he can eat his breakfast and prepare for school is also very useful. In our busy schedules, this may not happen every day, but it ought to happen at least a few days a week. The healthy eating rituals ensure that a greater amount of time will be spent in healthy eating.

If your schedule doesn't permit a family breakfast most mornings, perhaps you can call grandma or grandpa to have breakfast with the kids on some mornings. Perhaps there is a neighbor, good friend, aunt or uncle or nanny who can make sure your child has good nutrition and a calm routine while you are busy.

Overall it's crucial for parent-led teams to appreciate how all nutritional factors act on the learning brain. Whether you are caring for boys or girls, these issues matter. Especially in the context of boys and learning issues, nutrition matters a great deal, because boys start out with certain learning disadvantages today. Any obvious disadvantages we can remove from their daily regimen will be welcome to their learning brains.

Starting tomorrow morning you can take the nutritional piece of your son's life quickly in hand. You and your team can develop a plan for good nutrition and good eating habits. One place to begin is to look at how heavily you rely on fast food; this will serve as a barometer of how well your parent-led team is caring for the minds of your children. If going to a fast-food restaurant is a family ritual, you might want to reconsider this practice. Sugar, unhealthy fats, and unhealthy carbs dominate fast-food meals. If your family goes to a fast-food restaurant more often than you have a healthy family meal at home, your children may be getting set up for learning and behavioral difficulties. Like Terry, who read Eric Schlosser's *Fast Food Nation,* our culture is thankfully waking up to the neural and physical problems inherent to our present American diet.[16] One night a week of the fat and carb intake in fast foods will probably do our boy's brain little harm; but many nights a week probably will.

Making Sure Schools Are Involved in Dialogues About Nutrition

The nutritional needs and issues we've just discussed extend into our schools as well. Soda machines and the high-fat, high-carb content of lunch menus are problematic. Some schools and districts—including many with which the Gurian Institute has worked—are changing their lunchroom diets and the hallway soda and candy machine distributions. These schools acknowledge the near tragedy of asking our children to learn lessons that require a well-fed brain in school environments that systematically poison the health of that very brain through poor diet and nutrition. These schools are responding to the frightening obesity research by altering children's diets on school grounds.

Too many schools are not yet on board with significant dietary changes—for many schools, the costs of these changes are prohibitive. But while schools are getting on board over the next decade, parents can help children pack healthy lunches and share with teachers and community members the most current information on the effects of food and drink on the brain.

The Beauty of Brain Health

In this chapter, Kathy and I have brought you some of the newest research into learning stressors. With the help of some of our country's leading experts in each respective area, we hope we've given you insight and practical help regarding three potential major stressors on the health of your boys' learning brains. Although each of these applies to girls, we've featured these three because each stressor carries potential for boy-specific negative impact on learning. What your boy eats, drinks, watches, stares into, and hits his head on affects that growing and learning brain! To build optimal learning environments for boys, we must come together to establish rules and limits for screen use, nutrition, and physical activity.

As I ended my lunch with Daniel Amen that day in Spokane, he made a comment about his brain scans of children that is both poetic and clinical. He said, "When I look at a scan of a human brain that's really well taken care of, there's hardly anything more beautiful."

As you think about diet, screen time, and head injuries, you too may look at your child as if studying a scan. If you are dealing with a boy in your home or classroom who is having any kind of learning, discipline, or behavioral difficulty, we hope you'll feel the tug, the compulsion, to do just a little more to reduce the amounts of bad diet, soda, and sitting in front of the TV in that boy's life. Through these small changes you, your parent-led team, and your school will be doing just a little more to protect the beauty of that boy's brain.

PART

Teaching School Curricula in Boy-Friendly Ways

6

Helping Boys Learn Reading, Writing, and Language Arts

In reading and writing, girls outperformed boys by "significant amounts" in all industrialized countries.

—STUDY BY THE ORGANISATION FOR ECONOMIC CO-OPERATION AND DEVELOPMENT, 2003

Boys' imaginations are churning out fantastic stories, but getting them on paper is hard for them.

—NAN JORGENSEN, MOTHER OF THREE BOYS, SALT LAKE CITY

ON A COLD WINTER DAY I WENT TO PICK UP MY DAUGHTER AT HER ELEMENTARY school. Arriving about fifteen minutes early, I went into the school building and walked the hallway, enjoying the children's stories and drawings hung on the walls. "Chloe," "Jake," "Kristen," "Frankie," and hundreds of other names were written in child print or cursive at the bottoms of hundreds of little essays and pieces of artwork. I stopped at different offerings to read and admire the children's work. After I glanced over about twenty of these, something interesting stood out: there was a difference between what the girls wrote and what the boys wrote.

Pulling out my pocket notebook, I made a column for Girl and Boy. Then I counted the exact number of words in the girls' essays and in the boys'. After counting ten essays written by girls and ten by boys, I found the girls had written one-and-a-half times the number of words the boys wrote. This was a significant difference. I quickly scanned more essays from nine other classrooms. Not a single classroom showed the boys as a group to be using more words than the girls (though there were some individual boys who used equal numbers of words or more than the girls did).

Checking my watch and noting that I had three minutes until the bell, I made a new row on my notebook page. It stood to reason that the girls would use more words than the boys, knowing what I did about differences in verbal centers in the male and female brain. What about the content in the words themselves? Would there be a difference in that? I became especially curious about sensory detail—color, texture, sound, and tactile feeling, such as softness or hardness. I counted the number of times boys used sensory descriptors in an essay, versus the girls' use. Again I found a difference. Even when I included the boys who were clearly very verbal and who used a lot of sensory detail, the girls outperformed the boys in the essays by two to one in this "sensory output" category.

The bell rang, the classrooms became busy with activity, and soon the hallways were swamped. My spontaneous experiment had ended. Davita saw me, we reunited, and after we got to the car, we drove home chatting about her day.

But later that evening, I made calls and sent emails to colleagues, teachers, and administrators. I wondered if they could replicate my elementary school "experiment."

Over the next week, calls and emails came back. In Colorado, New York, Georgia, California—all over the country—elementary school walls were living proof of male-female brain difference in writing. The girls used, on average, more words and more sensory detail than the boys.

Since that afternoon at Davita's school, I have asked teachers, parents, and professionals in conferences and trainings to do this experiment on their own. This is an experiment you can conduct in any elementary school that puts children's work up on hallway walls. I feel confident that if you peruse the work of at least ten classrooms, you'll generally replicate my findings. You'll discover a dramatic way to understand what's going on inside the minds of girls and boys.

As we've noted earlier, boys' brains do not generally create as many words as girls'. They don't use as many verbal centers with as many neural pathways from the sensory centers to the verbal.[1] Boys do not, therefore, talk and write as naturally about sensory detail. They don't generally use as many words in their writing (or, during a given day, in their speaking). They don't gravitate as much as the average girl toward reading. This is "who a lot of boys are," yet it can be one of the most problematic aspects of educating them, for because of it, our boys are, on average, getting worse grades in language arts than our girls.

What Parents Can Do

This chapter is a very practical offering to all of you who want to improve male literacy both at home and at school. Reading, writing, and sensory detail are highly valued in contemporary education. If you know a boy (or girl) who does not excel in these areas, that child may well suffer from lower grades, test scores, and self-esteem.

It's no accident that in all the industrialized countries, including the United States, our girls significantly outperform our boys in reading, writing, and language arts. In the United States, the Department of Education reports the gap to be one-and-a-half years[2]; a first-semester freshman girl reads and writes as well as a second-semester sophomore boy. With the female brain better set up, in general, for word production, word connection to emotion and senses, and verbal processing, there will probably always be a reading and writing gap between girls and boys. But there are very practical means by which those one-and-a-half years can decrease to a few months.

This chapter will provide you with those means, celebrating the very "boyish" way males have of approaching reading, writing, and language arts, and also helping adapt and improve their performance in academic tasks, tests, and classrooms. We'll discuss home strategies and classroom adjustments that have worked around the country (and, in some cases, around the world), which protect and promote reading, writing, and language arts learning for boys. The strategies and adjustments are brain-based approaches to developing and connecting brain centers that enhance the use of words in reading, writing, and language arts. None of these strategies harm girls; in fact, some of them can be used to help girls too. But most of these strategies, techniques, and recommendations have been designed after years of research and field testing in the way boys' brains develop and learn.

All strategies in this chapter can be put to use right now to help promote development of verbal ability in the frontal lobe, temporal lobe, and other cortical areas. They can increase the performance of boys on those papers displayed on school walls, and indeed throughout their verbal learning experiences.

Encourage Early Childhood Word Use

As is true of so many learning issues, parents are "coteachers" for our children. Home and school are each most effective when the home is a center of reading, writing, and talking—a place that values the effective use of words from the child's birth forward.

In Chapter Three, we detailed how parents can set up a home as a healthy and pleasant learning environment for male learning, including verbal development. Because we focused on birth to kindergarten, we hope you'll explore that chapter in depth. In this chapter, we'll begin with some additional tips for helping preschool boys and then we'll focus more completely on strategies for verbal development in elementary school and beyond.

Helping develop verbal abilities in the brain is a matter of not only practicing words but also connecting word use to other brain functions. You'll notice that a number of the strategies we suggest are "whole brain" strategies of that type.

FOR TODDLER LANGUAGE DEVELOPMENT.   Make labels for items around the house. Some of these items may also appear in books you are reading to your child. Large Post-it notes or index cards work well for these labels. Use construction paper or poster board and one of the new "nonpermanent" adhesives to put the labels on the car, Spiderman figure, chair, table, cup, door, window.

It is fun to make labeling into a game that you play with your son. You can do this by challenging him verbally to place the words in the correct places. When he's done, congratulate him (and correct him as necessary), then ask him to collect the labels; shuffle them up and then play the game again. As your child's verbal skills improve, add new cards to the deck.

As your son becomes competent with a set of labels, use a timer and let him compete against himself to see how quickly he can place or retrieve the words.

When your son knows these words without any help, he can "collect" that word in a Ziploc bag. Once he has collected his entire original set of words, move on to a new set. You can expand this into the yard and tie it into a science lesson. You can do this at a grandparent's house, in the garage, in a cluttered basement—anywhere.

Throughout this game, enhance your son's fun and his whole-brain development by having him draw pictures of some of the items. This provides a visual reinforcement during the very early stage of learning.

FOR PRESCHOOL READING DEVELOPMENT.   Now let's say your son is able to read, even if it's only a little. Here's a way to keep reinforcing his verbal development.

Buy a set of magnetic words and put them on your refrigerator. (These words come in larger print for younger readers.) You might end up with fifty of these on one side of your refrigerator.

Create a "learning ritual" with your son by which, every day at a certain hour, you direct your son to these magnetic words. Ask him to move them around until he forms a sentence. Congratulate his effort and help him make corrections as needed. Then use the words to make your own sentence. Let him read your sentence. Talk to him about any elements of it he might not understand. Remember, keep this game fun! Keep your sentences age appropriate.

As you enjoy this game together, let it become increasingly challenging. Challenge him to use a minimum number of words in his sentences, adding one word then another then another as he masters each length. At each step, have him read and explain the sentence, and congratulate him and help him make corrections as needed.

This is an exciting brain builder than can also be enjoyed outside the ritual learning time. For instance, let's say you are cooking dinner: now you can use the words to build a menu. Your son can help you make a list of items you need for a recipe. He can help you prepare the meal from the written recipe and menu on the refrigerator.

Helping Elementary School Boys

Let's assume your son has learned to read. He may love reading, or he may not, but you can sense already how important reading is to his elementary school grades, socialization, and self-esteem. What can you do right now that will integrate improvement in verbal learning into your son's everyday life? Let's start with a few very detailed tricks and items.

START HIM OUT WITH LISTS: THE GROCERY STORE.   Before you go to the grocery store, challenge your son to sit down and make a list of some items he wants included on the regular list, including one special healthy treat. You might also have him rewrite, in his own letters and words, the family's grocery list—all of it or part of it, depending on his age and interest. If any of the words are misspelled (and if the boy is in third grade or beyond), model the correct spelling for him and have him copy it. If he is in fourth grade or beyond, pick a few misspelled words for him to look up in the dictionary (or electronic spell checker).

Once your son has all the words spelled correctly, he will get the healthy treat that he put on the list. By providing this incentive you are helping your son learn that "reward is part of effort."[3] He has an incentive to write these words. Ultimately, the good feelings he will get from being successful on his shopping-list spelling game will translate to pleasure for doing well on his school spelling tests, and he will seek that pleasure again and again.

Now let's say you and your son go do the shopping. You can let him read the labels of the foods and put the items he wrote down on his list into the cart. In this way, he has written the words, learned the correct spelling, and then integrated this verbal learning task into a physical task—finding the food on the grocery store shelf.

USE "VISUAL" DICTIONARIES.   Obtain a children's dictionary with lots of pictures, and play games that connect the pictures to the words. This kind of dictionary helps develop cross-talk in the brain between visual-spatial centers and verbal centers. Especially if you have a very visually or spatially oriented boy, this kind of dictionary can be a lifesaver.

USE THE LIBRARY.   Make a trip to the library as a regular family outing. Children's librarians can be great resources for directing boys to books that will especially appeal to them. (The book *What Stories Does My Son Need?* lists age-appropriate books that boys really like.) Take your son to reading and story times at the library, and watch for announcements that children's authors will be giving readings. Make sure a few of the authors you go to see are male authors—who can serve as positive role models for reading, word use, and books.

PLAY WORD GAMES AT THE DINNER TABLE.   During dinner, play word games. Each family member can select a word, and another family member has to use the word in a sentence. Your son gets to choose a word, and dad has to make up a sentence. Then mom chooses a word, and son makes up a sentence. This is also a good game to play in the car during long trips.

Word games, grocery lists, libraries, refrigerator sentence constructors—almost any activity that incorporates word use as a ritualized and fun part of your son's life can work wonders to enhance the connections he makes between sensory experience and words.

Rely on Your Parent-Led Team

Any brain development tool appropriate for parents can be used by any other member of the parent-led team At the very least, it's important for boys to write letters (and emails) to grandparents and other family members living out of town. This is a family's built-in brain developer. To make sure it happens, you might set up a regular time (perhaps Saturday mornings) for your son to do his letter and email writing. Boys often need these schedules, these routines, especially if they don't gravitate toward writing by nature.

In this letter writing, you can help the brain make verbal-spatial connections by having your son draw pictures for his grandparents that show them things he's learning. On these pictures (or in a separate text), make sure your son writes small annotations, even a tiny essay, which note sensory details in the pictures—the car is red or the sky is blue. If he draws a figure inside the car whose identity is not discernible to the eye, he can write, "That's my Daddy" or "That's my Mommy" and tell a short story that includes what they were wearing and whether they wore a smile (or frown!) on their faces.

When the weekly letter and drawing are finished, let your son help you mail them. Even in this small task, the boy's integration of words and everyday life can continue. He should address the envelope and take it to the post office with you. He can put it in the mail slot.

For this exercise to be especially powerful for your son's development, it's important that your relatives and other team members write letters and emails back. The more sensory detail you can get them to use in their return correspondence, the better for your son. When your relatives do correspond, encourage your son to read their letters aloud to you and to your spouse.

Art Technique: Put Language to Music

As we've already discussed, music helps children enhance their verbal skills. Musical activity is defined, in this case, as activity that activates music centers of the brain. Listening to the radio is a musical activity, but it is passive and thus not as effective as getting your son into piano, guitar, saxophone, flute, drum, or any other music lesson program. This was most recently confirmed by a study conducted at the Chinese University of Hong Kong. Children, specifically boys, who were given as little as one year of musical training tested out better in verbal memory than children who had no musical training.[4] The Chinese study showed that even a year after the musical kids had ended their music training, their verbal memories were still better than those of the nonmusical children.

A fun way to help younger children make music-learning connections is to get an inexpensive karaoke machine (usually available in toy departments of discount stores). Once your son has learned how to sing along with its musical accompaniment, you can challenge him to sing songs and tell stories. Make sure to be his audience for his songs and stories, asking questions to encourage expansion of sentences and lengthening of stories and songs. (Be sure not to criticize his singing—it's the process, not the product, that counts here.) Karaoke machines, like music lessons, not only use music-verbal connections but also have the added advantage of directly enhancing a boy's self-confidence in using words.

Helping Middle and High School Boys

If you are the parent of an adolescent who is already a strong reader, he may well like to read anything and everything. All he needs is time, an assignment, and a friendly book.

If your adolescent son isn't a strong reader, he may need help in these three specific areas, all of which we'll cover here:

1. Advocacy in his school for changes in the way language arts are taught.
2. Discovery of books and other reading items that are "readable" to him—the books he *wants* to read.
3. Focus of his time and energy on reading, homework, and learning tasks even when he doesn't want to do them.

In Part Four of this book, we focus specifically on helping undermotivated, underachieving, and underperforming boys, as well as boys with learning disorders. In this chapter, we'll assume that your son does not fit one of these categories—he just needs a little extra help to be a good reader and writer.

Try This
A Game for Youngsters

Write the letters of your son's first name in a vertical line down the left side of a sheet of poster paper. As a game, have your son find things that start with the each letter and fill them in. For example:

M   music
I   ice cream
C   car
H   house
A   apple
E   egg
L   leg

When he has come up with a word for each space, allow him a treat; make it something appropriate and appealing, such as a special trip to the park or a favorite food for lunch or dinner.

After he has completed the page, post it in your son's room; play again using the first name, with no repeats allowed! When you've exhausted the first name, switch to the middle or last name. Let him decorate his sheets with drawings or cutout pictures that match the words.

DO HOMEWORK WITH YOUR SON.   Many boys need you to do their homework with them—not *for* them, but with them. They need you to be their "focus coach." A seventh grader who is not turning in his language arts or other homework needs you and your parent team to spend at least an hour of his day helping him focus on the report he needs to write, the book he needs to read, the presentation he needs to make. This can be true even for a high school boy.

LINK SCREEN TIME WITH STUDY REWARDS.   If your son is not doing well with his language arts (or other) assignments—especially if he is not reading very much at all—he may be spending too many hours in front of video games, television, or the Internet. This indicates that he needs you to help him redirect himself to *essential tasks.* The visual stimulants, so much more comfortable to him than the reading-writing and verbal ones, must now become rewards rather than entitlements. He may be grateful for the help, or he may at first rebel against your strength on this issue. But if you handle it as a united family, and if you negotiate with him to see the positive results after a three-month trial period, you might be quite surprised by his response.

Provide Reading Materials That Boys Enjoy

There has been a great deal of argument over the last two decades about whether reading one kind of book is better than reading another. If a boy reads comic books, for instance, he is usually considered "an immature reader" or seen as "wasting his time." If he reads technical manuals but doesn't like fiction, he might be considered "not well rounded." If he reads science fiction novels but doesn't like anything else, he might be considered "a sci-fi geek." Our educational culture is, in general, quite judgmental about what kids read. To some extent, this is a good thing. We want children to be well rounded in their reading. But to some extent such an attitude is also a hindrance to a child's success in language arts, especially a boy's.

Department of Education researcher Diane Ravitch, an expert in the gender needs of children in our schools, has done extensive research and writing on what children are reading. Not surprisingly, she discovered a link between reading successes, the content of written works, and the reader's "right to choose."

Diane Ravitch has pointed out that books like those in the Harry Potter series show that American youngsters are willing to read good books, books that are exciting, mysterious, full of intrigue and show-downs between good and evil. In contrast to these, Ravitch has noted, history textbooks skim lightly over things, ignoring the drama and story of history.[5]

Michael Smith, of Rutgers Graduate School of Education, and Jeffrey Wilhelm, of Boise State University, corroborate Dr. Ravitch's findings. They conducted a study of boys in grades 6 through 12 and discovered that their reading and writing assignments were "divorced from their interests." Wilhelm and Smith reported, "We found that boys are totally cynical about how school doesn't relate to real life." One of their subjects, a sixteen-year-old boy, told them, "I just don't like reading fiction. I find myself sort of scanning." Another: "English is about nothing. It's about commas and rhythm. What does that have to do with anything?" These same boys, they reported, are very engaged when the book or writing assignment involves writing about skateboarding, or reading and using a motorcycle repair manual.[6]

After many years of research, these experts have noted something that is probably, at some level, instinctual to parents of sons who complain of boredom and lack of meaning in language arts, literature, history, and social studies classes. Boys will in general read what is interesting to them—what fits their hormonal, neurological, and psychological base. They will reject what is boring, what does not fit.

Given that the average boy may not read as many books over the course of a year as a girl, the books boys do read really matter. There is literature every child would benefit from having read—*To Kill a Mockingbird* or Shakespeare's *Romeo and Juliet* come to mind—but are all the books our children are forced to read, whether textbook or fiction, appropriate templates on which to base the success or failure of those children who are already not our best readers? This is a question parents of nonreading boys must certainly face. If you are one of these parents, you may notice what Diane Ravitch and other researchers have noticed: boys may need a faster-moving story line to stay interested. You may be compelled to advocate for "substitute" reading lists and "books by choice" in your son's classrooms.

You might also notice that many boys need more graphic-spatial content than girls in order to fully grasp all the content of a book. As boys move toward college, their brains move toward completion of their development, and the male need for more graphics and visuals than females dissipates to some degree. But still, on average, even adult male readers tend to gravitate toward reading material that is

- Filled with spatial-kinesthetic action—whether in thriller and suspense novels, science fiction, or sports biographies
- Technical and mechanical in content, such as instructional manuals and business books
- Graphic and visual, such as comic books and comics pages in newspapers

Given that the minds of boys and men lean in this direction, parents of sons are in a crucial position in this culture. Boys who read their school textbooks only dispassionately (if even that) might very passionately read Harry Potter books. Boys who are "bored" in school might very well read nonfiction books on cars. Boys who skim over the words in their history textbook might love to read a biography of a historical figure. For middle and high school boys, this reality is partly biological, as the next Did You Know? box reveals.

Given what is happening in the minds of boys, you as a parent of an adolescent male may find it necessary to become a parent advocate for all the adolescent boys in your schools. You can use this book and other similar resources to help schools notice these two foundational points:

1. In general, the male brain is not set up as well as the female brain for language arts learning; thus males will often need extra linguistic help, adjusted reading choices, and creative teaching to perform at par with females in this area.
2. Our school systems are actually contributing to the growing gender gap in language arts by denying boys the content, curricula, teaching strategies, and multimedia techniques they need in order to gain some parity in verbal learning.

Become a Parent Who Compels Change

For teachers and schools to help your sons succeed, they need your support in compelling change in educational institutions. Here are talking points—some ideas for dialogue and advocacy with your schools. If any

> ### ??? Did You Know? ???
>
> The dominant male hormone, testosterone, kicks into high gear during the middle and high school years (as the years of puberty take place). Boys during puberty receive five to seven spikes of this hormone through their brains per day. Testosterone increases male (and female) spatial-mechanical development and use of right-hemisphere brain centers. Boys have up to twenty times more testosterone in them than girls, so, not surprisingly, boys' brains in adolescence will differ from girls': at the very time that girls' hormones—estrogen and oxytocin—are enhancing left frontal lobe verbal development, boys' hormones are pushing the male brain toward aggressive-active, spatial-mechanical, and kinesthetic-physical life experience.[7]

of these are just plain impossible to accomplish, it's the wrong battle for you to fight with a school. But if it can be accomplished—even if it takes years—it might be the right one.

1. *Change curricula.* Encourage teachers and schools to check language arts curricula for male-friendly standards. (Of course, this should be done to help girls, too, in their areas of needs. For more on what girls need from institutionalized curricula, you might enjoy reading *Boys and Girls Learn Differently!*). If, for instance, the curriculum approved by the school district for language arts lacks substantial visuals and graphics, it should probably be shelved. If it never uses movies, videos, or other multimedia forms, it is probably not boy-friendly.

2. *Change reading requirements.* Some textbooks, like those described by Diane Ravitch, might have to be shelved. They simply may not be engaging enough to keep boys (or girls) interested. Perhaps even more important, schools may need your encouragement to allow children a personal choice of reading assignments. For instance, you might advocate

that Harry Potter books become acceptable for some students, while others read *Jane Eyre*. Not all preset reading requirements can or should be scrapped, but schools and communities can allow personal-choice reading assignments to become 30 to 50 percent of the classroom reading grade. Just this one adjustment may help a number of adolescent boys improve their grades in language arts.

3. *Increase the use of visual media.* It's important to expand use of visual and spatial media—movies, TV clips, CD-ROMs, PowerPoint, and the like—not only in curricula but also in student reports and presentations. These media often fit the minds of boys who are not as good at reading, writing, and literature.

4. *Encourage note taking and paper writing using laptop computers.* Financial issues make this innovation difficult in many situations, but for those families who decide to get one, the cost of a laptop may be worth a great deal in a son's classroom improvement. Many adolescent boys simply cannot take handwritten notes as well as the girls around them. If the family invests in a computer and in typing classes, the boy can improve his note taking immensely.

5. *Encourage, at home and at school, the use of physical movement while reading and writing.* Of course, a lot of physical movement in a classroom can become a teacher's nightmare. If parents advocate for students to be allowed to physically (and appropriately) move about in classrooms while they contemplate and accomplish parts of their writing assignments, parents must do their part to raise sons to respect this innovation with self-discipline. Although physical movement keeps the verbal centers of the brain stimulated and mitigates against boredom, performance anxiety, and rest states, it's a very different way of helping boys read and write than most schools now allow. Parents may even need to be volunteers in classrooms during the early stages of this innovation, just to help boys learn self-discipline.

6. *Initiate community discussions about school start times and class size requirements.* Research clearly shows that adjusting start times, especially for adolescents, has significant positive affects on performance and attitude. And reduced class size has been shown to be healthy for students at all ages.

Enhance Your Effectiveness as an Advocate for Your Son's Education

When Karen Teja completes her final term as a member of the Colorado Springs School District No. 11 elected school board, she will have served her term-limited eight years as a tireless advocate for children and their parents. We asked Karen—herself a parent and a former early childhood educator—how parents can become active advocates in their children's schools. Here is her response:

> Never give up! Start when your child enters school. Meet the child's teachers, ask how you can help, how you can support the teacher and the school in providing the best learning environment for your child— these are the questions to ask before there is ever a problem. Start at the beginning. In elementary school, volunteer. Get to know your child's teacher each year and develop relationships with the principal, and, just as important, with the school secretary. This is the person in an elementary school who regularly knows everything that is happening—and can be a great source of help and information, saving parents lots of time. It gets harder in middle and high school, because the opportunities for parents to work with the school face more challenges—not only from the schools, but also from the students. But, again, *never give up*. Our adolescents need us as much or more than our younger children.

Karen stressed that as parents you should

- Join and work for the parents' organization (PTA, PTO) at your child's school. As a member, you will get a list of other children in your son's class and school and their parents, a great networking tool when you need to develop grassroots support.
- Support the use of a portfolio to evaluate your child's progress—including *but not limited to* test scores—so that the focus on test scores alone doesn't continue to consume the kids, the parents, and the schools.
- Seek opportunities to serve on your local equivalent of "building accountability" committees and on various committees at the district level.

- Attend school board meetings, listening carefully to what individual members say so that you can get to know where they stand on important issues and policies. Then have coffee with the member of your school board who feels most approachable to you. Identify yourself as a registered voter!

Do all these things *before* there is a problem you need to address. That way you have already established a positive relationship, and you improve your chances of being heard when you need help as you work on behalf of your child. Karen recommends that parents peruse two helpful Web sites:

The official site for the National Parent Teachers Association, www.pta.org, features a great section on parent involvement, with a list titled "100 Ways for Parents to Be Involved in Their Child's Education."

The official site for the National School Board Association, www.nsba.org, has good information to help parents work with their local school board and work together with their representatives to effect needed change.

Colorado State Representative Michael Merrifield was a high school choral teacher before he retired and ran for state office. More than thirty years in the classroom gave him wonderful insights into helping children succeed, and he shared his thoughts with us about working with boys:

I always felt that I provided an important role model for my male students—I was an athletic, masculine guy who taught music. It seemed to say to the boys that they could like music and the arts, and still be men. I believe the boys felt more freedom to participate, and we had the freedom to interact as males. After the first couple of years, I always had large numbers of boys—fifty or sixty—signing up for the all-male choir classes, and many of my students would confide in me when they had friends who were having problems in school. I would encourage them to bring the friend around, and if we could get the boy interested in choir that would often be the hook that would keep him engaged enough in school to help him stick with it.

We asked Michael what advice he would give parents who want to approach their elected officials for help with problems they are trying to address in their children's schools. He had some concrete recommendations:

- Get your representative's phone number, preferably a cell number. (Michael always returns voice mail promptly, but can't respond as quickly to the hundreds of email messages he receives daily.)
- Identify yourself as a constituent—a voter. Better yet, identify yourself as spokesperson for a group (with more than one member!) of concerned constituents (parents), because your elected official has a vested interest in meeting the needs of constituents.
- Start with "I know you're busy" and then state your issues and offer to send information. Show that you have done your homework, and offer to email a summary (one or two pages) for review.
- Ask for a meeting—make yourself available at the elected official's convenience.
- When you meet, bring more information and be prepared to define specifically what it is you are asking the official to do. If you can partner with a local school board member, that adds more weight to your request.
- Recognize that elected officials don't know everything about every issue, so you will have to educate them and be willing to help them.
- Make sure the issue you want addressed isn't a municipal or county issue; it doesn't help to ask an elected state official for help with something over which the state has no control.
- Let your elected officials know you appreciate their help when they are able to help you resolve a problem or address an issue.

Michael shared these final thoughts for parents:

I was always sad when we had a concert or other event at school and the kids who participated didn't have family in the audience. It is so important that parents and grandparents attend events, join the booster club, volunteer in the school library. With the current budget crisis in many schools, volunteers are needed in more areas than ever before, and when you have a relationship with your child's school before something goes wrong, it's a lot easier to find allies and support when you do face a problem.

To Michael's comments, Kathy and I will add a recommendation that parents and parent-led teams seek out organizations in their communities that have already started making school-parent connections. A prime example is the Boy Scouts of America, who have developed a number of school- and parent-friendly programs to help boys become better readers. You'll find contact information and Web sites for these programs in the Notes section at the back of this book. Connecting your parent-led team, your son, and your community in already existing programs can save a busy family the trouble of reinventing the wheel. The Boy Scouts organization has made great strides in male literacy by forging connections between individuals and groups who are raising and teaching boys.

What Teachers Can Do

Corey Nussbaum is an elementary school teacher in Seattle. He came up to me after a teacher workshop and said something I've heard quite often: "People are beginning to realize that boys are really struggling in our schools, especially in reading, writing, and English. I think it's a good thing that the public is beginning to understand this, but I'm worried that people will blame teachers for the problem. I don't think teachers created this problem. And I don't think teachers alone can solve the problem. There's a lot we can do, but we can't solve this problem without parents."

We agree with Corey: parents are urgently needed! At the same time, when teachers enact specific changes and innovations, they can directly alter a boy's (or girl's) success in language arts. We'll focus on these now, but we won't repeat the strategies we encouraged in the preceding pages. If you are a teacher and have not read "What Parents Can Do," we hope you'll read it now. You can adapt all the strategies recommended in that section for use in the classroom. We also hope you'll read Chapters Three and Four, which covered infancy, the toddler years, and preschool. We'll begin this section with advice for elementary school faculty.

Helping Elementary School Boys

The first and perhaps most controversial thing you might look at as a teacher of language arts is the way you grade. If you are a teacher who emphasizes sensory detail in children's writing grades, you might notice boys getting graded down more than girls in this area. As we've noted earlier, the male brain does not naturally absorb or verbalize, either in writing or orally, as much sensory detail as the female. If you are seeing this brain fact at work right in your own classroom—or on the papers posted on the display walls of your elementary school—you might be inspired to rethink the educational theory regarding "good writing" that says sensory detail must be central to a B grade. Greater sensory detail is needed for an A grade, but perhaps not for a B. Perhaps by making this small adjustment, a child who has difficulty in the area of sensory detail could go from a C to a B.

Furthermore, in the same way that teachers altered grading standards for math tests to include more essay writing in order to help girls succeed at math, you as a teacher have the power to alter language arts toward less emphasis on male weaknesses and more on their strengths. If you know a boy is clearly not able to insert sensory detail into an essay in the same way as another boy or girl, perhaps he can be rewarded for his organization or his emphasis on logic. Perhaps these elements can become targets of teaching and grade enhancement for him.

Having said there might be wiggle room in grading and adjustments in essay writing, there is still no substitute for improving a student's retention and use of words, sensory detail, and other writing elements. Let's look now at some techniques that can help boys (and girls) become better at using their words.

ART TECHNIQUE: IMPROVING BOYS' WORD USE AND SPELL-
ING.   One of the most problematic areas for any child in word use is
correct spelling. Of the many fine strategies for improving spelling,
we've seen a lot of success in pilot schools that use music to help the
child's brain retain both the word itself and its spelling.

If you use melodies for language learning in the earliest grades, you
may still find fourth graders unconsciously humming while they take
spelling or other writing tests. A new set of studies by UCLA neuroscientists Elizabeth Sowell and Arthur Toga has begun to map when certain parts of the brain have "growth spurts."[8] These studies have shown
that at around six years of age children experience a growth spurt in the
frontal and parietal lobes, which support numerous brain skills such as
spatial tasking, language development, and musical attention. Thus,
establishing connections between words and music is key at this early
stage of brain development. Check out the next Try This box.

USING SPATIAL AND GRAPHIC AIDS.   Boys' brains have more
white matter in them than girls' brains do.[9] This is one of the brain differences that might explain why males tend to rely so much on their visual cortex. Not only do boys tend to rely more on spatial-mechanical
centers in their right hemisphere than girls do, but they may move
more neural material more quickly from and to their visual cortex via
the increased white matter. Teachers can use this information to design
appropriate strategies for implementing language arts curricula. The
overhead projector is a tried-and-true visual-spatial teaching tool. The
boys (and girls) can be called to the front of the class to practice words
and sentences through writing and manipulation of letters on the overhead. Seeing the words projected on the screen or wall is visually reinforcing for any child's brain, and may especially help boys who are
visually and spatially oriented.

The most immediate and useful graphic aid is of course a child's
own artwork. Reading and writing improvement often directly follows
art and drawing. Just as many boys' brains respond well to connecting
music to words, many boys also do better in their writing when they
draw their subject, both before and after doing the written work.

Try This

In your own first-grade classroom, five-letter spelling words can be sung to the tune of "You Are My Sunshine." The five syllables of the song phrase get mimicked in five-letter words, such as

H-A-N-D-S
G-R-E-E-N
S-T-A-N-D

Six-letter words can be sung to the six syllables of "Happy Birthday to You." Following are some examples of six-letter words:

F-O-R-G-E-T
C-A-R-P-E-T
M-O-V-I-N-G

One of the most popular innovations in our Gurian Institute schools is the use of artwork for brainstorming. If you are teaching fourth or fifth grade, you have probably taught your students to brainstorm before they write. Generally, when teachers teach brainstorming, they teach written brainstorming.

"Go ahead and just write for fifteen minutes" you might instruct the kids. "Just write freely about any details that come to you."

A male-friendly modification of this instruction might sound like this: "Some of you would rather draw a lot of your brainstorming. Go ahead and do that. Draw the cars, houses, airplanes, and everything else that is a part of your writing assignment."

If you make this option available, you'll find over a period of a month that generally more boys than girls will choose it. You'll also find that the children who do choose it will refer back to their drawing for a lot of sensory details they might not have been able to write down in the verbal brainstorming. This is a strategy that uses the male predilection toward spatial, graphic, and visual stimulants to improve the child's "verbal product," his writing.

This innovation is very popular among the schools working with male-female brain difference theory. It has the potential to bring males toward some parity with females in writing assignments, especially if the boys use colored pencils (or crayons) for their drawings and especially if they are allowed to "follow the drawings" into not only their written words but also the making of booklets and small, word-annotated comic strips. These "writing products" are self-esteem boosters, especially for boys who tend to write essays with few words or minimal detail.

USING TEAMS AND COMPETITION.   Some boys are loners, of course, but most boys either like teams or wish they were on a team of some kind. As teachers, you can take advantage of this "team instinct" in boys for language learning. If you supervise it carefully, you can inspire boys to learn to write by having them compete with each other in teams. Essays and writing assignments can receive a "team" grade—everyone on the team gets the same grade. This creates a good-stress kind of peer pressure for the whole group to write a more detailed, more logical essay. If the teams are not too large—three or fewer members—there's little chance that one of the boys will "totally slack." In fact, generally, if one boy does begin to act like a slacker, it will be obvious to you, and the other boys will probably call attention to it as well.

For boys especially, competitive individual and team learning can be the stimulant they need to really care about learning, reading, and writing. It can breathe life into their lesson. But classroom competition can be daunting for some teachers, especially female teachers who do not have sons of their own or who rarely experienced competition in childhood. If you find yourself in this situation—or if you just don't like the idea of competitiveness among elementary school children from a philosophical point of view—you might enjoy calling together a meeting with both male and female teachers in the school. In this meeting, you can air your concerns, figure out where your colleagues stand, and get support from colleagues more experienced with competition. You can even ask for someone to be a "competition mentor" to you, someone to lean on when you're not sure how much noise or movement or how many student jibes are normal for a competitive environment. You may find that many of the male teachers in your school dialogue will immediately cry, "Yes, let's have more competition in our learning." They may have been brought up with a lot of competition or just gravitate toward it naturally. Their support will be especially helpful in using competition and creating male mentoring when necessary.

We are not stereotyping here—many women like to compete more than many men—but at the same time, in our experience with schools, we find a larger number of male teachers pressing for more "fun, competitive" learning strategies.

USING PHYSICAL EXERCISE AND ATHLETICS.   You have probably noticed by now that in our innovations for elementary school teachers is a "subtext" about getting other parts of the brain than the verbal centers involved in language learning. Because a lot of our sons have spatial, kinesthetic, visual, or musical brain centers that are better developed than the verbal ones, we can improve their verbal and language learning by connecting their "strength" centers with their somewhat weaker centers. This practice is good for all boys and girls, though it might be grade saving for the boys whose brains operate at the very "male" side of the brain spectrum.

The physical body is not separate from the brain. The physical body can be a strength center for boys, and in fact for any child's brain. The male brain has more spinal fluid in the brain stem than does the female.[10] This is one of the reasons that boys are "so physical." With more spinal fluid in the part of the brain that connects learning with physical movement, boys are "primed to move." You can use physical activity and athletics to not only release energy so that the kids' brains can focus and concentrate but also to stimulate the brain toward greater potential for language learning.

A beautiful illustration of this came to the Gurian Institute from a teacher at Robert Ogilvie Elementary School in Fort St. John, British Columbia, who wrote to us a few months after we did a male-female brain difference training there: "Following the training, I began taking my class down to the gym and letting them run laps before our spelling tests. The boys especially showed marked improvement in their test grades. And they were better able to work at their desks following the period of exercise." Where the body goes, so goes the brain. For many boys, getting the body to prime the brain's functioning can inspire learning improvement.

As you and your school staff absorb information about the male brain, you might carry on a discussion in your school about how to organize class times to best use sports and other physical activities. Given that there can potentially be a great deal of grade and performance improvement after the kids play soccer or basketball or run track, you might want PE classes to come just before language arts classes.

Helping Middle and High School Boys

What we have advocated in the preceding section, as well as in earlier sections of this chapter, carries over into a boy's adolescence. His brain is growing by leaps and bounds, but it is still a male brain. To whatever extent a boy has had trouble with reading, writing, sensory detail, or language arts, that trouble may travel with him into middle and high school.

The issue of reading choice is mentioned by many middle school and high school teachers in our trainings. Many teachers want desperately to give more choice, but they also feel nervous about what will happen if they do. Will they be called "unfair" if one student reads a harder book (*Oliver Twist*, for example) and another student an easier one (one of the Harry Potter books)? Will their workload increase because they will now have to familiarize themselves with all sorts of books—nonfiction, technical, fantasy, sci-fi—in which they may have no interest?

Greater reading choice is an innovation that must be discussed throughout your faculty. It can work only if the school's administration agrees to it. It often works well for one classroom to lead the "experiment" and to collect data on how (and why) grades improve over a year. Fortunately, how the teacher handles the fairness issue seems to resolve the problem. Teachers are smart and intuitive—they are not going to allow one student to read a Harry Potter book and the other *Oliver Twist* without making assignments that require equal amounts of work, research, and care. Fortunately, a teacher can get on the Internet and usually find out something about the new book a student has selected. No matter how arcane, the book and its subject are generally listed on some Web site (and the student can be required to furnish that Web site) so that the teacher can familiarize himself or herself with the material without reading the whole book. The smart and intuitive teacher will require the student who writes about a skateboarder's biography to write a heck of a good paper!

This is the case at the Webb Schools, in Claremont, California, where all tenth graders are required to read *Frankenstein, The Wars, Catcher in the Rye, Great Expectations, Othello, Antigone,* and a selection of poetry, but there are also single-gender lists from which students can choose their own reading assignments. The girls select from *The Gardens of Kyoto* and *Girl with a Pearl Earring;* the boys might choose *Into the Wild, The Picture of Dorian Gray,* or Jack London short stories. These lists are constantly being added to by students' choices. By letting boys and girls choose gender-specific "elective books," the teachers at the Webb Schools have innovated in the direction of allowing more choice to kids.

Reading choice is a curricular change the Gurian Institute advocates wherever we go. Here are some other, more specific techniques for getting more and better writing out of your boys.

USING PHYSICAL MOVEMENT.   For middle and high school boys, physical movement during writing and reading is often crucial for brain alertness and performance. Some adolescent boys will suddenly flourish as writers once they are allowed to write as they move around within an appropriate and agreed-on space in the class or outdoors and without bothering classmates. Allowing adolescent boys who seem to be "zoning out" or "getting bored" in class to squeeze a Nerf ball in the nonwriting hand can keep the brain stimulated to read and write.

Here's a good way to test this theory. Before making any changes, observe your present classroom for a week—even keep a diary—and note whether you are seeing discipline problems during writing or reading tasks. Do you notice boys tapping pencils, nudging each other, talking out of turn? If you have a middle or high school classroom in which a few students (generally male) are tapping pencils or even bugging and nudging their friends to the point that it is bothersome, their brains may be going into a rest state during language learning tasks, and the tapping and nudging may be a way the boy is trying to keep himself stimulated.

Squeezing a Nerf ball or moving around the classroom (within set limits) can really help. The teachers trained by the Gurian Institute find that it does not lead to discipline issues and can help the boy write and read better. To test your own results, continue to keep your diary—but now, institute supervised physical movement and the use of Nerf balls. Note changes in discipline and in language arts learning. You might be pleasantly surprised!

ART TECHNIQUE: ACTING AND DRAMA.   Margaret Buehler is a middle school English and literature teacher at the Regis School of the Sacred Heart, in Houston, Texas. I met her when I visited her boys' school for a training. Later, when I asked her what innovations she had put into effect to improve her boys' language arts performance, she wrote, "In response to your suggestion that the boys act out characters in order to better remember them, the eighth grade literature class put on *Julius Caesar* for the entire school. They thoroughly enjoyed it and learned the plot very well. In fact, they were the only students at the Main Street Theatre performance of *Julius Caesar* who understood what the director was trying to do with timelessness, and that made me very proud of them. The students' understanding of the play definitely improved when they had to act out the parts." Anne Carty, the head of school for Regis, confirmed Margaret's observation and noted an improvement in these students' grades.

Margaret told another story:

When the seventh grade boys were preparing [the song] "White Christmas" for the Christmas program, I had them take on different character traits. First I had them show disdain for singing. The

second time, I had them act like rock stars. They did well on both oc-
casions. I think their variety of performance taught them staging and
character in a way no lecture could. Now, as we read other pieces of
literature, I have the boys stand up and show me the physical pos-
tures of the characters in the story. They will show emotions through
physical actions instead of just staring at me when I ask them to articulate emotions. It has been a very good technique for teaching literature.

From learning about how boys' brains work, Margaret and others
in her school have rethought the teaching of language arts and literature. At first, Margaret wondered how "crazy" it would get for middle
school boys to be doing all this acting and physical play in their learning. Would it be too rowdy? Her school and classes are all boys, so would
the situation get out of control?

Margaret, like so many middle school teachers, discovered that
authority could be maintained while the boy's minds were freed to learn
in ways natural to them.

LEARNING THROUGH INTERVIEWS.   Earlier we noted the studies
that showed male learning levels to be higher when written material
was integrated into their areas of personal interest and success. This is
especially true for early adolescent boys.

You can use this understanding by sending the boys (and girls)
home to do interviews. Learners who have trouble writing with adequate
detail will often write better after they have interviewed someone of
interest. To this end, you can instruct your students to interview five
people in their lives (parents, extended family, older siblings, teachers,
coaches, community leaders) and collect a list of each of the person's
favorite words. This emphasis on words is also a way to keep building
word use in the student. The student can print interview sheets with
simple questions like these:

- What are your five favorite words?
- What does each word mean to you?

- Why do you like those words?
- Do the words bring to mind any special memories?

These are just some of the questions students can ask. Often the interviewee will use words such as "love," "justice," "peace," "courage"—these are words with a lot of potential for classroom work. After the class has collected all the words and answers, you can have students write sentences using each word; you can have them illustrate the words (and their meanings) by making posters and hanging them in the classroom. Students may already do this kind of activity with character traits, if your school has a character development program. The students can write the words in large letters on poster paper and survey the lists to see which individual words appear on the most lists, how many are nouns, how many are verbs, how many are descriptive. These words will often generate lists of other words, and all of this activity inspires dialogue.

This "Five Favorite Words" activity gets boys talking to people who are important to them. It gets boys to focus on words and meanings. It builds team cohesion in a classroom that uses learning teams. If and when the boys are given a writing assignment that uses these words, the writing assignment will be all the stronger because of the boys' "buy-in" to the interviewed individuals and the subject matter.

CONNECTING FEELINGS WITH WORDS.   The next Try This box describes an activity you can do over a period of time with your students. It integrates feelings, words, sensory details, and visuals.

USING SINGLE-GENDER STRATEGIES.   At Woodland Middle School in Taylor Mill, Kentucky, teacher Sean Detisch joined with colleagues in trying a controversial but effective strategy for improving male performance in language arts: the use of single-gender groups and classes. Sean reports, "Woodland is about twenty minutes from downtown Cincinnati. It is a combination of public housing projects and upper-middle-class subdivisions, with a huge range of abilities in one classroom. Last year, we separated boys and girls in order to discuss

Try This

Challenge your students to create two boxes of picture files, then label the first box "Tasks" and the second box "Thinking or Feeling." For the Tasks box, have your students collect pictures of people doing things. These pictures can be from magazines and newspapers or from online pictures of people engaged in some task or activity. Encourage your students to find unique and diverse pictures—you don't want a whole box of NBA or NFL players, although there can be some.

For the Thinking or Feeling box, have the students focus on pictures of people's faces and expressions, posture, and other signs of nonverbal communication. Research shows that adolescent boys have a tougher time than girls in reading nonverbal cues,[11] so this activity will help them practice expressing how they think people are feeling and thinking. Some of the pictures might be appropriate for either box, so have the students really contemplate what it means when a picture gets placed in the Thinking or Feeling box.

Once this collection stage is complete, have your students close their eyes and select a picture from the Tasks box and a picture from the Thinking or Feeling box and use them together to write a one-page story about the two. The subject of the story doesn't have to be the person in the pictures—rather, the story is about the task and the thoughts or feelings about the task. The same two pictures can easily end up being the catalyst for a variety of stories. It is especially interesting to look at the similarities and differences between the stories created by boys and those created by girls.

their writing pieces. The difference in quality of response (from both sexes) was amazing. The boys would actually talk, and if allowed to sprawl on the floor, not one of them was a behavior problem."

In Chapter Eight, we will explore the single-gender classroom in more depth. It is being used effectively all over the world, especially for greater male participation in language arts classes.

A High School Innovation

Patricia St. Germain, a Gurian Institute–certified trainer in Colorado, created her own innovation at her high school after becoming proficient in male-female brain difference theory. Her innovation is called Mindworks. It is an elective she now offers that has attracted as many boys as girls. Patricia created the program to help students find innovative ways to be creative and engaged with each other. She makes sure to pack her course with good language components. Students must do a great deal of writing in this course, but the writing is so completely connected to things student are interested in that Patricia finds the written work very powerful.

Patricia reports:

> The students in the class spent the 2002–2003 school year asking 250 people at their high school two questions: "What do you look for in someone you want to date?" and "What do you look for in someone you want to marry?" Each student asked 10 males and 10 females and recorded their responses. They recorded the responses in categories of:
>
> What do guys say to guys?
> What do guys say to girls?
> What do girls say to girls?
> What do girls say to guys?
>
> The class then promulgated a Top Ten List and spent time analyzing the results in discussions and in their writing.

Knowing that we were writing this book on boys, Patricia sent us a number of the boys' papers. She wrote, "In some classes, girls really do outwrite boys, but in this class, the boys were so engaged in the topic, I got incredible papers from them."

You'll hear more about Patricia's innovation in Chapter Twelve, where we discuss helping undermotivated boys. (Contact Patricia for details on her Mindworks program—you will find contact information in the Certified Trainers section of www.gurianinstitute.com.)

Do Heroes Read and Write?

Ari Goldman, a language arts teacher in San Diego, said to me, "Have you noticed how in TV shows and in movies, the heroes rarely read or write? When did you last see an Arnold Schwarzenegger character sit down and write a letter? When have you seen Superman read a book? In the ancient world, to be literate used to be heroic. If you could read and write, you were a king or great man. Now, to read and write is something most boys' heroes think or do little about."

Ari's comment startled me. I hadn't noticed that truth before, nor had I been looking for it. Since he mentioned it, I've watched movies and TV shows that target boys, and sure enough, the acts of reading and writing are rarely incorporated in their scripts or characterizations.

We as parents and teachers can do a lot to help our boys get better at reading, writing, and language arts. We can show them role models—founding fathers and heroes like Ben Franklin, Alexander Hamilton, Thomas Jefferson, and Abraham Lincoln—who loved to read and write. We can be the heroes who read and write. We can get them books written by Michael Jordan or other sports heroes.

At the same time, perhaps it is time to ask our culture and our "hero" makers—the writers of our movie and TV scripts—to protect the minds of boys better than they are doing. Would it hurt the script of an action movie to include a few more books in the backgrounds, or even in the hero's hand? Would it hurt the script to incorporate more scenes in which the hero engaged in letter, email, or other correspondence?

Let us all put out a specific "literacy call" to those parents and teachers who make our graphic and visual media, asking them to remember how valuable a small adjustment in their creative output can be. Let's all work toward a culture in which our heroes read and write quite well. This would help our boys—subtly, powerfully. If television and movies are becoming—or have become—major arbiters of modern culture, it is time they enhanced the culture of boys by making it heroic to be smart, learned, and literate.

Helping Boys Learn
Math and Science

Natural numbers are better for your health.
Decimals have a point.
Calculus has its limits.
Geometry is just plane fun.
Polar coordinates aren't just arctic fashions.

—POSTER ON A MATH CLASS DOOR

I used to love science when I was in elementary school, then it just
became a bunch of memorizing. By high school, I just checked out of
science. I wasn't even there. Now that I'm in college, I wish I had done
better in science. I wish science had been interesting.

—AARON, 22, COLLEGE STUDENT

"MY SON REGULARLY TELLS ME HOW MUCH HE DISLIKES—NO, HE SAYS HATES—
math," writes Ron, a dad from Tennessee, about his high school sophomore, David. "But he plays outside linebacker on his high school
football team and has memorized a whole complicated playbook! He's
using math every day, and doesn't even know it. If his geometry teacher
would help him learn math by using diagrams of football plays, he'd eat
it up!"

Math can be a four-letter word for lots of students. Science can be "boring." Yet few areas of study are more important—and for many kids, more natural to the learning mind—than math and science. Throughout human history, boys and men especially found organic self-development through the spatial-mechanical tasks of hunting, the mathematical tasks of economics and trade, the scientific tasks of invention. This male brain is a beautiful maze of connections just waiting to link numbers, distance, size, orientation, and direction. The minds of boys are curious and inventive, wired to question how far it is to the sun, how water turns into ice, what causes tornadoes, what will happen if you shoot a bottle rocket off inside a garbage can, how hard one object can hit another without causing a bruise.

For many decades, boys outscored girls consistently in the areas of math and science; boys' standardized test scores, such as the SAT, were consistently higher than girls'.[1] The innate spatial-mechanical tendency of the male brain provided a strong foundation for male success in these areas. Because our educational culture was not doing enough to help girls achieve parity, the American Association of University Women and other researchers spearheaded changes in the teaching of math and science to girls, and girls have now made great strides. The gender gap favoring boys in certain areas of math and science has virtually disappeared. Also, girls now make up the majority of students in math and science classes (with the exception of computer science and some advanced placement courses),[2] and they get a higher number of the high grades (A's and B's) in many of our states.[3] The 2003 report of the OECD shows this advancement of girls' scores and grades to be a worldwide phenomenon. In the industrialized countries, boys are no longer outscoring girls in math and science at high statistical levels, and girls are even outperforming boys in some of the countries included in the research.

Those of us who are parents of daughters and advocates for girls have much to celebrate. Those of us who are parents of sons and advocates for boys find ourselves celebrating the success of girls, but we are challenged to compel our civilization to help the boys too. This chapter provides strategies, tips, and analysis for helping boys learn math and science in ways that take advantage of how boys really learn and develop. These methods are specifically designed to improve boys' success without negatively affecting girls. When we find either gender getting more of the A's and B's in any area—whether it is reading and writing or math and science—we know we've got a job to do: not a job that hinders girls, but one that makes sure boys learn math and science too. For every boy outperforming a male peer or a girl in math or science, there is another boy not doing so.

Relevance!

The ultimate goal of math and science teaching should be to turn a child's everyday world into a laboratory of learning experiences that make math and science *essential*—not just interesting, exciting, or fun, and certainly not simply boring, but so needed by the child, so *relevant,* so organic to the child's natural brain development that the child will become a "mathematician" and a "scientist" throughout his life. When our boys are playing with their friends in backyards or scrub lands or wheat fields; when they are adding up the numbers of their marbles in the street; when they are trying mischievously to see what happens when you hang shoes from a power line (a practice not to be condoned!), they are organic learners of these disciplines. How can we help them integrate their wonderful learning energy in this area with, specifically, the home and the classroom?

What Parents Can Do to Help Boys Learn Math

A father told this story of lying on the grass with his four-year-old son, Kevin, who asked, "Daddy, how high is the sun?"

Dad said, "Really high."

Kevin asked, "How high is that?"

Dad said, "I think I remember learning in school that the sun is ninety-three million miles away from our Earth."

"How far is that?"

Dad remembers saying, "Well, Grandma lives fifteen hundred miles from us, so to get to the sun we would have to drive the same distance as going back and forth to Grandma's house a whole lot of times." Dad tried to do the math in his head, but couldn't, so he pulled out his Palm Pilot. He showed Kevin the screen and said, "Sixty-two thousand times."

Kevin squinted at the Palm Pilot, his little mind working. Dad tried to help out by saying, "Do you remember how long it takes to drive to Grandma's house just one time?"

Kevin didn't, so Dad said, "It takes three days. So it would take us 186,000 days to get to the sun. So if we drove to the sun in our car, you would be 512 years old by the time we got there."

This father told us, "It seemed to me that even though Kevin didn't get the numbers and all that, he still was getting something out of it. What he said next either proves me right or wrong, I don't know. He said, "Whoa, that's too far. What about the moon? Could we get there sooner?"

This father, though clearly not a professional at making math make sense to a four-year-old, nonetheless understood something very fundamental and important about a parent's (and school's) best method of teaching math: to use things in the child's daily life that he already understands as a way to help the child identify and understand the role that math plays in the world itself. For each of us, in whatever our present employment, math (like science) is used when it is relevant.

Fortunately, to a great extent, conventional education knows this. A lot of our math and science classes and methodologies are quite sound. Unfortunately, however, conventional education—and our own everyday busy lives—are often not working well in the areas of learning and relevance. When our educational system is malfunctioning, it is generally doing so because of old methods and ideas, most of which began over a hundred years ago, when "relevance" was a matter of rote learning. Most children merely needed to be able to perform industrial tasks that were relatively uncomplicated by mathematical processing— tasks in factories and assembly lines. Some of our math and science education is still set up to serve this old way of thinking about math, science, and future work.

For all of us today, it's crucial to make a commitment to the relevance of math taught in school. We no longer want our children to be cogs in an industrial wheel. The minds of boys, when fully activated, cry out against being cogs. As parents, we can do something about this. Even if, like Kevin's dad, we teach our sons awkwardly, the relevance of a "Grandma example" will bring the lesson home. And there's more.

Before He Starts School

You'll notice starting shortly after his birth that your son focuses his attention on objects in space, such as the mobile hanging over his crib. While your son is watching the mobile, you can count the number of airplanes in the mobile while singing a tune, such as "Twinkle, Twinkle Little Star" ("one two three four five six seven, that is how many planes there are"). Repetition of the song and the counting can help build the boy's math brain.

You'll will be setting up, from infancy, a mind that wants to count, so that as your son grows up to focus on playing baseball or basketball, skateboarding, climbing, jumping, building, and ultimately on working with computers and playing video games (all of which are spatial-mechanical tasks that often feel comfortable to boys' brains), he will intuitively count how many times he hits the ball, or jumps off a wall, or beats his last score.

When your son is very young and you are choosing what children's toys to buy, you can even focus your purchasing power mainly on those toys that include sorting by size and shape, counting like and unlike objects, and matching items. Movable puzzle pieces inherently involve spatial, mechanical, and math development.

Let's look even more closely at specific things you can do with your son.

MAKE AN "ALL ABOUT ME" RECORD BOOK.   With your son, keep an "All About Me" record book, like a baseball statistics book, but in this record include "statistics" about him: height; weight; number of teeth; size of shoes and clothing; and age in weeks, months, and years.

There are creative ways to gather this information. You can, for instance, get a large roll of butcher paper and have your son lay down on it, legs slightly apart and arms down and slightly out at his side. Draw around his body, then cut the "body" out and hang it up in his room. Repeat this activity at regular intervals. Do the same with his foot size. Soon you will have a "picture" of your son's growth for both of you to look at and talk about:

"Look how much longer your legs are than they were! Two inches looks like this."

"Wow, no wonder you needed a bigger size shoe! Look how fast your feet are growing! Here is your size three shoe. Now look how much longer your size four is."

Your little son's teeth are another built-in record-keeping topic. In his record book, provide your son with a diagram of how many teeth he can expect to have during his life. You can get a generic diagram either from the Internet or from your son's dentist. Encourage your son to color in which teeth he already has and to add to them as new ones appear—talk about "adding" new teeth and "subtracting" baby teeth that are then replaced by adult teeth.

Height, teeth, weight, and any number of other items and interactions can be housed in the record book so that your son constantly refers to this math learning all in one place. If he does a lot of activities on different sheets of paper, they can get lost and forgotten. Having one book for math, at least for a few months, is good practice for organizing math projects and textbooks later in life.

Another fun and brain-building item for record book work is a tape measure—a fabric or plastic one at first to avoid accidental cuts, one that is your son's and his alone. With it he can measure things and compare the numbers. You can show your son how to use his tape measure to "collect numbers" of items around the house, the yard, the park. All of these get entered into the record book.

MAKE A CALENDAR.   Time is a mathematical concept that children learn as they grow, and a calendar can be a concrete, fun way to help reinforce the concept. Include things on the calendar that will provide anticipation and whet your son's curiosity. Together you and your son can count how many days until his birthday, a pending holi-day, a grandparents' visit, and so on. Use different-shaped stickers to "count off" the days. Pick a week and record the time the sun goes down each day and comes up the next day, reinforcing the concept of time and seasons.

For each month, and for as many days as you can, post interesting holidays or celebrations in the larger community or culture. Your local library can be a great source of material, with such resources as "Chase's Calendar of Events."

You can continue the calendar activity as your son starts school. It can be especially useful in reinforcing homework and learning projects that will now become part of your son's world. Boys on average have more trouble organizing their learning than girls do, especially their homework. But your son, prepared in the use of the calendar, will be ready to know exactly when his homework is due—and be on time. The calendar also helps your son develop self-discipline and punctuality, an important developmental benchmark during the elementary years that will serve him well when he encounters the challenges of early adoles-cence.

Patricia St. Germain, of Monument, Colorado, found that parent-assisted calendars improve male students' performance in school. "Keep-ing a calendar at home and at school almost always improves performance. The calendar is tangible, visual, spatial. Boys can see where they have to go, and measure the time they have to get there. Calendars really work."

Helping Elementary School Boys

Now let's say your little son is bounding off to elementary school. You can continue building his math brain in your family life, while sup-porting what the school is doing. Here's how:

ART TECHNIQUE: USE MUSIC!   It is important to expose your son to music—recorded music, live music, classical music, pop music, and music he performs himself. You may say, "Wait a minute—we're talking about math here, right? So what does live music have to do with math?"

In fact, many of the parts of the brain that build math skills are the same as those that react to music.[4] Music can "wake up" the brain for math learning and keep it awake. This is one of the reasons your children may enjoy listening to music in the background when they do their homework.

Much research has shown that music often correlates directly with math success. The craft of music is built on a mathematical framework of scales, chords with prescribed intervals, timing, rhythm, cadence, and beat. If your son learns an instrument and practices it daily, this simple exercise can lead to improved math performance.

PLAY GAMES AS A FAMILY.   Many popular and fun games use math concepts and language. Dominoes, Parcheesi, Sorry!, Monopoly, Yahtzee, and a variety of card games encourage counting and strategy that help build mathematical skills in elementary school kids. The added bonus to playing games with your son is that it provides great opportunities for stimulating conversation, supporting verbal skills as well. It is one of those attachment times in a family that create learning relevance, for every child implicitly feels the relevance of a learning skill when it coincides with attachment within families.

If your son is not playing games with you but is playing video games on his own or with his buddy, you may want to make family game night a ritual. To play video games without playing mathematical games is a waste of a good brain. Video games, in moderation, are not harmful, as we explored in Chapter Five, but nor are they brain builders. They are not generally "games" in the sense that we use the term in this chapter—activities that have immediate relevance and build important parts of the brain.

Helping Middle and High School Boys

By the time your son goes to middle school, he has an adolescent brain that is undergoing dramatic growth. Children's abstract math skills are now ready to blossom as they are challenged with higher levels of math. If they have been well prepared—with calendars, music-math connections, lots of games, and lots of math relevance in their early years—their concrete abilities to grapple with math are established, and now they can really enjoy abstract math.

Yet even if they are "brain-ready" for higher-level math, many boys have a specific problem in middle and high school: doing their homework *and* handing it in. In the science section of this chapter (and in other areas in this book), we focus on the problem of our boys and their homework. Our adolescent boys need extra encouragement in this area. They need you to "interrogate" them on whether they handed in their homework. They may need you—or another parent-team member—to help them with their homework (even well into high school).

Adolescent boys also need all of us to advocate for schools to allow more physical movement in math classrooms—as well as other innovations you'll read about in the "What Teachers Can Do to Help Boys Learn Math" section, later in this chapter. As your son meets the challenge of learning complex math, one of your primary jobs may well be act as "boy advocate."

Here are some very specific things you and your team can do to help your son become more successful in math.

CONNECT ATHLETICS TO MATHEMATICS.   Bill, from Colorado Springs, began taking his son to minor league baseball games when Josh turned twelve. Bill told Kathy:

> Josh wasn't that keen on math homework, but he loved being the one to keep track of all the stats in the program whenever we went to a ball game. I took advantage of his interest to start showing him where the box scores and stats were listed in our local paper. I showed him how important it was for the players to keep track of their batting averages, to know how many more hits or runs they needed to exceed their personal best, things like that. He was doing math, and enjoying it, and not even realizing that's what it was!

Like Kevin's dad, Bill hoped to keep making math relevant to areas of a boy's innate interest.

There are many other ways that we can connect math to being either a fan or a participant in sports and athletics, because so many numbers, records, and statistics are involved. Whatever sports you follow or enjoy, make math a part of it.

"Did you see that, son? That was Ichiro's 256th hit! He broke an eighty-four-year-old record. What do you think? Do you think it was the same back then? Should there be two records, one for the old days and one for now? You think so?" On and on the applications and discussions can go. Sports love numbers! Challenge your son to make a case, using numbers.

MAKE HIM RESPONSIBLE FOR HIS OWN FINANCES.   Our world runs on money, yet many of our children spend little time learning how money works. They get an allowance and spend it on a pleasure item. That's that. But money and finances are fertile areas for mathematical development. If your adolescent son is getting an allowance, and if he's having trouble doing math in his schoolwork, make that allowance contingent on his development of math skills—specifically, he must keep a financial record of every penny he receives and spends. He must add up totals. He must create debit and credit columns. If he doesn't keep this "portfolio," he doesn't get paid. Of course, you have to help him learn about debits and credits. If creating and maintaining a financial portfolio is not one of your strengths, this is a great chance to let a member of your parent-led team help out—especially if you have relatives or friends who work in a financial field.

If your son is ready to get a car, you have a number of opportunities to enhance mathematical learning: saving for purchase; comparing prices; understanding down payments and interest on car loans; and calculating miles per gallon, cost of gasoline, repairs, and insurance. You can elicit the help of your insurance agent (who can become a member of the parent-led team) by asking for a meeting between you, the agent, and your son. The agent can spend some time mentoring your son in all the ins and outs of how insurance works—much of which is mathematical.

If your son is going to college, he'll need help with projecting budgets, gathering cost information, and analyzing various financial aid opportunities. Although you may be tempted to do as much of this as you can, it would be a lot better for your son if you let him take the lead. These are not things for adults to do *for* adolescent boys, but *with* them.

HELP HIM UNDERSTAND THE "MEANING" OF MATH.   A teacher in New York shared this wisdom: Children learn what they have decided to learn. They learn what has meaning for them. By this she meant to call attention to the brain's prioritizing of specific learning tasks. The brain learns what it has made into a learning priority, and whether a task is given priority is guided by the human individual's search for meaning. Adolescent boys may need you and your team to help them understand how much math can mean to them.

If your adolescent son has prioritized entertainment above learning math, he has forgotten how much math means. Now, you as parent have the hard task of repositioning his priorities and helping him understand the value and meaning of how he spends his time. To help him prioritize math work above entertainment, you may well need to create reward charts and checklists. These could include entertainment—watching TV, playing video games, going to the mall—as rewards for work and grades accomplished.

Driving this vigilance is your desire to show an adolescent boy how important a comfortable level of knowledge and skill with math can be— it affects every aspect, both professional and personal, of his future life as a man. Your son can also benefit if you take him to work with you, specifically to see how you use math. You and others in your parent-team can give math relevance for him. You have the job of helping your son realize that math isn't an option—it's crucial!

Students who are already doing well in their classes probably don't need this kind of hands-on attention. But any adolescent struggling in school will generally not succeed if personal entertainment has become a higher priority than the work of measuring life's meaning one integer at a time.

PLAY CHESS.   If you have a son or know a boy who is very good at math, playing chess could be a wonderful entertainment for him. Once he learns the moves, he might find it very easy. If you have a son or know a boy who is having trouble in math, playing chess might be a way to help that adolescent brain develop greater mathematical intelligence.

Chess playing, like music, uses many of the same parts of the brain as mathematics. Chess is not the only game that does this—checkers, cribbage, and many card games do too—but chess is, for some boys, the most rewarding. It is highly competitive; it requires any player to master his own impulses and emotions; it challenges mathematical intelligence; it can bond players together and builds friendships; and it is a worthy substitute for TV, video games, and endless Internet surfing.

What Teachers Can Do to Help Boys Learn Math

When participating in training at our Gurian Institute, math teachers often express frustration at figuring out how to make math more interesting and relevant to boys in their classroom.

"Some things a kid just has to learn," said a geometry teacher in Connecticut. "Maybe it doesn't matter if it's interesting or relevant. It's kind of like going to church. Church can't be interesting every Sunday. It's just . . . church."

This comment led to a wonderful discussion, and many people agreed in theory with the teacher's analogy. Yet most teachers ended the workshop noticing how the human brain retains the most math learning when it can connect new learning to natural curiosity about the world in which it lives. This is especially true in early childhood and elementary learning.

Helping Elementary School Boys

Just as parents of young boys are charged with helping boys love math by loving its applications to their lives, so too are early education teachers.

USE MANIPULATIVES.   As an elementary school teacher, you probably hope that a boy's home life and preschool programs have included the use of blocks, puzzles, finger plays, nursery rhymes, rhythm instruments, games—all the kinds of educational materials we explored earlier in this chapter and in Part Two.

One manipulative that brain-based research finds especially effective for teaching numbers and counting is *number rolls*—connected beads in iterations of ten that come in packs up to one thousand. Children can use number rolls to learn numbers and foundational mathematics through physical and kinesthetic activity. This takes the learning of numbers off the page and into the physical body, which especially helps kinesthetic boys.

The Montessori method for teaching mathematics uses number rolls even in preschool. You can acquire number roll kits from Montessori catalogues, though many other catalogues include them as well.

USE PLAY AND HUMOR.   Human play is an organic method of learning all kinds of academic skills. Studies completed in 2004 by researchers at Hofstra University corroborated findings over the last decade that physical play actually stimulates growth of the brain.[5] There is a direct link to physical play and the problem solving needed for math success.

Human play is not only a matter of physical playtime or movement. It is also a matter of humor. When you develop math problems for your boys to solve, you might try to make them "playful." If the boys are chuckling while they're solving the problems, they just might retain more. Check out the next Try This box.

GROUP YOUR STUDENTS INTO TEAMS.   As you know, not every child's brain has reached the same point on the developmental continuum by the time the boys sit in your class to learn. Between the ages of three to twelve, the human brain develops in spurts of growth that create "unevenness" in individuals in a class. This is a good reason for team learning—groups of three or four. Each child must do his part in the research project or learning activity. A team is not an excuse for an individual to slack off, but the loneliness of "feeling behind" in a certain kind of learning dissipates when the boys can rely on each other to help them learn.

In dividing your students into groups, you can build on math learning. For instance, you can ask them to sort into groups based on what quarter of the year they were born in. This activity requires them to think about how many months there are in a quarter, which months

Try This
Math to Laugh

Here are some examples of humorous "math" questions you can have your students ask and answer.

1. I had 37 ants. I put 9 in my sister's bed, dropped 14 in my mom's pancake batter, and fed 3 to my pet frog. How many do I have left?
2. My teacher talks 60 miles an hour. How many miles does she talk in 25 minutes?
3. To win a game of basketball, I need to score 21 points first. If I score four 3-point baskets, how many 2-point baskets and 1-point foul shots do I need to win?

Boys can make up their own problems and drop them in a suggestion box. When you read one you think really works, give the boy verbal credit in front of the class.

they are, and how many quarters there are in a year. The activity allows them to interact verbally to figure out who else is in their month and quarter and then to move as they divide into their groups. This kind of activity, though simple, is a nice template for others that you develop over the course of a year, in which physical movement, verbal communication, and math concept processing are all integrated as a learning activity.

MAKE PHYSICAL MOVEMENT AND RECESS A PART OF LEARNING MATH.   Anne Carty, the head of Regis School of the Sacred Heart in Houston, modified her school's punishment policy to fit the needs of the male brain. She told me a story of a math class in which some boys were constantly in need of discipline intervention. They were not completing their work, and one of the discipline techniques suggested to teachers was to withhold recess from them. The students sat through recess period to finish their work.

After learning about the physical needs of the male brain, however, teachers began the practice of having the boys exercise—by raking, picking up leaves, running track, and the like. The boys were still "punished" in that they were not allowed to socialize on the playground with their friends during recess. But in this new mode of discipline, the boys now got the physical boost of energy they needed to return to their work engaged and more likely to succeed. Carty reported an increase in student performance from this "movement" innovation.

The Regis School has gone further: the children take one-minute physical "brain breaks"—standing and stretching during class. These too have helped stimulate students' brains toward greater learning. In the school's second-grade classrooms, Carty reports, "We now have the students learn while walking (moving) in mid-afternoon, as much as possible. This is a time when their brains have, in the past, been generally 'sleepy.' But since we've gone to a greater emphasis on this 'walking method,' their schoolwork has improved."

Helping Middle and High School Boys

Brain breaks and physical movement, like many of the other innovations appropriate for elementary school, can also help middle and high schoolers. At no age is the human body begging to spend its whole learning day sitting in a chair. Boys' bodies and brains especially want to be "on the move!" For middle school boys whose bodies are now experiencing between five and seven spikes per day of the aggression hormone, testosterone, physical movement is crucial. Every school at which the Gurian Institute has trained teachers has reported back to us that the use of physical movement, the squeezing of stress balls, and the physical brain breaks have been crucial in increasing adolescent boys' academic success and especially in lowering discipline problems.

Here are some other things to try:

PLAY MATH OLYMPICS.   Kristy Bateman, a middle school teacher at Lewis Frasier Middle School in Hinesville, Georgia, implemented what she learned during a Gurian Institute all-staff training, going beyond simply "increasing movement" to make her math curriculum even more experiential. Influenced by the 2004 Olympics, she led her students to create a "Math Olympics." Kristy observed a fascinating set of differences in how the boys and girls engaged in the activities.

There were three events: measuring water squeezed from a sponge, weighing marbles, and measuring the length of steps. Kristy shared her experience:

> The water event was the most interesting. [Students were given a soaked sponge, a gauge, and a bowl and asked to measure the amount of water contained in the wet sponge by squeezing it and collecting the water in the gauge.] The boys would figure out on their own to hold the gauge over the bowl (to catch excess water) but I had to put plastic bags under the bowl area for the boys because they managed to get water further away from the bowl even though the gauge was over the bowl.
>
> Instead of thinking through how to keep the water off the floor, the girls immediately picked up the sponge from the bowl and started to squeeze the water into the gauge. It never initially occurred to the girls to pick the gauge up and hold it over the bowl to catch the excess water not going into the gauge.
>
> In the marble event, I am sure you can guess—the boys had to be reminded that the event was to weigh marbles not *play* marbles!
>
> All these student exercises created "messes," but both the boys and girls learned a lot!

Kristy developed another innovation for teaching measurement. She had her students do a scavenger hunt. She noticed something interesting.

> They had a sheet telling them to find certain items that matched the measurement requests on their sheet. They were told that the items to measure should be items from their purses or book bags.
>
> Among the girls, the items they pulled from their purses got verbally shared with their group. They would tell where an item was bought, who gave it to them, why they liked the color of it, etc.
>
> The boys did not take anything out of book bags to measure but measured things on the posters on the walls in the classroom. The boys found no need to discuss what they were measuring.

LINK ARCHITECTURE AND MATH.   A physics teacher who participated in Gurian Institute training in Cullman County, Alabama,
shared this activity:

> I wanted my physics class to do some hands-on learning, so I gath-
> ered the materials similar to those that a tribe of Native Americans
> who lived in our part of the country might have used to create a
> teepee. Each group got three long poles, some rope, and material to
> cover the structure.
>
> The poles were really long, about 12 feet. I got them loaned from a
> local lumber company. The students struggled with how to get the
> poles into a position that would remain stable while they covered the
> outside with fabric. We did the activity out on the football field so
> they had plenty of room between groups. It was fascinating to watch
> them and see how the different groups figured out what to do. We ac-
> tually spent three days on this activity. The groups that did some out-
> side research on construction did the best job—and helped the others
> after they got their teepee built. They learned more about measure-
> ment in this exercise than they've learned in a long time. Some great
> peer mentoring happened as a bonus.

USE SINGLE-GENDER CLASSES.   At Breckenridge County Middle
School in Harned, Kentucky, Missy Critchelow and her colleagues
hoped to improve grades and test scores and to lower the numbers of
discipline referrals. With the lead of their principal, Missy and her colleagues received training in male-female differences from the Gurian
Institute. They instituted single-gender eighth-grade math (and science) classes in 2003.

Missy reports significant improvement in academic performance
from this innovation.

> Before the switch to the new methods, the boys had several F's and
> the average was a low C for all of the classes. The girls generally had
> better grades—only a few F's—but the overall girl average was high C
> to low B. In these particular classes were all of our special education
> students, because we don't have a resource class for seventh- and
> eighth-grade students.

After the change, both classes had higher grades. And, by the end of the school year, the boys' average was within 5 points of the girls' average. In total, at the end of the year, out of 180 students, I had only 3 boys with the F average and 2 girls. I credit this outstanding improvement to the gender specific classes.

Missy and her colleagues also noted a significant reduction in discipline referrals: "Discipline was also a big change. I sent two students to the office all this year, and that is outstanding. With the boys especially, using gender specific methods was helpful for decreasing discipline problems. Boys had to take on leadership qualities."

Single-gender education is a very powerful innovation for math, science, and many other subjects. Chapter Eight focuses exclusively on it.

STIMULATE VISUAL CONVERSATIONS.   Ann Brock, a math teacher at Lewis Palmer High School in Monument, Colorado, created a poster for her classroom that the students found funny. It also generated good conversation about how math relates to the real world. Ann used the "visual conversation starter" in the next Did You Know? box, and she encourages you to try it in your high school class.

What Parents Can Do to Help Boys Learn Science

Like many boys, my brother, Phil, and I grew up feeling like natural scientists. When our family lived in Honolulu, Phil and I explored the ocean reefs, collecting shells and learning about anemone and jellyfish. When we lived in Colorado, we explored the mountain worlds. In Laramie, we got into bottle rockets. We wreaked some havoc but learned a lot. Then, as a freshman in high school, I learned about Albert Einstein from reading the encyclopedia. I also began to read science fiction avidly. I've had a love affair with science from early on.

Often, as I train parents and teachers in learning science, I wonder why my brother and I both loved (and both still love) science so much. Why is it that much of my written work and professional philosophy is

??? Did You Know? ???
Top 10 Reasons to Become a Statistician

10. Deviation is considered normal.
9. Estimating parameters is easier than dealing with real life.
8. Statisticians are significant.
7. I always wanted to learn the Greek alphabet.
6. The probability that a statistician will get a job is > .999.
5. We do it with confidence, frequency, and variability.
4. You never have to be right, only close.
3. We're normal, and everyone else is skewed.
2. The regression line looks better than the unemployment line.
1. No one knows what we do, so we're always right!

built on scientific understanding of the human brain? Why does my brother, who is now a Web designer and inventor, use science every day in his work? Why did these two boys, two brothers, both get so much out of science and science learning?

From research in genetics and other areas I can now see that my family's love of science was both a genetic and a learned affection. My father, a sociologist, integrated the biological sciences into sociology. My mother, an anthropologist, had a keen mind for science. Clearly our family had a "science gene." But my parents also modeled and nurtured a love of science in my brother and me from our earliest years. They cared about science, so my brother and I did too.

Now we're the parents, and our job is to help the next generation appreciate the mysteries and wonders of science. And once again, the techniques and activities we're suggesting here may in some cases apply to girls too, but we've developed most of them specifically for boys—their unique brains and the way their unique brains develop.

Helping Boys Before They Go to School

Much of what we've said earlier, especially in Chapter Three, is useful for setting up good science learning. Let us add the idea of *science mentoring* from an early age. When children are infants and toddlers, parents are natural science teachers—involving boys in housework, gardening, digging for worms. As the boy enters preschool age, everything is "science" to him.

By science we mean, at this age, "discovering how things work." A scientist like Einstein is born with great genetics for it, but he still needs people to tell his little boy mind how things work. Each of us can spend a piece of every day making sure to explain to our child how something works. It is very rewarding to do so. As your son's eyes light up with understanding, you can see a young scientist finding his way.

Helping Elementary School Boys

With elementary school boys, nurturing an affection and aptitude for science continues to be a family affair.

INTEGRATE SCIENCE MENTORS INTO YOUR SON'S LIFE.   You don't have to love science or even be good at it to help your little boy care about science. You just have to give your son the tools, encouragement, and guidance to use science in his everyday exploration. If you don't feel qualified to do this, you most certainly have access to someone in your family or parent-led team who does. In churches or other faith communities you might belong to, there are likely to be retired people who worked in the sciences and would now love to mentor a child. Given how important science and technology are to our boys (and girls) today, it is crucial to provide your K–6 son with "science mentors"—grandparents, family friends, tutors—who can help you prepare him for a life of science and technology.

INTEGRATE SCIENCE INTO DAILY LIFE.   Your own kitchen is a very scientific place, for science happens just about every time you prepare a meal. Include your son as much as possible, as soon as he is developmentally ready. Measuring, mixing, freezing, thawing, boiling—during these processes, talk about the changes that happen to the things you prepare. Talk about where the different foods come from, what salt is, how yeast makes dough rise.

Personal hygiene and nutrition are science lessons waiting to happen. Why do we need to take a bath or shower? What happens when we brush our teeth? What is protein, and how does it help us grow strong?

Boys' brains love the stimulation of interacting with the outside world. Plants, animals, weather—everything you encounter in the yard and the park will serve as opportunities to introduce science into your son's world and language.

GIVE HIM THE TOOLS.   A microscope makes a good birthday present and will last through the elementary years and beyond. A laptop computer, if you can afford one, will help your son in his science classes. Internet access helps a child learn science (though this access needs to be supervised until your son is well into his teens).

When your son is in elementary school, set aside time to peer through the microscope with him. Discover the wonders in a drop of water, the veins of a leaf.

EXPLORE YOUR LOCAL ECOLOGY.   No matter where you live, there are sure to be issues relating to the local environment and ecology in which you can become involved—with your son—that will not only bring the rewards of social service but also spark his interest in science. With your son, ask and answer these questions:

- Where does our water supply come from?
- How long will it last?
- How does it get cleaned up?
- How much does it cost our family?
- Where do they dump the oil from our car when we get it changed?
- What do they do with the trash they collect each week from the end of our driveway?

These real-life questions can lead your family to "field trips." County and city engineers often enjoy taking a few minutes to show you around the local water treatment plant. Trips like this bring science alive in a young mind. After such a trip, your son might say, "I want to be an engineer when I grow up." The seed of success has been planted in the young boy's mind. Who knows how it will grow?

Helping Middle and High School Boys

By the time a boy hits puberty, his interest in science will probably already be sparked by personal curiosity and family and school innovations. By now, we can hope that he's decided that science is an important part of his life. If he is completely disconnected from science, then we must go back to basics: make science a priority over entertainment, and identify science mentors within the family or community who will work with your son.

By puberty, your son will enter science classes that are challenging in ways he couldn't have dreamed of in elementary school. High school science classes can shock our sons with their quantity of abstract theory, empirical data, lab experiments, memorization, and homework. There's a lot we can do as parents.

BECOME A HOMEWORK COACH.   Parents and members of the parent-led team often need to become homework coaches if their sons (or daughters) are going to succeed in middle and high school science.

If a grandparent, uncle, or family friend is a retired engineer or other "science-minded" person, this might be the individual you ask to become your son's tutor and homework coach. Once or twice a week, the coach-mentor and your son can meet to review your son's homework. They might talk about homework and assignments on the telephone during the week, as needed.

If your son is having any trouble in science classes, this one intervention may prove to be the most immediately helpful.

BECOME A MEMORIZATION COACH.   Because of the immense amount of memorization required in high school science classes, and because the adolescent brain develops its memory centers in varied and uneven ways, adolescents of both genders often need help from "memory coaches." Here are a few ways to weave memorization practice into your son's daily life:

- While you and your son are driving somewhere together in the car, you can "test" him on his chemistry homework tables.
- You can set limits on screen time. "Until this assignment is memorized this evening, you have to turn off the TV."
- Even at the dinner table, you can provide memory testing and coaching. "What are the three major parts of the brain?" "How many stars are in the galaxy?"

Memory coaching is a very good time to help a student get his daily science work to "stick in his mind."

USE APPRENTICESHIPS.   Much of the science a boy in your ancestry learned came from his work as an apprentice on a farm or shop under the tutelage of a master. As we've seen in earlier chapters, establishing a one-on-one master-apprentice relationship is still a very powerful learning strategy for our children, especially for boys who may not naturally "reach out" for as many relationships as girls do, or learn as much verbally—from written words in books.

In the past, parents and other important family members negotiated and set up the adolescent male's apprenticeship to a master. Today, many of our adolescents find masters on their own: a boy who likes computers finds an uncle who is a computer designer; a boy who likes animals finds a family friend who is a farmer, and works for him during the summer; a boy who wants to master tennis seeks out a good coach.

A mother of three in Oregon wrote this email:

My son Dayne has never been a great student, but he was always interested in cars. Even as a little boy, cars and trucks were his life! When he turned sixteen, he worked to earn enough money for his own car. He wanted a Ford Fairlane with a very "souped up" engine.

Dayne's father and I were scared that he would drive this car too fast and hurt himself—Dayne doesn't always think so clearly before he acts. We tried to get him to just get a normal car, not something with a huge engine. He was offended, said we didn't trust him, and insisted on his own car. Dayne wasn't unreasonable in his request for his very powerful car, and we weren't unreasonable in our fear of what could happen to him. Finally, we came up with a solution. He could get the car as long as he worked on weekends with Carl, the husband of my good friend, Tracy. Carl is a mechanic and races old cars at the racetrack.

Carl and Dayne agreed to the deal, and Dayne has really learned a lot from Carl, not just about cars, but about hard work in school. Dayne's father and I have nagged him about his homework and grades for years, but somehow now that Carl insists he work harder in school, Dayne is doing it. We probably should have tried to help Dayne and Carl get together years ago, but just didn't think of it until Dayne scared us with that souped up car.

Dayne has entered a master-apprentice relationship with Carl. In this relationship, he is actively engaged in scientific learning. His brain is engaged in discovering practical applications for science and technology. He has also discovered a bond that challenges him to do what his parents always hoped he would do: find success in school.

Teaching the Science of Puberty

From 1986 to 1988, my wife, Gail, and I taught in Ankara, Turkey. It was a wonderful experience, filled with many kinds of learning for both our students and us. One thing that struck me immediately was Turkish honesty about the adolescent's changing scientific body.

In Turkish families, there is much less "Puritanism" than in American families—much less of the sense that the physically mature human body is inherently sexual and thus must be avoided in discussion. Turks more often say to adolescents, "Here are the parts of your body; here are their functions." Americans often think of Muslim countries as being more "repressed" than America, but in this science of puberty, they are not as repressed as many parts of the United States. In fact, if you have traveled overseas and observed how adolescents are taught the nature of their changing bodies, you might notice a natural and comprehensive attitude toward sex education often lacking in an American boy's home.

The human body is a crucial area of scientific exploration. Indeed, *The Minds of Boys* is a scientific examination of the male body and brain. Fortunately, parents and members of parent-led teams can use the science of the body with middle and high school boys who are in puberty. Studies show that if parents neglect to teach the science of puberty to their sons, the boys are more likely to act out with earlier sexual behavior in order to learn their own natural science. The science of puberty involves four crucial elements of natural development: physical changes, emotional changes, psychological changes, and social changes. All of these topics need comprehensive attention.

A wonderful resource for parents is Jane DiVita Woody's book *How Can We Talk About That?* My own book for adolescent boys, *From Boys to Men,* specifically details the science of puberty, and engages boys and their families in a "science lab" approach to puberty.

What Teachers Can Do to Help Boys Learn Science

In the earliest years of scientific learning, water tables, sand tables, field trips to farms or zoos, and outdoor climbing equipment all lend themselves not only to actual science lessons but also to the spatial-mechanical brain development that aids in science learning. In this next section, we'll feature innovations that can enhance what you are already doing with early learners.

Helping Elementary School Boys

Science in elementary school is often an everyday matter. Many elementary school classrooms allow the children to help care for a class pet, such as a rabbit or guinea pig, which allows regular opportunities for being "scientists." Other classrooms use the arts. Arts? Yes! The arts can teach science. They are just one of the innovative ways to make science work.

CONNECT THE ARTS WITH SCIENCE.   When educators in Hamilton, Ohio, decided to make sure their students learned the solar system fully, they teamed with the Fitton Center for Creative Arts, a community center for the arts, to choreograph a modern dance routine based on the planets and moons. Artists helped elementary school students sculpt and paint the solar system. Art made science experiential! This collaboration of arts and sciences was adopted in response to low standardized test scores among Hamilton elementary students, and it is now raising scores![6] This should not surprise us—the more experiential the learning, the greater a student's success.

A number of the Gurian Institute trained schools have used arts techniques for improving science learning in the same way they have improved math and language arts success. Whenever you as a teacher "hit a wall" in teaching any aspect of science, a good fallback pedagogical method can be to use visuals, graphics, drawings, paintings, drama, music, dance, or any other artistic medium. Especially for boys from three to twelve, the link between spatial-mechanical and other brain development lends itself to collaboration between arts and sciences.

RECRUIT MENTORS.   Science is a hands-on affair, and thus it is "done" by somebody. That somebody can't always be the teacher. It can often be a peer—in the case of "peer-assisted mentoring"—or a volunteer, especially a retired volunteer who comes into the classroom to help out. At Trentwood Elementary School in Spokane, Washington, sixty-nine-year-old Bob Stapleton corrects the work of youngsters in a third-grade class, and he also sneaks in a game of cribbage now and then (a very scientific and mathematical game, when Bob breaks it down for students). The students enjoy having his elder male presence, the teachers find him an essential part of the classroom and of the after-school games club, and Bob gains great satisfaction from being a part of the children's lives.

Because science is the academic expression of kinesthetic human interaction with the natural environment, it makes a great group venture. Certainly, it can be explored alone, in the backyard, or in the basement with a chemistry set, but when able peers or senior citizen volunteers are available to make it alive and rich and rewarding, they can become a part of the science "core" staff. Boys especially are hungry for peer male mentors and elder male mentors. Any elementary school science teacher who is trying to teach science without the use of these classroom volunteers and mentors may be missing the opportunity to make science a part of his or her students' lives forever.

Helping Middle and High School Boys

Middle and high school science teachers already pack their classes with content. Especially in an educational environment that pressures teachers toward standardized testing, teachers are already overwhelmed with work to do. Adding boy-friendly innovations into science classes can seem, at first, like a burden. Nevertheless, we hope you'll find the innovations in this section to be uplifting. They are success-driven strategies, as you'll see. We hope too that you'll review the innovations described in the section about elementary school, for you can easily and effectively adapt many of those for use with older boys. The next Try This box is an example.

MAKE SCIENCE EXPERIENTIAL.   Monica Gutierrez, a middle school math and science teacher at the Regis School, shared with us how she now makes science more experiential for her seventh-grade science class: "While learning parts of the cell (both plant and animal), the students made giant size cells, the main body and each part of the cell cut from bulletin board paper and then glued in place. They were very big, bright, and colorful. Each group of students was very engaged in the activity and was very proud of their masterpiece in the end. After the cell was completed in its entirety, each person in the group took turns telling me what they worked on, and how the parts of the cell functioned. They really had a great time."

Regis, a school for boys, is a wonderful testing ground for new innovations in learning. Anne Carty, the head of school for Regis (featured earlier in this chapter), altered her school's methods for teaching many of the disciplines, including science, after engaging the Gurian Institute to train teachers in how boys learn. She reports, "We now have students construct what they study in science, bringing new excitement to science classes, and improvement in academic performance in these classes."

Try This
Connecting Words with Science

Print the word *SCIENCE* in a vertical line along the left side of a large piece of paper, such as a flip chart pad. Have the boys brainstorm and give you a word that starts with each letter. Ask the boys how each word can be connected to some kind of science. Develop a lesson plan to use each of the words in a science learning experience. For instance:

S   sun
C   carrot
I   Indians
E   eyes
N   nuts
E   energy

For sun: Perhaps you can talk about solar power and let the students experiment with photosensitive paper to show how the sun can burn an image onto it when they leave it exposed to sunlight.

For carrot: You might talk about how carrots are really roots, and grow under the ground. Your students could read the book *Tops and Bottoms,* by Janet Stevens (a great book about the rewards of hard work!).

For Indians: Here is an opportunity to talk about Native Americans and their lifestyles, what they ate, how they made clothing. There was a real science to Native American survival in nature. If

Perhaps there is an instinct among all science teachers to use physical construction in order to teach scientific lessons. There is also, however, an inertia common to a busy school year. This inertia tugs at teachers to give up large and potentially noisy construction projects when it would just be easier to provide verbal instruction to students.

your students research tribes from your own part of the country, it might be more relevant to them. You might have a Native American among your students, or you can invite a local resident to visit and explain his or her culture and folklore.

For eyes: In a discussion about eye color, you might let the students make a chart showing how many in the class have blue, brown, green, and hazel eyes. Your students can survey their family members and then figure out whose genes were likely to be responsible for their eye color.

For nuts: You might have nuts for a snack and talk about where various kinds of nuts grow. (Let us assume that all classroom allergies are accounted for.) Peanuts grow underground; walnuts grow on trees. Your students might want to try growing a peanut plant.

For energy: Your class can discuss how to "fuel the body." Your students might design a menu plan for eating an energy-packed breakfast, focusing on protein, which "wakes up" the brain and makes it ready to learn.

This activity can be repeated any number of times, generating a new list of words and inspiring new lessons. As your students participate, they will learn that if they share words on a topic they are interested in, they will have a chance to learn more about it. Because we know that the brain's capacity to remember visual images is nearly unlimited, this exercise is enhanced by adding an art element: let the students create posters to accompany each word, using pictures they draw or find in magazines.

Carty, Monica, and the Regis staff fight this kind of inertia. Carty writes, "At an all boys school such as ours, a tremendous amount of energy abounds. The boys are all over the place! And yet we've found that increasing the kinesthetic and physical construction work has not caused a problem. In fact, now we have to correct and discipline the boys less than before. We also find that if (when!) they start to get out of hand, it is easier to calm them down. We've seen a significant decrease in discipline problems this year."

REARRANGE YOUR CLASSROOM.   In the *Australian Journal of Middle Schooling*, researcher Michael Nagel, a Gurian Institute associate, reports on innovations for boys in Australia.[7] After providing training to middle schools in Queensland, he found teachers moving immediately toward allowing greater movement in science classes and reconfiguring classrooms to support that movement. He describes an example:

> A Year 7 teacher decided to incorporate greater movement and autonomy in an effort to meet the needs of her male students. She did so by reconfiguring her classroom so that one desk for each student was situated in a U-shaped format in the center of the class. Outside this configuration were a number of other desks set up as single spaces, paired working stations, and group tables. The simple premise of the classroom was that while she or anyone else was providing instruction and/or information and standing in the middle of the "U," all other students needed to be seated in the desks of the "U" and be attentive. At all other times, students could choose to sit wherever they pleased and move as often as they liked. The results of this simple exercise were interesting, to say the least.

Michael discusses a number of positive outcomes, but perhaps this one is the most important: "Disruptions and behavior issues diminished, impulsive behavior appeared to subside and all students relished their newfound autonomy. . . . It is significant to note that the overall teaching and learning environment improved for not only the boys, but also for the girls, due to the fact that the teacher spent less time managing behavior and more time working with students."

INVITE GUEST SCIENTISTS.   Our schools have guest artist programs—painters and paints. What about inviting guest scientists too, especially in high schools? Hydroelectric engineers, sewage engineers, doctors, dentists, nurses, nutritionists, health consultants, artists working in metal sculpture (in other words, expert welders), therapists—the list of possible scientists goes on and on. You can find nearly all these human resources among your students' parents and parent-led teams. These guest scientists are not the science teachers or mentors the students see every day—these are scientists in the field who come into class to share their expertise. One guest scientist a month is probably all you will have time to organize, but if you can create a "guest scientist committee" among your students, that committee can organize more than one visit per month. This practice of organizational leadership will help each member of the committee gain life skills, and the committee will provide your classroom with enough guest scientists to stimulate even the most difficult students!

RECRUIT STUDENT ATHLETES.   At a training in Princeton, a high school teacher pointed out, "All around our adolescent students are 'scientists' disguised as athletes." She continued, "These athlete-scientists are often already idolized by our students. I've put these scientists to work by giving them special assignments. In these extra credit papers, my athlete-students study their sport in 'scientific terms.' The athletes have to explain their sport using science."

Teachers often report feeling a "disconnect" with athletes in their classes—the athlete often is self-absorbed in his physical prowess and craft. He may neglect academic learning. A research project on "himself"—or, more substantially, on the athletic and physical life he has chosen—can reconnect him with his science. An effective report from him on the science of his athletic endeavor—using PowerPoint or an overhead projector, words and graphics, testimonials and personal experience—can help him design a part of his own grade success. The popularity often attached to student athletes can be broadened by allowing them to present themselves as student scholars too.

The Importance of the Arts and Athletics in Academics

You may have noticed that a number of the innovations in this chapter (and in many of the other chapters) involve the integration of arts and athletics into children's learning. Arts and athletics are good for all kids.

For boys, there is a special case to be made for integrating both into academic learning. Graphics, visuals, dramatic self-expressions, and physical movement and athletic exercise all have positive affects on children. Boys need to move their bodies, they need to stimulate their minds, they need to maneuver their learning toward the visual cortex as much as possible, and they need physical exercise to keep their brains alert. These activities may help boys bring C's up to B's and B's up to A's.

In our very difficult and test-driven contemporary landscape, our educational system often finds itself cutting arts and athletics programs. Many schools are focusing almost exclusively on raising standardized test scores so that they can keep or increase their funding. They are in survival mode, and some arts and athletics are seen not as "survival enhancers" but as "fluff" or as burdensome. There are even some schools that have eliminated recess in order to spend more class time raising test scores.

Teachers and parents who base their classroom teaching and child rearing on knowledge of the human brain find themselves creating physical and artistic innovations to keep boys engaged and learning. Our sons' educational issues today are in part linked to industrialization's emphasis on sedentary (nonphysical) learning and its de-emphasis over the last century on the artistic pursuits of higher learners. We must reverse this trend now. In your own community, you can renew the wisdom of the ancient Greeks, who believed that a boy could not be educated fully unless he was an artist and an athlete.

Contemporary research on the male brain supports this ancient wisdom. It calls on our homes and schools to look at the visual, graphic, and physical nature of boys (without leaving girls out) to see how relevant arts and athletics are in an educational landscape in which boys are continually falling behind.

If your community engages in a dialogue about giving up recess or ending male sports programs or cutting funding for relevant arts education, you can bring logic to bear on that dialogue by referencing the research, testimonials, and success data of schools featured in this chapter and the last. These schools are helping children succeed in math, science, language arts, and other academic rigors through sports, drama, drawing, and music.

Our boys live in their bodies, in their eyes, in the hidden emotional expressions of the heart that many times cannot find a voice in words or on the page alone. They need sound, color, and movement in order for the words to become real and relevant in the world.

Using Single-Gender Classrooms Effectively

The controversy over single-sex schooling simply revolves around two concerns: whether it is legal within public schooling, and whether it produces educational benefits for girls or boys.

—ROSEMARY C. SALOMONE, AUTHOR OF *SAME, DIFFERENT, EQUAL*

A young frog fell in a tub of buttermilk. After calling for his momma, yelling "FIRE!" and having nobody come to save him, he just kept kicking until he kicked up a lump of butter that allowed him to hop out. We'll just keep kicking!

—JACKIE DYE, PRINCIPAL, RUDD MIDDLE SCHOOL

IT BEGINS WITH AN EMAIL OR PHONE CALL. THE WRITER OR SPEAKER SAYS, "We're noticing some issues with our boys [or girls]. Can your Institute train our school [community] in how boys and girls learn differently?" Kathy or I or others from the Gurian Institute go to the school district, community, or state education board. We provide training in male-female brain difference and how to teach so both boys and girls can learn better—the kind of material you've been learning in this book— which we think can help them confront the issues they're facing in their school.

Then, at some point during the training, someone will say, "What about separate-sex classrooms—are they useful?" Now a side discussion begins. Some parents are for trying this, some are not. Some administrators are leery of it, some are not. Some teachers immediately buy into the idea, some are opposed. The training day or days are over, and the community is left to experiment in the many ways available; then, often, we get another phone call or email.

"Our school has decided to try single-gender classrooms," the superintendent, principal, teacher, or parent reports. "Can you help?" This phone call brings a second adventure in learning and teaching that can reap immense rewards if practiced effectively. The Gurian Institute has helped schools and school districts set up a number of single-gender pilots that have provided success data. Because the single-gender classes are such an obvious structural alteration, student statistics either show improved grades and discipline in single-gender classrooms within a few months or they don't. These separate classes either work or they don't. If the boys in the single-gender class are getting better grades and having fewer discipline problems than peer boys in coed classes, the new policy becomes an increasingly significant part of a school's life.

The Gurian Institute understands that coeducation is the norm in American and democratic schooling. Most of our work as trainers is with schools that are coeducational. Nevertheless, the effectiveness of single-gender classes is clear, as we'll show in this chapter.

In this chapter, we'll focus our information on the use of single-gender *classrooms* to help boys (and girls) improve their educational success. Although there are a number of very effective single-gender schools in the United States and abroad—one of them, The Regis School of the Sacred Heart, an all-boys K–8 school in Houston, has been featured in other chapters of this book—this chapter will focus on single-gender classrooms within coeducational school systems. Establishing single-gender classrooms in coeducational schools is a relatively easy method of piloting a new strategy. Altering a whole school from coeducational to single gender is more difficult and less common.

If single-gender classrooms are an alternative you want to consider for your child or for your school, this chapter will introduce you to schools, teachers, and communities that have used it effectively. Some of the school results you'll find reported here are, we believe, really remarkable.

The Essential Search for Equality

There is a history to single-gender education. Although coeducation has been the standard for public education in the United States for most of the last one hundred years, single-gender schools have existed historically in the form of private schools for girls only or boys only for many years before public education was widely available. During the Industrial Revolution in the nineteenth century, our society began supporting the concept of free, public education that would help promote development of a disciplined workforce and raise up "poor children." Wealthy families were expected to pay for their children's education, and private schools sprang up everywhere as a result.

Whether children went to school at all was up to parents until 1851, when Massachusetts passed the first law making education compulsory.[1] The right to a public education was legislated many times in the years that followed, including the government's legal sanction of racial segregation of some groups of children. Despite numerous private schools for boys only and girls only, landmark rulings such as *Brown* v. *Board of Education* in 1954 showed that the doctrine of "separate but equal" needed to be rethought.[2] The court found that "in the field of public education, the doctrine of 'separate but equal' has no place."

Equality for Girls

This formal declaration against racial segregation was used later in the 1960s by advocates for female equality to argue (rightly) that girls were not receiving schooling equal to that of boys. Girls too often found the path to higher education closed to them, especially if they wanted to pursue the same opportunities as boys to become doctors, lawyers, or scientists—professions that offered economic and social rewards and that required girls to have all the educational opportunities boys did. Advocates for girls fought and, on many fronts, won the battle to provide clearly defined opportunities for girls to gain better access to quality education equal to that being offered to boys. With the passage of Title IX of the Education Amendments of 1972, the law of the land was again clarified, declaring that, "No person in the United States shall, on the basis of sex, be excluded from participation in, be denied benefits of, or be subjected to discrimination under any education program or activity receiving Federal financial assistance."[3]

Title IX was a welcome piece of legislation to all who cared about our nation's daughters. It was applauded by women's groups as finally providing the basis for girls to receive equal opportunities in the education system. And it has worked. For example, more women than men are now applying to law schools and medical schools, a trend that should expand career opportunities for women in those previously male-dominated professions.[4] Women now outnumber men in higher education, representing nearly 60 percent of undergraduate degrees and a majority of graduate degrees in many fields. Prestigious academic institutions throughout the country have increased their recruitment of outstanding female scholars, and girls now attend traditional all-male institutions, such as West Point, Annapolis, Virginia Military Institute, The Citadel, and elsewhere. Thanks to court rulings and legislation, equal coeducation has improved opportunity for girls.

Although many of us agree that there's still work to be done for our daughters, there is a great deal to be proud of in the past half century of advocacy. But where do boys stand in the search for equality? In Part One of this book, we looked at the ways that industrial education before *Brown* v. *Board of Education* and Title IX created obstacles to teaching many of our boys: it brought boy energy out of the natural and excitable world of movement and confined it to the closed, sedentary world of the classroom. We saw a problem in the making, one that in our new century has become a crisis. We are now in a different historical moment than we were in 1954 or 1972.

Equality for Boys

"We've seen a cultural shift in many communities," writes Mary Broderick, president of the Connecticut Association of School Boards, "that makes it downright un-male to be studious, while we've celebrated the academic achievement of girls. The pendulum has swung too far . . . it's time to find balance—perhaps for the first time."[5] Broderick's words reflect a new consciousness that our culture now needs to allow innovations that protect boys' equal right to quality education—innovations proven to work.

As part of federal No Child Left Behind legislation, public schools are allowed to provide single-gender education if they believe doing so will help both sexes improve school performance. Our culture has come to understand that the act of dividing boys and girls into separate classrooms and even separate schools is not inherently bad for girls. In fact, there is a great deal of research to support the idea that for many girls, separate-gender schools and classes are quite helpful in opening up opportunity for girls in all areas of success, including engineering, law, and medicine. The pendulum has swung back to an interest in single-gender education—and the job of educators and parents today is to make sure that the "new" (actually quite ancient) innovation of single-gender schools and classrooms works for both boys and girls.

For boys in particular, schools around the country are exploring the potential for single-gender classrooms not only to bring up grades but to bring down disciplinary referrals (in which boys consistently outnumber girls, sometimes as much as ten to one). At the beginning of the 2004–2005 school year, the National Association for Single Sex Public Schools identified 113 public schools as offering some single-gender classes.[6] Those classes are most commonly language arts, math, science, and social studies.

Although the list of schools offering single-gender classrooms includes all school levels, from kindergarten through high school, many are middle schools, which include some combination of grades 5 through 8, depending on the state and community. In *Boys and Girls*

Learn Differently! my colleagues and I showed that middle school was a very important time to separate boys and girls for some classes, given the hormonal, developmental, and social difficulties our young males and females face during early to middle adolescence. We've found that implementation of single-gender classes is initially driven by the need to improve standardized test scores that measure competency in math, language arts, science, and social studies. As school districts, principals, teachers, and parents look for academic and behavioral options, especially in middle school, they see good opportunity in single-gender classrooms.

In our work in these schools, the Gurian Institute has generally found improvement in grades in core classes that are single gender, as you'll see in a moment, but we've also found something else worth highlighting. Boys who have suppressed their creative side in the competitive pubescent coeducational environment often become more engaged in creative arts, music, and drama when offered single-gender classes in those subjects.

The Success of Single-Gender Classes

If a strong case is to be made for a certain kind of educational strategy—especially one that's been as controversial as single-gender classes—outcomes need to speak for themselves. Major studies around the world (including the United States, Canada, England, and Australia) have demonstrated that single-gender education can help both boys and girls. The Australian Council for Educational Research studied more than 250,000 students over six years, in fifty-three academic areas, and found that students in single-gender classrooms scored between 15 and 22 percent higher in academic performance than their coed counterparts. A British study looked at test scores from eight hundred public schools and found that the students in single-gender education not only demonstrated improved performance but also had better attitudes about school and learning—both the boys and girls.[7]

Here are some specific outcomes from around the United States.

Rudd Middle School, Pinson, Alabama

In 2003, Carol Crawford, director of programs for the Alabama State Department of Education, initiated statewide training by the Gurian Institute for Alabama administrators, school principals, and a team of trainers assigned to help schools across the state improve performance. From this training, administrators then took Gurian Institute resources and methods into their individual schools. This training led to the piloting of single-gender classes by a number of Alabama schools.

It was through this process that the Gurian Institute became acquainted with Jackie Dye, the principal of Rudd Middle School (sixth, seventh, and eighth grades) in Pinson, Alabama. In summer 2004, Jackie brought Kathy to her middle school to train faculty, administrators, and parents in how boys and girls learn differently. According to Jackie, "We immediately saw teachers reporting decreased disciplinary referrals and improved academic performance for both our boys and the girls." Jackie's school piloted single-gender classes for language arts, math, and science.

Lewis Frasier Middle School, Hinesville, Georgia

After reading *Boys and Girls Learn Differently!* and pursuing research on single-gender alternatives, Dr. Yvette Keel, assistant principal of Lewis Frasier, contracted with the Gurian Institute to provide on-site training on how to implement gender-specific strategies in the classroom. Kathy provided that training, augmenting faculty training components with an evening session for parents on how boys and girls learn differently. Lewis Frasier opted to use single-gender classes as one of their innovations and have provided us with their results from the 2003–2004 school year, the first year of the new classes.

Table 8.1 shows the percentage of Lewis Frasier students who scored below state standards at the end of the 2002–2003 school year.

Testifying before the school board in 2002, Keel discussed not only the worrisome percentage of low test scores in sixth grade and the disturbing trend of boys' scoring well behind girls in all areas, but also the overall decline by eighth grade, for both boys and girls. The school board agreed that gender-specific teaching strategies might well be helpful

TABLE 8.1   LEWIS FRASIER MIDDLE SCHOOL TEST SCORES, 2002–2003.

GENDER	READING (%)	LANGUAGE ARTS (%)	MATH (%)
6th grade			
male	23	36	32
female	7	16	18
8th grade			
male	27	26	47
female	18	16	46

throughout the curriculum and that sixth grade would be pilot-tested with single-gender classes in language arts and in math. Approximately half the students, 120 out of 277, were put in single-gender classes (called the Gender Team). When the next year's test results came in, Keel and her colleagues looked to see (1) if there was general improvement in test scores due to new understanding in all sixth-grade classes of how to teach to the minds of boys and the minds of girls and (2) if there was specific improvement in the single-gender classes (the Gender Team).

Indeed, Lewis Frasier immediately saw improvements in both over-all class performance and in the single-gender classes. At the end of the 2003–2004 school year, only 12 percent of all sixth-grade students did not meet state standards in reading, and only 18 percent did not meet state standards in language arts. In math, only 19 percent did not meet standards. (If you compare this to the results shown in Table 8.1, you can see this was quite an improvement.) According to Keel, these results were largely due to new teacher sensitivity to male-female brain and learning difference. Keel shared with me that teachers applied the new gender-specific teaching methodologies and strategies even in coed classes to meet the specific needs of boys and girls.

Even greater improvement in test scores in language arts and reading occurred among the students in single-gender classes. Table 8.2 shows the percentage of students in single-gender classes who scored below state standards at the end of the 2003–2004 school year.

Because of these positive results for both boys and girls, Keel and her colleagues are preparing to go before the school board to recommend

TABLE 8.2   LEWIS FRASIER MIDDLE SCHOOL TEST SCORES, 2003–2004.

GENDER	READING (%)	LANGUAGE ARTS (%)	MATH (%)
6th grade Gender Team			
boys	7	7	11
girls	2	2	8.5

that more grades at Lewis Frasier Middle School become single gender in the next school year.

Keel told us, "Just learning about how boys and girls learn differently has had a significant effect on how we teach in our coeducational classes. At the same time, what is prompting us to go forward with our appeal to the school board for more single-gender classes is the significant improvement in test scores, grades, teacher comfort, parent and student buy-in—most parents and students really like this program—and our improvement in school discipline."

Lewis Frasier Middle School saw a 50 percent decline in discipline referrals in the Gender Team. Furthermore, the number of discipline referrals for sex-related and sexual harassment referrals decreased to zero in the Gender Team students.

Beaumont Middle School, Lexington, Kentucky

This middle school instituted a single-gender initiative with the start of the 2002–2003 school year. The Fayette County public schools, of which Beaumont is a part, contracted with researchers Patricia Stevens and Neal Gray at Eastern Kentucky University to do an independent study of the single-gender innovation. That study reports grade improvement for both boys and girls. Scores on the Scholastic Reading Inventory (SRI) also improved: the girls' class showed a 134-point increase, and the boys' class score went up by 169 points.

Two California School Districts

In 1999, the Jefferson Leadership Academy, in the Long Beach Unified School District, began separating sixth- through eighth-grade students for core subjects, under the direction of principal Jill Rojas. She reports, "What we have seen is that grades and test scores improved for both boys and girls at Jefferson." Phil Duncan, principal of another California school, the San Francisco 49er Academy in East Palo Alto, echoed Ms. Rojas's enthusiasm for this innovation, explaining that before the school decided to use single-gender classes, "Our boys had more attendance and disciplinary issues and they were more likely to become involved with the criminal justice system." Now, however, he reports, "We have not had a single expulsion in seven years. That's because we have the magic here."

Main Street School, North Branch, Wisconsin

Teachers David Balzer and Susan Howard approached their principal, Sara Svir, in May 2003 with an idea: let's try single-gender education in some of our fourth-grade classes. Howard became interested in the innovation after reading *Boys and Girls Learn Differently!* and having noticed positive results in other communities. He showed Svir that in an elementary school in a low-income area of Washington, D.C., test scores shot up after the switch to single-gender classrooms. Specifically, 88 percent of students at the Washington school now tested in the top two categories of math (previously only 49 percent had). In reading, 91 percent tested in the top two categories (previously, only 50 percent had). Svir gave the okay for the single-gender classes, and David Balzer reports that he is especially excited by what happens with boys' greater engagement in literature classes.

Thurgood Marshall Elementary School, Seattle

At this elementary school, located in an economically disadvantaged area, students are being separated by gender. Principal Ben Wright, honored as Washington State Distinguished Principal of the Year in 2003, provided the vision and leadership when his school was challenged to boost academic achievement.[8] The class sizes didn't change, teachers were the same, and in fact initially nothing changed except the single-gender grouping.

Students at Thurgood Marshall have made impressive academic progress: the number of students meeting state reading standards jumped from 27 percent to 51 percent; those meeting math standards rose from 13 percent to 35 percent the first year. Boys made the most pronounced improvements. Disciplinary problems, which had been sending a nonstop parade of students to the principal's office every day, were primarily between boys and girls: hitting, harassing, teasing, touching. These incidents nearly disappeared when single-gender classes began.

Teacher Lihn Le says, "I see the boys just get stronger, and I see the girls who are shy and timid speak up—especially in math class. They would speak up and be themselves." In this elementary school, both boys and girls are doing better.

Letting Boys Learn as Boys

The results and positive outcomes we've been featuring from our pilot schools and other schools around the country are transferrable elsewhere. They show that boys learning as boys can work well. And "boys as boys" is not a stereotype, not a detriment. According to Graham Able, master of Dulwich College in England, boys in boys' schools consistently outscored their counterparts in coed schools during his research, suggesting that single-gender environments are especially advantageous for boys and dispelling the popular myth that boys do better in coed classes where girls set "a good example."[9]

At the 2003 International Boys' School Coalition Conference in Sydney, Australia, Dr. Bruce Cook reported, "In boys' schools we can concentrate on their learning style. In co-ed, boys tend to adopt a quasi-masculine attitude because girls are there. They feel they have to demonstrate their emerging masculinity by gross macho over-reaction. In boys' schools, they can participate in anything irrespective of any perceived gender bias, whereas in co-ed schools you get boys who don't even try moving into those areas, the choir or debating, because they're fearful of being labeled gay or a sissy."[10]

Diane Ruble, professor of psychology at New York University, has studied the single-gender innovation and argues that these positive results stem from boys' greater freedom to be themselves in single-gender environments without the constraints of gender stereotypes that prevail in coed settings.[11] In the single-gender settings that the Gurian Institute has piloted or assisted, Ruble's theory is borne out: boys become more engaged in art, music, drama, and foreign languages.

The Importance of Teacher and Parent Buy-In

There is something very important happening in all these schools: an innovation that fits the needs of students is being tried and is succeeding. If your community is thinking about trying single-gender education, here are some issues to look at closely: teacher training and buy-in, what parents are saying about single-gender classes, and the socialization of boys and girls.

Teacher Training and Buy-In

One key determinant of success with single-gender classes is teacher training in how boys and girls actually learn. When schools and teachers receive training in how male and female brains learn differently, things get better even for coeducational classes; and very important, trained teachers are best suited for (and come to enjoy) teaching separate groups of boys and girls. If teachers don't get training in male-female brain difference—or when they just don't buy into the concept—things go less well, especially in the single-gender classrooms they have been "forced" to take on by their school district's or community's innovative zeal.

One of the schools trained by the Gurian Institute contacted Kathy just recently to report difficulty a teacher is having in a single-gender (boys-only) language arts class. In the words of the principal: "This teacher hates the concept of having only boys in the class, and she is politically against the idea of boys and girls learning differently. We're having a lot of trouble with her class—her students are not doing well." These are stark words (and we aren't naming the parties involved in order to protect the in-school review process); they are important words, however, for all of us to hear, because they speak of a definite reality among many individuals and in many schools.

If teachers don't buy in and aren't trained, things can go less than well—indeed, the whole innovation can backfire. A room full of twenty-eight boys and a teacher who is not happy with their energy—or is untrained to handle it—can hurt rather than help the educational system and the students. In all cases, we have found that the single-gender classes need to be given to teachers who have been trained in how to handle them and who have no deep belief or conviction against them. It's clear to us that in a community where there are no teachers who want to have single-gender classrooms and there's no support from the administration or school board, such an initiative simply won't work and should not be attempted.

In any case, our Gurian Institute results support the success of single-gender classrooms when there is buy-in and commitment. Joining us, Michael Younger, who directs research on single-gender teaching in England, has observed that "where the idea has been sold to staff, pupils and parents" single-gender teaching is working very well. In schools where staff is less committed, "it is not."[12]

Similarly, at Jefferson Leadership Academy, featured previously, both boys' *and* girls' grades and test scores improved by statistically significant percentages (for seventh and eighth graders who had attended the same school the year before). School staff attributed these improvements to the single-gender innovation, adequate training of teachers, and to yet another element in success: involvement of parents.[13] As with so many innovations in schools, parents and families need to be part of the process.

What Parents and Kids Say

What are parents and kids saying about single-gender classes? We asked some of our pilot schools to report not only on their increased academic success in the classrooms but also on parent reception of single-gender classrooms.

Dr. Yvette Keel, assistant principal of Lewis Frasier Middle School (whose successes we discussed earlier in this chapter), tells us, "Parents told teachers during open house that they love the idea of single-gender classes and that they are looking forward to their children coming to school to pay attention to their lessons and not each other."

Peggy Daniels, middle school principal at Carolina Day School shares, "In regard to what is happening in sixth grade . . . we are now four weeks into school, and I must tell you that our single-gender classes are being well received. Our early impressions are that students are happy, and so are parents! Many positive comments are floating around in our school community. The teachers and parents remain excited, and they are quite pleased with what they are experiencing so far."

One parent of a sixth-grade boy recently told Peggy that she was "'sure the boys in sixth grade are enjoying their single-gender classes, even though they might not be open about discussing it.' I'm hearing such positive comments from other parents, and single-gender instruction at CDS is such a nonissue now."

A father who attended the Gurian Institute parent training session at Carolina Day School admitted that he had concerns before the session and was really worried that "this single-gender class would be just another way my son would get the short end of the stick. But now I see that's not the case—this will benefit my son every bit as much, if not more, than the girls. It really makes sense; I'm convinced."

A mother whose son moved from a coed to a single-gender setting shared, "This is great. So many problems we had last year stemmed from girls. My son just told me he likes the girls not being in his class this year—he doesn't worry about them now. He just does his work and stays out of trouble."

For this mom, the case for single-gender classes was made very simply. Her son's performance in school improved, his grades went up, and behavior ceased to be a problem. He is getting more out of his time at school, and a lot of the difference is that the distraction of girls has been removed during the period of his school day when learning is the focus.

And how about the girls? A teacher from North Carolina shared one of her female student's recent writing assignments with us: "I thought that single gender would be horrible, but I really think it is a great thing. It makes learning a lot easier, and I am not as shy to raise my hand in class because I was scared someone might laugh at me because I got the answer wrong. I also like single gender because there are smaller classes."

Of course, there are some boys and girls that want to be in classes with the opposite gender, and some parents question the strategy of single-gender education. One parent came up to Kathy after a parent evening and said, "No matter what you say, I don't think this is a good idea. I'm not going to change my mind, and I don't want my children participating." It is crucial that this point of view be heard, and there certainly are cases in which parent buy-in is not possible. Fortunately, the school this parent's children attended had both coed and single-gender classes, so they were able to find a class that offered a coed alternative.

Socialization: Will Boys Get Enough Interaction with Girls?

Even when their grades improve or they're getting in trouble less often in single-gender classes, some students say they miss the social aspect of coed classes. One Rudd Middle School male student told a local reporter of the *Birmingham Post-Herald,* "I'm not ready for it [single-sex classrooms]."

One concern that is always expressed by at least one parent in every training session is that boys and girls who are separated in their classrooms will miss out on socialization opportunities that are important to prepare them for building successful relationships down the road. If your community is thinking about single-gender classes, this is a question you may well be asking yourself.

Fortunately, this question becomes a "nonconcern" once the single-gender classes are implemented. It becomes clear to parents that today's world provides a multitude of opportunities for boys and girls to interact with members of the opposite sex. In schools that have single-gender classes in core subjects, boys and girls often still mingle during electives (such as art, music, and foreign languages) and during lunch and extracurricular activities. Away from school, boys and girls interact at home, at church, in community activities, at the mall, and so on—and in these venues parents can exercise their judgment in how those interactions develop.

What Young Adults Say

In earlier chapters, we told you about Patricia St. Germain's unique course, Mindworks, that allowed boys to explore male-female brain differences and express how they felt their own individual male selves did or did not fit into the expected and accepted patterns in their high school environment. In essays at the end of the class, many boys wrote insightful comments about their single-gender experience.

One boy, seventeen, wrote, "Now I look at how I react to situations and I definitely know I am a bridge brain guy [see Chapter Twelve]. There are many, many times in movies where I have cried. In public, also. I have always felt I am more in tune with others, but have not ever talked about it like this before. Being with just other guys really helped me."

Another student, eighteen, shared, "This class happened at an opportune moment for me, because I was nearing a point where being possessed of a fast, male brain was causing me a lot of problems that were very perplexing to me. The class being kind of like an owner's manual to the male brain, allowed me to look at what was happening and help me to know how to deal with it."

Although single-gender classes can help test scores, grades, and discipline referrals at any age and grade, these students' comments reflect a hidden gain of boy-only classes for middle and high schoolers: the depth of human dialogue between the boys can often increase, as working within single-gender groups allows the boys to ask questions of their own maleness, their own developing masculinity, they would not have thought of asking among crowds of girls and boys together.

Single-Gender Sex Education

When we think of single-gender classes these days, we tend to think of innovative high school classes like Patricia St. Germain's or middle schools and elementary schools that are raising test scores and grades. We often forget about a very important single-gender venue: sex education. Almost without exception, the schools the Gurian Institute works with, both single gender and coed, public and private, report (much to the expressed dismay of many teacher and parents alike) that they offer incomplete "sex education" to their students. Even those schools that have a section on human development as part of health classes (often as early as the fifth grade) admit that they are woefully inadequate relative to the broad societal problems of early adolescent sexual activity and increased numbers of teenagers suffering from sexually transmitted diseases. In the Harrison School District in Colorado Springs, Colorado, middle school health classes were eliminated from the schedule because of budget cuts, despite the district's consistently high teen pregnancy statistics.

If your school or school district is thinking about single-gender classes for language arts, math, science, or other core curricula, but wants to try something that seems more logical or intuitive first, your sex education components (or their revival if you've lost them already) may serve as a ready-made opportunity for this research.

Most schools already know that both boys and girls benefit from a comfortable, single-gender peer group in which they can ask questions and discuss topics like sex and hygiene that would never be addressed—at least not seriously—in a coed group. Your school can offer a single-gender sex education class for one week (or more) with a same-sex observer on hand to watch the interactions, the physical movement of the boys, the pencil tapping, the way the boys talk to each other and the teacher, and other male-specific body and verbal language we've discussed in this book. You may well notice a justification for single-gender core classes in the behavioral improvement (and verbal success) you see in your "study" of the sex education class. You will also be initiating a crucial human dialogue about sexuality among the young men of your community.

At the Presbyterian Day School in Memphis, headmaster Lee Burns and upper school head Mark Carleton created and implemented a program called Building Boys, Making Men. This program allowed them to reach positively into young men's lives, while also evaluating how single-gender groups work. Developed for fifth- and sixth-grade boys, the program helps boys develop a vision of manhood. "We have parent lunches," writes Susan Droke, head of the lower school and a participant in Gurian Institute training delivered through the Tennessee Association of Independent Schools, "to discuss topics such as peer relationships, drugs and alcohol, girls and dating, mothers and sons, father and sons. We do this in single-gender groups. Another part of the program involves father-son retreats, trips and dinners."[14]

By providing boys with male identity models and mentors, involving fathers and other male extended family, getting male teachers and coaches involved—all the while studying the boys and their interactions—you can help boys address their sex-related questions. At the same time, you can evaluate the character and developmental goals of sex education and prepare your school for the implementation of other single-gender classrooms.

Bringing Single-Gender Innovations to Your School

This chapter has provided a success-driven argument for adding single-gender classrooms to the list of strategies you might try in your school. If you as a parent, teacher, administrator, or other concerned citizen see the possible use of this idea, you'll find *The Minds of Boys* to be a helpful resource. Every chapter of this book contains elements that can be applied in single-gender classrooms. Each of these elements has created success in coeducational settings and does not require single-gender settings, but their benefits are often very observable when there are only boys in the room.

- More physical movement occurs.
- More stress balls get squeezed in boys' hands.
- More diagrams, graphs, and pictures get used.
- More art and music techniques achieve strong academic results.
- More boy-friendly books get read.
- More men become involved as teachers and as volunteers.

If you as a parent are convinced of the usefulness of single-gender classes, you may want to form an advocacy group that meets with the school principal. You can show the principal the success outcomes discussed in this chapter. Before your meeting, you might want to get some key teachers on board, teachers who would welcome piloting single-gender classrooms in their schools.

If you are a teacher or administrator who is holding off on advancing the single-gender option for fear of Title IX or other parental concerns, we hope this chapter has allayed some of those fears. For further success data, you can go to www.gurianinstitute.com, where you'll find descriptions of more pilot schools and programs that have applied the "minds of boys" program not only in their coeducational settings but also in single-gender classes.

Can a school bring about positive results for boys without single-gender classes? Of course it can. As the success data in other chapters indicate, just training teachers in how boys learn and applying good male-friendly strategies create better learning. At the same time, the successful results of single-gender classes are strong enough now that they provide another tool for the community's toolbox: an exciting way of applying all we've learned about boys in settings that give boys both a crucible for innovation and the emotional safety to "just be themselves."

Now let's move to the last part of this book and discuss boys who are learning-disabled, undermotivated, underperforming, and emotionally sensitive. In these next chapters, we won't repeat discussion of the potential for success in single-gender classes, but we placed this chapter here, before the final section of the book, so that you'd keep it in mind. Single-gender classrooms, study groups, and school clubs can help you help undermotivated boys, special education students, and our most sensitive sons. Keep this innovation in your toolbox as now we focus together on those boys who need extra help.

Helping Boys
Who Need Extra Help

9

A New Vision of Learning Disabilities, ADD/ADHD, and Behavioral Disorders

The brain is an organ that can go wrong just like any other.

—DANIEL AMEN, *CHANGE YOUR BRAIN, CHANGE YOUR LIFE*

Boys consume 80 percent of the world's supply of Ritalin. That is an increase of 500 percent over the last 10 years.

—MICHELLE CONLIN, *BUSINESS WEEK*, MAY 26, 2003

IN SPRING 2003, *BUSINESS WEEK* PUBLISHED A COVER ARTICLE ON WHAT WAS happening to boys in our educational system. Over the last decade, the Gurian Institute has been involved in providing information on children's educational health to most of the major media, but rarely had a business magazine taken on the topic of our sons' educational health. The *Business Week* cover story was a corporate wake-up call to the crisis boys face in education, especially to the rates of male brain disorder diagnoses in the last decade. It was telling businesses to pay attention. Corporate health, ultimately, depends on community health, and all health begins with the health of children.

Thankfully, corporations and businesses are beginning to pay more and more attention to the problem of male brain disorders. In May 2004, Medco Health Solutions, America's largest prescription benefit manager, reported on a study of medication use among children in its annual analysis of drug use trends. Some of Medco's findings are listed in the next Did You Know? box.

These are sobering statistics, especially when coupled with the fact that estimates of the number of children diagnosed with attention deficit problems has now risen to 10 percent of all American children, according to the National Center of Health Statistics. The number of children ages three to seventeen diagnosed with ADD/ADHD has risen from 3.3 million in 1997 to 4.4 million in 2002.[1] Quite sobering also is the fact that the use of behavioral medications, especially among our youngest children, might well have lasting physical and psychological effects.

Can the new science help us get a handle on what is going on here? Studies performed over the last decade have noted that the brains of children with brain disorders have what some specialists call "brain anomalies" and others call "brain atrophy." Medications can work wonders to treat the anomalies and combat the atrophy, but some specialists believe that the very medications used to treat brain disorders and anomalies can cause other anomalies and other atrophy.

It is important to remember that parts of the brain needed for effective learning—such as the corpus callosum, the right frontal lobe, and posterior lateral ventricles—are often shrunken, or atrophied, in a brain struggling with a disorder like ADD or ADHD. When we talk about "brain anomalies," we are usually referring to this shrinkage. Once a disorder like this is clearly diagnosed, the physician, psychiatrist, family, and the community are charged with treating the brain-in-distress by whatever means are safe and effective. But what exactly should parents and professionals do? How much treatment via medication is appropriate?

In support of the use of medication, Dr. Howard Schubiner, of Providence-St. John's Hospital in Detroit, recently told me, "Medications are so effective in treating both child and adult ADD that not to use them

??? Did You Know? ???

- Annual spending for behavioral medicines (such as Ritalin) has *eclipsed all other categories of children's medicines,* including antibiotics and asthma medications.
- Specifically, 17 percent of total drug spending for children in 2003 was for behavioral medicines, compared to 16 percent for antibiotics and asthma medicines, 11 percent for skin conditions, and 6 percent for allergy medicines.
- Use of ADHD medications in particular *by children under five years old* rose 49 percent between 2001 and 2004, with spending on these drugs increasing 369 percent in the same time period.
- Use of these medications among all children increased 23 percent a year (the increased use of these medications for children under five being considered the most startling statistic).
- An estimated 5.3 percent of children (more than six million) in the United States took some kind of behavioral medication (including Ritalin, Adderal, Strattera, Concerta, and Prozac) in 2003. Of that 5.3 percent, three fifths take attention deficit/conduct disorder medicines and the remaining children take antidepressants (the percentages include boys who take both).[2]

is a cruel mistake. Medication is the single most effective intervention for children with ADD, ADHD, and other behavior and brain disorders like anxiety and depression." Dr. Schubiner, coauthor of the article "Attention Deficit/Hyperactivity Disorder in Adolescent Males," reminds us all of the benefits of medication.[3] Dr. Schubiner is well aware of the fears parents and others have of medication—that it could cause problems as it is trying to relieve them, but he points to a study reported in the *Journal of the American Medical Association* in 2002, which found little cause for alarm in the link between medications and brain atrophy. A study of 291 children and adolescents over ten years found that medication did not cause brain atrophy.

Yet that study is surrounded by other studies questioning the role that medication plays in the developing human brain. Regarding whether medication can cause new problems for the brain it treats, neuropsychiatrist Daniel Amen recently told me, "The atrophy question has not been completely answered." Researchers at Harvard University, including psychologist William Pollock, are at present trying to determine whether some children's brains are actually losing the potential for genius because of prolonged use of medications. Parents and such professionals as the physician Peter Bergen—an outspoken critic of Ritalin—and the psychologist David Stein, author of *Ritalin Is Not the Answer*,[4] worry that if medication is in fact negatively affecting the brains of some children in significant ways, we as a culture will look back on this era of constant medication of youngsters with deep regret. The obvious need of many children for medications like Ritalin is further confused by a recent study at the University of California, which found that the use of Ritalin and similar drugs might negatively affect *physical* growth.[5] This study was funded by the National Institute of Mental Health and headed by Dr. Stephen Hinshaw. Other researchers also warn that when children younger than five years old take the drugs, the risk of long-term harm rises exponentially, in both the physiological and neurological areas.

What should parents and teachers make of all this? Overall, it's clear that something is going on among our children, especially our sons, in the areas of brain disorders, diagnosis of these disorders, and medical treatment. Considering that 70 percent of learning disorder diagnoses as well as 85 percent of ADD/ADHD diagnoses are of boys and that males make up the majority of special education students, this is an area of crisis for an ever larger group of boys, families, and schools.

This chapter offers a new perspective on this issue. First, we'll look with you at the present clinical process for diagnosing causation in brain and learning disorders among males, as well as the possible consequences of overdiagnosis. Then we'll present evidence of a dangerous stereotype, not supported by actual brain science, that afflicts our culture's ability to diagnose and treat learning disabilities. We'll also suggest a new method for diagnosing brain disorders more accurately—and how to avoid stereotypes and bad diagnosis. Finally, we'll offer both parents and teachers strategies that work with boys who actually do have learning and behavioral disorders.

The Inherent Fragility of the Male Brain

"Boys are naturally fragile as learners," wrote Helene Crouper, a high school math teacher. "I can see the fragility in their eyes when they don't understand something, or think they've failed. In fact, when I stop seeing it, I really start to worry. When their eyes go blank or 'too cool to learn,' I know they've crushed their own vulnerability or they've had it crushed. That's when I know we've lost them as learners. In our special education classes and learning disability teams, I see a lot of those lost boys. I don't see tough guys, I see fragile minds."

Over the last decade, many of us have learned about men's vulnerability in areas of physical health—how much more likely males are to get various diseases (especially when ethnicity is also a factor) and how much earlier than women our men are dying (seven years for white males, twelve years for black).

We've also heard a great deal in the last decade about how emotionally fragile boys and men can be; we've seen that fragility expressed in suicide, homicide, and other violence. We've learned that boys do, quite often, have tough exteriors, but have profound and powerful feelings in their hearts. As Jamal, sixteen, wrote in a paper on gender roles in his social studies class in a Michigan high school, "Boys are tough, but we get hurt like anyone else. I cry a lot—just not with tears."

Now that our culture has opened the door of understanding to men's and boys' bodies and feelings, we are ready to understand a crucial element of human brain biology: *the male learning brain is inherently fragile.*

Neurally speaking, it just isn't as tough as our cultural myths and stereo-types tell us males are or should be.

Neural Vulnerability in the Male Mind

Metaphors about porcelain dolls generally describe girls, not boys, yet a good gender-bender metaphor would be this one: "The male learning brain is more porcelain than the female; the female learning brain is more steel."

Although girls experience their own unique kind of painful vulner-ability, consider this research on the male brain, summarized in the next Did You Know? box.

When Belsky, Rappaport, and other researchers share these results, some people are skeptical. Our culture is so accustomed to the stereo-types of tough males and fragile females that it's often difficult to believe the new brain research. Fortunately, however, MRIs and PET scans allay skepticism, especially when we localize our discussion to *learning fragility.* A picture, as the saying goes, speaks a thousand words.

When the brains of boys and girls are scanned, researchers see not only less attention activity for a greater number of boys than girls but also less blood flow in the learning male brain between the parts of the brain that control impulse. The frontal lobe, a part of the brain crucial to general learning and to impulse control, grows later in the majority of males and is more vulnerable to disruptions in infant and toddler development in the male brain than in the female.

The Cerebral Cortex

The development of the cerebral cortex has taken up a good portion of this book's time, and we return to it here, for it is the fragility of the "thinking brain" that led to Nancy Bayley's findings in the late 1990s.[6] At UC Berkeley, she studied the effect of attachment (nurture) on boys' and girls' learning brains, discovering that daughters of mothers who had problems forming secure attachments to their children as infants did not test out significantly lower in intellectual functioning during

??? Did You Know? ???

- According to Dr. Judith Rappaport, chief of child psychiatry at the National Institute of Mental Health, MRI results show the male brain to be more vulnerable than the female to certain psychiatric diseases and learning disorders.[7]
- Males are diagnosed with the majority of brain disorders in our schools, predominantly ADD/ADHD (seven boys for every one girl).
- Over two-thirds of children labeled learning-disabled and 90 percent of children labeled behaviorally disabled are boys. As the learning or behavioral disability becomes more severe, boys constitute an increasingly higher statistical number.
- Neurobiologist Jay Belsky, who has studied the whole life span, has summed up the gender-bender conclusion we face as a society: "Actually, males have a more vulnerable biology than females."[8]

adolescence than daughters of securely attached mothers (though these girls did have other emotional and relational problems). In contrast, sons of insecurely attached mothers tested out *significantly lower in high school intellectual markers.* Bayley's studies indicate that in the area of educational learning in the cerebral cortex, the female brain seems, in some ways, stronger than the male.

New Genetic Research

Male neural fragility goes beyond the cognitive and intellectual brain centers in the cerebral cortex, as geneticists have discovered. New genetics research shows us neural fragility of the male brain at a *cellular* level. In the last five years, DNA research has revealed a cellular fragility in male development that affects the educational ability of the male brain. As the geneticist Bryan Sykes has researched and reported in his book *Adam's Curse,* the Y chromosome itself (the single chromosome out of our forty-six human chromosomes that creates the male gender and brain) is more fragile than the X chromosome of the female. He points out, "Ironically, although the Y chromosome has become synonymous with male aggression, it is intrinsically unstable." Sykes reports that damaging changes "are ten to fifteen times more likely to happen in male chromosomal cells than in their female counterparts" and that DNA is better protected in the cells of the female body and brain than in the male.[9]

The impact of genetics and brain research on male vulnerability is important for the whole culture. One parent, one teacher, one person at a time, we are each called to help our civilization absorb this impact and use it to break down the "tough male" stereotype. In few places is this more important than in our diagnostic and treatment procedures for male brain and learning disorders in schools.

Boys constitute the vast majority of our school's learning disorder, brain disorder, and behavioral disorder referrals in our school system, but the school system is diagnosing and treating boys for these disorders without understanding the male mind.

Many boys diagnosed with learning disabilities are "learning-fragile," not "learning-disabled." The starting point for addressing these disabilities lies here, in convincing our educational culture to pay attention from the outset to this inherent male vulnerability—to understand, be sensitive to, and accommodate the needs of learning fragility, without labeling boys as learning-disabled. Boys do not need any more pathologizing—they need understanding.

Why the Fragility of Boys Matters, Even in a Male-Dominated World

Thus far in this chapter, we've made a case for the educational fragility of boys. Recently I made the same case at a workshop, and a very important discussion ensued.

Carla Bates, a middle school teacher, said, "But does it really matter if boys have 'learning fragility'—men succeed anyway?" She fleshed out her point, rightly mentioning that from Bill Gates to Warren Buffett to George Bush and every president, men dominate the highest ranks of society. Tiger Woods, Donovan McNabb, Barry Bonds—most sports figures are male. Others in the workshop joined this teacher in wondering whether, given the ways in which life is stacked in favor of males, any early learning fragility just evens out later, and we don't have to worry.

Three important responses to this quandary emerged.

1. Some men get to the top, but most men struggle like anyone else. Being male is not in fact an assurance of future success. As we noted in Chapter One, new studies show that boys need good schooling and then good mentoring, college, or continued education (or all three) in order to succeed at all.

2. Standardized testing and other rigors of schooling make it more likely now that if a boy starts failing early in his education he will remain one-down the rest of his career. Fabian Napolsky, a thirty-year teaching veteran, put it this way: "We've tended to think 'Boys will get by, they'll figure it out, they'll end up successful anyway,' but this is old thinking. Now, with the new testing, it's make-or-break for our kids, boys and girls. With the testing, failure at a young age begins a labeling process. The boy gets labeled and then there are long-term consequences in the boys' self-esteem and in his future success."

3. Men, not just boys, are biologically fragile and socially vulnerable in ways we tend to avoid in our social dialogue about men and women. As Judith Nance, a high school teacher, pointed out: "About five years ago I read a book by Warren Farrell called *The Myth of Male Power*. It really affected me. Until then, I thought of men as just naturally successful, but that's not true. Men are more likely than women to commit suicide. The unemployment rates for men are getting very dangerous. The

majority of mental hospital patients are men; so are the majority of the homeless. We think of men as being so tough and successful. We forget that they are very fragile."

Whether for rhetorical or political reasons, some observers argue that "men succeed anyway, so why does success in school matter?" Embracing the assumption that all boys grow up to be successful men makes it easier to continue our ongoing struggle to get more women in Congress, more women as CEOs, more women in governor's offices, and more equitable pay for women—certainly all important goals. At the same time, if you are a parent of a son or a teacher of boys, you know how incomplete this argument is.

As we ended this workshop, we returned to the theme of fragility. Males are more fragile than we think, we all agreed. Boys are not necessarily wrong, bad, disordered, or pathological, nor are they "tough guys" who can "succeed in life just because they're male." Boys and their brains are quite fragile. Not to realize this is to continue approaching men and boys either as presidents or comic book heroes or as inherently defective—rather than as who they are: people who struggle in life like anyone does and who need clear and appropriate aid, from the very early stages in their lives.

Changing Our Course

"We have to change course," Terry Schultz, a social worker and school counselor of thirty years, told me. "If we don't, the number of pathologizing diagnoses for males will just keep rising. Before we know it, a third of our schoolboys will be labeled with a brain disorder, learning disorder, or behavioral disorder. We'll keep misjudging fragility for 'disorder,' or we'll miss the ways in which boys really are fragile. On both sides, we'll be setting up more and more boys to fail in school and then in life."

Terry's projection—including the one-third statistic—is not as far out as it may sound. Right now, 17 percent of our schoolchildren are in special education programs.[10] Nearly 10 percent of our children are labeled ADD/ADHD. Most of these latter students are not in special education programs, but even with some overlap in the two categories, just under one-quarter of students in our schools are labeled with a learning or brain disorder, of whom approximately 70 percent are boys. Although many boys succeed in life because they received an accurate diagnosis and therefore the right help, the quality of many boys' lives can deteriorate because they have been incorrectly "labeled." Terry hopes for a future educational system in which boys are diagnosed the right way.

Terry Schultz came to the Gurian Institute's summer course at the University of Colorado-Colorado Springs, one of a growing number of educators who have devoted their energy to the specific study of boys' needs in schools. "What has to happen first and foremost," Terry told us, "is that policy and procedure must be based on the fact that boys and girls can't do the same things in the same ways at the same times. I would estimate that half of the learning disability diagnoses and special education referrals in my schools over the last ten years would not have been made if we dealt with male-female difference."

A New Vision

Terry is among a growing group of longtime educators working to raise awareness. He joins the Gurian Institute and others in working toward a new vision of boys' education.

As Terry and I discussed, if you think for a moment of every country and culture you know, you'll notice that structured into all of human civilization is the protection of the female body from aggression. Although war, male chauvinism, rape, and other forms of violence mitigate the protections, nevertheless, all civilizations strive to protect the female body from physical harm and brute force. As Warren Farrell showed in his multicultural analysis of gender issues, *Why Men Are the Way They Are,* it's the male body that has historically been considered disposable and sent into harm's way—in infantry combat, in the most physically dangerous jobs in our cities and towns—while the female body has been considered essential and has been protected.[11]

In our schools, this cultural protection of the female body is nowhere clearer than in athletic activities. Our girls, almost without exception, do not play football or soccer or even run track against our boys. The difference in muscle mass between girls and boys is obvious to us, so we give girls protection from the boys. Inherent in this protection is also a different physical standard for athletic success. We do not expect a 150-pound girl with lower muscle mass to lift weights at the same standards as a 200-pound boy with higher muscle mass. We do not expect a smaller girl to compete with a bigger boy (even though in some cases she might compete very well indeed!). Because in most cases it would be unfair for her to risk the possibility of physical damage caused by that competition, and because in many sports the male's larger muscle mass gives him an unfair competitive advantage, we protect girls' bodies (and self-esteem) by ensuring fairness of standards through mostly girl-only athletic grouping. We reward female fragility with its own playing field, so to speak, and protect our young girls against damage to body and mind.

If you agree that there is an inherent male-female brain difference in the same way there is an inherent and natural male-female body difference, then perhaps you'll see immediately where this athletics analogy is going. Using this analogy, ask yourself: *Why does our school system respect female physical fragility but not male neural fragility? Why do we punish boys for their inability to compete with girls who are mentally more developed in certain areas of education?*

If we didn't have PET, MRI, and SPECT scans now, which show us the physiological differences between the male and female brain, we could not make a powerful analogy between brain and body or even ask ourselves this question. It would still be possible to say, "Yes, the bodies of girls and boys are different, but the brains aren't." However, because of scientific technology, that myth is no longer tenable. Physical differences in the body are visually obvious through our naked eyes; physical differences in the brain are obvious through brain scans. Male learning fragility is an established fact in the same way, we argue, that female physical fragility is an established fact.

Therefore, when Terry Schultz or Helene Crouper see "something in boys' eyes," they are seeing a fragility that needs our greater compassion as a culture. As we've noticed thus far in this book, educational models of the past don't usually protect male neural fragility—they often create an unfair playing field for neurally fragile boys, emphasizing artificial environments over natural learning; cutting out the physical movement that was once known to be organic to male learning; placing great emphasis on reading, writing, and verbal-emotive functioning, which is difficult for many boys who don't have as much or as early development of Broca's and Wernicke's areas as girls; and giving the vulnerable male brain too little emotional and intellectual care at home and at school. Meanwhile, that same school-home system, believing the myth of gender plasticity, tries to change the way the boys' brains work. When the boy can't fit or doesn't change, he is often diagnosed as defective and labeled with a brain disorder.

Is there a better way to treat our fragile boys? Yes! That way begins with changing our diagnostic and treatment standards for learning and brain disorders. Our culture now has scientifically proven diagnostic techniques (with accompanying treatments and adjustments) that can accurately differentiate boys with bona fide brain disorders from boys who have been incorrectly labeled, so that next generations of learning-fragile boys can find a better way.

Getting the Right Diagnosis

When Kathy's son Karl Michael was a boy, his problems in school inspired his teacher to ask for a special needs assessment. The teacher suspected that he suffered from ADHD and one or more learning disabilities. Kathy took her son to a psychologist, who spoke for an hour with the boy, looked at some of his written work, and listened briefly to Kathy's story regarding her son's experience in school. At the end of that appointment, the psychologist diagnosed her son with ADHD and another learning disorder. The psychologist prescribed Ritalin, and ultimately Karl Michael was put in special education classes.

In retrospect, Kathy looks back at the diagnostic aspect of her son's educational journey with both grief and pain. "It's been seventeen years since then, and I know things are getting better for parents of boys like my son, but it's still amazing to me that the diagnostic process is so faulty. Karl Michael may have had brain disorder problems, but how could we ever really know, given how little was done to diagnose him?" Kathy, an advocate of diagnostic strategies we'll present later in this chapter, concludes, "Fortunately, now, we can diagnose with much better clarity. Our new tools for helping children with special needs and attention disorders, whether boys or girls, work today in ways they didn't seventeen years ago."

Kathy is referring to brain disorder diagnosis via neural imaging technology—PET, SPECT, and other brain scans—as well as neuropsychological and other assessment techniques. These new tools constitute an exciting new wave in diagnosis.

New Possibilities

If your child has recently been diagnosed—with a learning disability, ADD/ADHD, bipolar disorder, or behavioral disorder—brain scans may now provide a corroborating cutting-edge diagnosis for special needs children. An interview between a psychiatrist and your child, a verbal or written test, and a teacher's (and your own) social observations are important steps in the process, but seeing an actual picture of your child's brain might be immensely helpful in confirming a diagnosis. You and your physician can explore this new possibility. Diagnosticians have to be very careful when using brain scans with small children, so it is important to discuss all possibilities openly.

Remember, among the key indicators of ADD/ADHD diagnoses in psychiatric manuals are "short attention span, impulsive behavior, difficulty focusing and sitting still." If you've read the previous chapters of this book, you know that each of these "symptoms" is actually quite normal for millions of young males. If a teacher, parent, counselor, or other medical professional is "looking for" these symptoms and determined to classify them as pathological or "sick," he or she can make painful mistakes regarding the future of the boy.

A brain scan does not look for these symptoms. It takes a photograph of the brain. What might the image show?

1. You and your doctor may see temporal lobe damage. Perhaps the boy has been injured without your realizing it, and the

sharp inner edges of the cranium have cut into the temporal lobe. If a scan shows this, you will know with greater certainty what mental disorder your boy suffers—whether bipolarity or a learning disorder.

2. You and your doctor may see frontal lobe inactivity or atrophy. By seeing the lack of blood flow to certain areas of the frontal lobe, you can better see that your son has ADD.

3. You and your doctor may see low levels of prefrontal cortex activity. Especially if you also see low levels of cingulate gyrus activity in the limbic system—which causes lowered ability to sit still and concentrate on tasks—you may see in this neural image the brain of a boy with ADHD.

Many of the diagnoses for ADD, ADHD, and other brain disorders that emerge today through our educational and psychological resources turn out to be quite accurate. Many psychologists and school staff can, within a few hours, apply external diagnostics or just good instincts and know that a boy suffers from a particular disorder. The existence of brain scans does not negate the work of psychologists, psychiatrists, school staff, and concerned parents; however, if integrated into a diagnostic model, brain scans can, if needed, give you a crucial tool. Here is the integration model we recommend.

What to Do When You Hear "Your Son May Have a Brain Disorder"

There is a useful chronology to follow when a teacher calls you and says, "Your son may have ADD" or "Your son may have a learning disorder."

First, we suggest that the diagnosis process be a family-based process—specifically, that the parents and parent-led team look carefully at the child's learning fragility and the possibility of neglect in the school or home educational system. You and your team can do a "learning fragility diagnosis" by observing the boy's study habits and learning time and by researching his family genetics for possible causes of the disability. This home-school learning fragility research might take up to three months and often takes the form of answering questions along these lines:

What are we doing right or wrong at home in terms of learning?
What is the school doing right or doing wrong?
What is my son doing to sabotage learning?
Who else in the family has had learning problems?
How did they solve those problems?

Taking this kind of time before investing in medical assessment is of great value in the diagnostic process. It allows parents and teachers to see if the boy's negative behavior or "symptoms" are simply a normal phase of his particular experience growing up and will disappear on their own or whether the classroom and school can make adjustments like those offered in this book to solve the problem. It allows the school staff to see if a number of boys in one class appear symptomatic, in which case the school might find a different teacher for these boys or try creating the kind of single-gender learning environments we looked at in the previous chapter.

If, however, the symptoms in the boy are not group symptoms and are not a "phase"—if they do not decrease or diminish within a few months—the boy now needs to be taken to a diagnostician who specializes in male brain disorders. This could be a designated "special education" diagnostician on the school psychologist staff, or an outside psychiatrist, psychologist, or neuropsychologist. This professional will have assessment tools at his or her disposal.

Here are two tools neuropsychologists use that can garner very fine results:

• The Halstead-Reitan Neuropsychological Test Battery
• The Luria-Nebraska Neuropsychological Battery

If a professional spends only an hour with your son and then gives a brain disorder diagnosis, you will probably need to ask the professional to spend more time, complete more diagnostics, or recommend a professional for a second opinion. If the professional does spend enough time to satisfy you of your son's diagnosis, you may want to simply proceed with interventions.

At the same time, this may be a moment when a brain scan is useful. If the diagnostician, using external and observational diagnostic methodology, diagnoses the boy with a learning or behavioral disability, you can request a brain scan, or you may need to find a facility that has brain scan equipment. The facilities we've mentioned in this book, the Amen Clinics, take referrals from doctors all across the continent (their Web site lists these doctors). You can contact the Amen Clinics or one of the referral physicians. You can also call psychiatrists, psychologists, and other professionals in your area to see who specializes in brain scans for childhood diagnosis. It is important to remember that many doctors are not likely to suggest scans or utilize them. There is not 100 percent agreement in the medical community on the need for scans.

If the brain scan confirms ADD/ADHD, a learning disability, or a brain disorder, the boy can be set on a treatment track within the home and the school that specifically fits the diagnosis made available through the initial verbal, observational, and neuropsychological diagnoses and through the brain scan.

Does it happen that a professional will diagnose a child with a brain disorder but a scan will show no such disorder? Yes. In these cases, parents may (with the school's help) need to confront issues of mismatch in the school system, or problems at home—in other words, learning fragilities and environmental neglect by those in the school or at home that are being masked in the boy as "symptoms" of a learning or brain disorder. Treatment may involve family therapy, the school's reassessment of how it provides education to boys, or both. The boy may not, in this case, need invasive treatments.

Can it happen that a brain scan is wrong? A child has a disorder, but somehow the scan or the reading of the scan missed it. Yes. This can happen. Anything can happen. There is no absolute miracle or magic bullet. This is why we suggest that diagnosis involves *both* the many hours of external methodology used by one or more professionals *and*, if needed, the brain scan.

Protecting Boys with Brain Disorders Throughout the Treatment Process

Earlier in this chapter we mentioned that children with brain disorders show anomalies (sometimes called *shrinkage* or *atrophy*) of brain tissue in crucial learning areas. These areas include the following:

- The corpus callosum (involved in helping the brain talk between hemispheres and thus more quickly process different kinds of emotion and cognitive and sensory information)
- Prefrontal cortex (involved in impulse control)
- Left caudate (involved in feelings of reward and success)
- Posterior parietal (involved in movement)
- Cerebellum (involved in task accomplishment)
- Right frontal lobe (involved in attention span)
- Gray matter volume (also involved in attention span)

If your son has a brain disorder that manifests in these areas, a brain scan is a very visual diagnostic way to diagnose your son. It may be useful to get a brain scan *before* putting your son on medication, then another within a few months *after.* A trained diagnostician can compare the two scans to see how medication and other treatments (to be discussed later) are affecting your son's brain. In this way, brain scans can show you the before-medication and after-medication structure of your child's brain, which can help you make the best decisions possible about whether and how to continue to medicate your child. Without the scans, you won't know if the medication is solving one set of symptoms but negatively affecting other parts of the brain. With the scans, there is no absolute guarantee of anything, of course, but at least there can be pictures of your son's brain.

Throughout this process, these are a few key things to remember:

- ADD/ADHD and other brain disorders are overdiagnosed in the United States. It is crucial for parents and parent-led teams to be vigilant during the diagnostic process. If your son does not have a brain disorder, he need not be labeled with one.
- Some cases of ADD/ADHD and other brain disorders go undiagnosed in the United States, however. Our system is immensely imperfect at this time, so many boys with brain dis-

orders are not getting the treatment they need. Parents must therefore beware of both overlooked diagnoses and false diagnoses.

- Clear and accurate diagnosis and treatment require a multifaceted approach: trained professionals must lead families in their areas of specialization, and families must ask a lot of questions and support progressive methods of diagnosis, such as scans.

If you have read a book or article, viewed a media report, or heard a speaker who tells you there is no such thing as ADD or ADHD, you are hearing an extreme opinion, not supportable by available research. By the same token, if you see a physician or other medical professional who favors Ritalin or another medication over all other treatments or who does quick diagnosis (a one-hour interview) with no other supporting tools, you may have met a busy professional who is not taking enough time with your child. At minimum it is important to insist your diagnostician spends adequate time with your son and fulfills neuropsychological battery protocols such as the ones we listed earlier. All of us must combat the "quick diagnosis" of our sons.

Paying for a Brain Scan

Recently I discussed the value and importance of brain scans with a group of parents; quite logically, many raised the question of money. "How are we supposed to pay for a brain scan?" I asked Daniel Amen, founder of the Amen Clinics, which specialize in brain scan technology for diagnosis. I think his answer makes a lot of sense.

> First of all, our clinics find that about half the time, insurance companies will pay. It's in their long-term interest. But even when they won't, parents and communities might be inspired to use these technologies by potential savings that offset the cost of the scan. These savings occur in the amount of money spent on repeated diagnostic visits to professionals that don't lead to certainty of diagnosis.
>
> Here's an example of how this can happen. My studies have found six types of ADD, but without a scan, it is difficult to know

which one a child has. Without a scan, it can take many visits to a practitioner, in which medications are changed over and over again. This can cost thousands of dollars in doctor visits and medication trial and error. Using the scan can eliminate that expense by providing a diagnosis. There may still be need to test various medications, but with the scan, you are often best prepared to get the right medication and the right treatments for the individual child.

Only you can determine if the case for scans makes sense in your specific insurance and financial situation. As parents ourselves, Kathy and I hope to inspire all parents of potential special needs students to base their treatment choices on many hours of diagnosis, with all available tools, *in addition to* scans. We hope also that brain scans will continue to decrease in cost as more and more people explore their use in the service of children. At the same time, we are well aware of studies indicating that brain scans, though useful, are not a panacea for parents (please see the Notes section at the back of this book).

The approach of Gurian Institute staff is middle of the road. Kathy and I have studied the available research for over a decade and have seen various school and parent responses to children with disorders. We maintain that there is clearly a problem in the United States with diagnosis and with disorders; all the research is not in agreement, and ultimately it falls on individual parents and families to use a multifaceted approach to diagnosis and treatment.

Treatment

However a boy is diagnosed in his learning fragility, his treatment for a learning or brain disorder will need to begin immediately. Following are the five major treatment tools, all of which should be used under the supervision of a professional trained in brain function:

1. Pharmaceutical medications, such as Ritalin, Adderal, Concerta (the newest specifically for ADD/ADHD), or Prozac
2. Alternative medications and dietary changes, such as cutting

out sugar and increasing omega-3 acids (more on this in a moment)

3. Talk and art therapy, as well as other hands-on therapeutic techniques already used by your local practitioners in the field
4. Special education modalities and protocols in your school system
5. Parental and parent-led team adjustments for care of the boy

If you have a boy with special needs or are teaching children with special needs, we hope you will challenge yourself and your school system to consider the course of treatment inadequate if even one of the listed components is not in play.

If you have a boy on Ritalin but you have not altered your home life to accommodate the treatment of his brain disorder, we hope you'll challenge yourself to make some of the adjustments we're about to discuss. Similarly, if you are a teacher or other professional who has one or more children on Ritalin or a similar drug in your classroom but you have not made any other adjustments in the school, we hope you'll consider more comprehensive care of the boys.

Although many of the following suggestions are good for any learning-fragile child—and some are just good for children in general—this is a short list of those that are essential for boys with learning disabilities.

What Parents Can Do

Commit to one-on-one care. This boy will need an increase of parental and parent-led team one-on-one attention throughout the week. The more challenged the child, the more the need for increased one-on-one care. The mother, father, grandparents, tutors, and any others close to the child can provide the increased personal attention. It's often helpful for each person to assume a somewhat differentiated role—one person might be the hands-on homework coordinator; another might be better at providing discipline.

Emphasize the idea of a caregiving *team* rather than a super-parent. If so far only one parent has been dealing with the learning-disabled or brain-disordered boy, it is time to set up a team of caregivers. Mom, dad, grandparents, everyone must now get further involved. Should financial resources permit, a tutor who can work long term with the boy might now be hired for twice-weekly coaching. The whole team needs to get trained in how to handle this kind of fragile boy so that within the team there are consistent learning expectations and discipline techniques.

Obtain a nutritional diagnosis—for food allergies, effects of sugar and junk food, and other dietary factors—then cut out brain-stressing foods. Many symptoms of ADD/ADHD are exacerbated by junk food, sugar, and caffeine (including the sugar and caffeine in soda pop).[12] Hypoglycemia can play a part, as well as a child's individual food allergies—to gluten, yeast, or dairy. A pediatrician or other professional trained in the link between brain disorders and food is an essential ally in setting up your home-based treatment program, which eliminates unhealthy foods and substitutes healthy foods. The nutrition professional can provide you with a diet plan that helps this boy's brain. The boy may need more of the omega-3 acids (often found in fish) that help fight learning disabilities. The boy may need more protein intake just before he performs learning tasks. Every member of the parent-led team must consistently apply the new nutritional standards. This avoids "poisoning" the boy when he's away from home. Educate your son's teachers and school system on his particular needs by putting everything in writing and using written information—emails, books, and pamphlets. Quite often, teachers are so busy that mentioning something on the phone doesn't produce solid action.

Once you've developed a plan for treatment, make sure to share it with your son's teacher—in writing. If, for instance, you have cut out soda pop at home but your son drinks soda pop at school, you might find problem behaviors erupting in the hour your son just comes home from school. Let the teacher know, in writing, what the plan is and when it has been violated.

Cut down television, video game, and computer time. Screen time increases attention and focus problems. A little bit of screen time—especially educational computer use—is generally okay, and most parents want to pick their battles, so they don't cut out all video games or television, but research clearly shows ill effects in brain-disordered boys from too much screen time. More than an hour a day in front of a tube might well constitute a problem.

Avoid fights or confrontations with your son in favor of calmer relationship strategies. If your son does have ADD/ADHD, his brain is an "adrenalin-seeking" brain system: his brain needs extra adrenalin stimulation to reach a level of focus others come to naturally. ADD/ADHD children often try to keep themselves stimulated by creating relational anxiety and conflict situations within families—fights, arguments, confrontations, rebellion. Certainly, parents and caregivers set healthy limits that can sometimes result in arguments and conflict. But if conflict is occurring consistently, then get the help of a therapist to bring other communication strategies into your parenting. Constant conflict will make the lives of everyone in your family worse, not better.

Cut out the chaos of "busyness" in the home by creating more structure, more highly disciplined expectations of performance, and alterations in the physical environment of the boy's room. As much as possible, make his walls and floor space less filled with bright colors and images. ADD boys especially need sensory destimulation rather than increased sensory stimulation. Almost all learning-disabled children benefit from greater emphasis on structure. If that structure is too rigid or authoritarian, it can lead to rebellion and conflict. But if it's fair and appropriate, more structure can lead to better behavior and learning.

Model and teach personal responsibility and independence, but don't overemphasize individuality. For parents and parent-led teams, one of the most difficult aspects of caring for an ADD/ADHD child is the need for creating a balance between independence and responsibility. The ADD/ADHD boy is generally more dependent on caregivers (even as he rebels a lot) than another boy might be, and a parent's instinct, especially with adolescents, is ordinarily to increase the boy's independence. If that increase involves personal responsibility—taking out the garbage, mowing the lawn, cleaning his room—it's probably healthy. But parents who say, "go ahead and do what you want; you're your own boss," are probably not helping. This casual approach to individuality can imply that parents don't care and can leave children feeling isolated and lonely. Worse still, it can lead to selfish, irresponsible young men.

Make sure the boy gets a lot of exercise. Physical exercise is essential for these boys. It helps calm them, helps them sleep at night, and helps them perform learning tasks. When physical exercise can be linked to contributive tasks (like mowing the lawn), it is especially good for family life and for the boy.

Help the boy see his condition not as a disability but as a matter of character development, of challenge, even of hero development. Sometimes, finding a strong religious life for him can help. Connecting and framing his condition with character and with religious heroes can help the boy see that his situation may be creating at-risk and inappropriate behavior that he need not address alone but with the help of inner resources (God, prayer, meditation). Even if he has no religious tradition or context, he can still see himself as being on the hero's journey. He can reflect on his "flaw" as the thing that can make him stronger.

It's a fascinating aspect of brain science that many boys with ADD/ADHD or other learning disabilities have flaws in temporal lobe functioning.[13] The temporal lobe is a brain center linked to identity development. For a child with a learning or behavioral disability, who receives years of treatment, identity development will be crucial. Gradually, painstakingly, those who love this boy must help him notice how his identity won't be crushed by his condition, but instead will be fed by its challenge. An obvious functional flaw in the self, such as a learning disability, can and has become the essence of success for many boys, such as Charles Schwab, who is dyslexic yet has become one of the most successful businessmen in America. It can be for your son, too.

What Teachers Can Do

Most school systems already have a number of strong and effective protocols in place for dealing with special needs kids. On any short list we hope you'll find the following:

• Rely on experienced teachers as coaches and mentors. The challenge of working with a child suffering a learning disability or brain disorder is difficult enough that no teacher should go it alone. A mentor-teacher or teacher-coach should be close by.

- Use teacher teams. They can make or break a special needs program. Weekly teacher team meetings and regular contact between families and teachers for problem solving can help individual teachers care for special needs children.

- Make sure teachers in your school are trained in the gender issues, especially male and female brain factors, that you'll encounter in your special needs children. Understanding the gender issues will inspire your own innovations. For instance, nearly every special education teacher who has received training in male brain fragility allows more physical movement in his or her classes.

- Use single-gender classrooms and learning teams. If you haven't read Chapter Eight, please check it out now. Single-gender strategies are very effective in cutting down discipline problems and improving learning for special needs children.

- Provide peripatetic (talking while walking together) counseling and other alternative formats for special needs boys. These should involve spatial-mechanical stimulation as well as exercise. Counseling that takes place while the boy is sitting in an office is often listless and ineffective. Walking with the boy can stimulate his limbic system so that he can access more of his emotions. Art therapy, which involves use of spatial-mechanical processes, can also be helpful.

- Stimulate and destimulate the boy's brain with Nerf balls and other objects he can squeeze. Use music for the same purpose. You can use these tools when the boy needs calming or when he needs to rev his brain to refocus.

- Rely as much as possible on multisensory analysis of the boy's special needs. Some boys with ADD have trouble with visual processing and may need more oral processing. Others have trouble with oral processing, so a teacher talking to them may be ineffective. Boys in general tend to be better at visual processing than oral processing (using more white matter in the brain to direct neurotransmission to the visual cortex) and often tend to compensate for any learning disability by relying on their visual cortex.

- Alter the classroom and school environment to cut out distraction, fast-moving images, and busy sound. Boys with learning disabilities tend to need things to be slowed down. They tend to need fewer drawings and posters and objects on the walls. The busyness of a class-room or other environment "revs up" their adrenalin, which ruins their lesson.

• Emphasize hands-on learning. As much as possible, teach math through number rolls and other physical objects rather than through talk or small written symbols on a blackboard. Use experiential strate-gies in every content area possible.

• Give every learning-disabled boy a peer or adult mentor. One-on-one attention has always been and will always be the most effective treatment for brain-based disabilities. There is an inherent feeling of loneliness in a child with a brain disorder, an emotional complexity that affects all aspects of learning. The peer or adult mentor can not only help the child with his lessons but also help the child move through the complex loneliness that affects any learner who is acutely aware of his own difficult inner challenges.

Moving to Optimism

When I was a boy diagnosed with hyperactivity and put on Ritalin, a dark cloud fell over my family. Happening as this did in the 1960s, little was known about how the male brain worked, what effects the medica-tion would have, what was "wrong with Mike," and what the future held for me.

When Kathy's son Karl Michael was diagnosed with learning dis-abilities and put in special education, a similar cloud fell over his fam-ily. Though his diagnosis and treatment occurred more recently than mine, in the 1980s, there was still sadness, a stigma, a feeling of hope-lessness among those who loved him.

Among all the grim statistics available to us now—the increase in male brain disabilities, the acceleration of medication use, the overflow of boys in special education classrooms—there is also, thankfully, less need for the hopelessness. Because we can now understand male brain fragility, because our assessment tools and medications are getting bet-ter all the time, because our culture in general is talking about brain and mental health issues openly, we can now face a brain disorder in our sons with more optimism.

New vision and new techniques are now available to help your son deal with a mental or cognitive disability that often makes him (and you) feel defective and alone. There is good reason for an optimism that you can take into the schools and into your pediatrician's and psychologist's offices—an optimism that involves diagnostic and broad-based treatment methods. Further, we hope that you will be able to insist on change in your school or other educational environment, especially if it's one of those that constantly misdiagnoses boys.

Individual parents and teachers are particularly important in keeping the optimism alive. Often it happens that doctors, psychologists, and other professionals are not trained in male-female brain difference. Often it happens that parents and teachers, well armed with knowledge of what is happening in the mind of the child, become wise and heroic in their insistence that their boys' needs get met.

We hope this chapter's discussion of learning disabilities will spark public dialogue on male learning fragility. By correctly diagnosing boys with verifiable disability, we can better help those boys who are also troubled at school but whose brain scans appear normal. These are the boys we call undermotivated or underperforming or sensitive learners. Let's turn now to the challenges for these boys and the strategies that work best for them.

Confronting Undermotivation and Underperformance in Boys' Learning

Restless thoughts came to him . . . Siddhartha felt the seeds of discontent.

—HERMANN HESSE, *SIDDHARTHA*

"ALL THROUGH SCHOOL I FELT RESTLESS," WROTE BARRY, TWENTY-FOUR. "I didn't really know who I was or what I should be doing. My parents called me 'unmotivated.' Some people called me lazy. They were right. Sometimes I tried my best, like in sixth grade, but a lot of the time I didn't do much in school. I guess I didn't really live up to my potential as a student. I dropped out of high school during my junior year."

Sheri, in Seattle, expressed a similar story, in even more detail: "My husband and I are concerned about our fifteen-year-old son, Jeremy. He is very bright, attractive, and has natural athletic ability. But he does not work even close to his ability level in school. He chooses not to study. He did well in football last year but now says he doesn't like the 'rah-rah' aspect of his school. He prefers to get on his computer, watch TV, and play video games. He calls himself 'lazy,' almost like it's a badge of honor."

Paul Marcus, a school counselor in Albuquerque, told me, "I'm seeing a lot of boys underperforming and unmotivated. It's as if they don't feel any worth in themselves or what they're doing in school. I think they lack a sense of honor, but I know it's more than that, too. The problem is so big in our school, we started a program to meet these boys' needs."

It comes on slowly, the loss of the boy's mind to some yearning other than education or to no real yearning at all. Perhaps, first, the boy decides not to join this or that club or sport. That's okay, you think; he has that right. Then the grades begin to fall. You can tell he's a smart kid, but he's just not "working to his potential." If you're his teacher, you might wonder what could be happening at home to traumatize him. If you're his parent, you might wonder what could be wrong with his school. His grades slip further. You lecture, cajole, encourage. He seems discontented. He pulls out of another extracurricular activity, then another. Perhaps he watches more TV, plays more video games, spends more time on the Internet.

You start to notice he's becoming a little lonelier every day. "School's not cool," he starts saying. "School's a joke." Perhaps he starts making fun of the kids who are learning well. Or maybe he just seems to keep everything to himself. He might perform just enough to squeak by, disappointing to himself (though not admitting it), disappointing to his parents and teachers.

When you confront him, he might complain, "I just can't do it. I'm stupid." Or "I'm doing my homework. Back off!" even though he isn't. Or "You can't make me get good grades. It's my life." He seems to feel that something is missing. What it is, he does not seem to know. Nor do you. Unlike the main character in Hermann Hesse's classic novel, *Siddhartha*—who sets out on an epic search for the missing elements of life— the boy you know lives not in a book but in your own personal world, a non-epic reality of lackluster learning.

Undermotivated, Underperforming Boys

"Undermotivation" and "chronic underperformance" are not clinical diagnoses recognized by either the American Medical Association or the American Psychiatric Association, but they are painfully familiar to parents and schools everywhere. For male students they manifest not only in lower grades but also in lower participation in school activities.

At this point it is impossible to quantify the number of undermotivated and underperforming boys in our educational system, but some related statistics could help us understand the problem. We introduced one of those earlier—that boys receive the majority of the D's and F's and hand in less homework than girls—but there are many others. The National Center for Education Statistics released findings in 2004 that outline other components of male performance and motivation issues in our schools. As the following statistics show, girls outnumber boys in all areas of school extracurricular activities except athletics:

- Student government:
  Girls: 13 percent
  Boys: 8 percent
- Music/performing arts:
  Girls: 31 percent
  Boys: 19 percent
- Yearbook/newspaper:
  Girls: 13 percent
  Boys: 6 percent
- Academic clubs:
  Girls: 19 percent
  Boys: 12 percent

Life at school can be a wonderful haven for our children, an inherent motivator, a place of learning and activity. But many of our boys find themselves struggling with both academic and social motivation. Why is this happening? What can we do about it? These questions are the subject of this chapter.

Some Causes of Undermotivation—and Some Cures

If your son is chronically underperforming, it may be because of undermotivation, a condition whose causes will lie in one or more of four areas of the boy's life:

1. The boy's brain itself (including biological and social changes at puberty)
2. The school system, because of a particular school's ineffectiveness in teaching him successfully
3. Family dynamics, especially if there has been family trauma, such as divorce
4. Other social stressors, such as poverty, malnutrition, peer pressure, violence

Now let's look at each of these areas more carefully.

Within the Boy Himself

The undermotivation and underperformance of some boys are directly caused by a learning disability. Chapter Nine was devoted to clinical diagnoses of learning disabilities, as well as advice for special education programs. If a boy has a clinically diagnosed learning disorder, parents and teachers often will have noticed learning problems in the boy from his early elementary years. There might be a genetic component. The disability will be exacerbated as learning tasks become more difficult, so the diagnosis may not occur until fourth or fifth grade; but the disability will most likely show up early because it will have been indigenous to that boy's brain.

What we are calling undermotivation, however (which can be disguised by diagnosis and treatment as ADD/ADHD or other disability), generally begins evidencing itself in later childhood or in adolescence. This condition generally does not have a single cause in the genetics of the boy's brain, but instead is an amalgam of brain-related elements.

Motivation works in the human brain like a chain reaction of light. At one end is the prefrontal cortex, the decision-making part of the brain, which can be stimulated by a learning task; a school, home, or natural environment; or a book or other symbolic text. This stimulation begins a neural journey toward internal and external treasures of emotion, memory, and understanding that also involve the limbic system. "Wow, that is neat!" the prefrontal cortex might "say," "Let's learn about that." This decision-making light starts burning through the lower pathways of the brain because the highest brain center, the prefrontal cortex, has ordered it to do so. It burns in the dorsal striatum, a part of the limbic system that lights up when a person is feeling enjoyment and satisfaction. It burns further down into the limbic system, through emotion and memory, then back up toward the top of the brain—toward meaning and understanding in the frontal and temporal lobes. "Give me more, more, more of that book [or learning task or athletic task or game]," the limbic system might say, "I want more of *that*." These emotion centers are chemical reactors—adrenalin, cortisol, dopamine, and endorphins are rushing through. Then the prefrontal cortex and frontal lobes say, "Yes, here's how to get more of that!" This whole process, which began with a spark in the prefrontal cortex, ends up lighting up the whole brain. Motivation, then, is a complex and also fragile brain process in which biochemistry, neurotransmitters, and neural tissue work together to seek meaning, understanding, accomplishment, achievement, and success.[1]

In understanding the brain's functioning in motivation, we can come close to defining undermotivation: it is an underfunctioning of a person's prefrontal cortex and emotion centers, as well as of the neural connectors between them. One of the key connector areas, the cingulate gyrus (housed in the limbic system), can seem to shut down some of the boy's "motivation centers" when your son or your student appears to lose his "want, want, want" of learning. His brain becomes listless; his internal ideas and dialogue take on a quality of meaninglessness. An undermotivated boy often becomes learning-depressed—initially he may not be depressed in other aspects of life. He may be only situationally depressed in his learning functions. After a few months or years, his learning depression can spread into other parts of his life. Some of his "neural light" starts going out.

Looking at the undermotivated boy as a child whose neural functions in motivation compare to those of a depressed child is a first step in discovering how to help him. As we explore the other causes of undermotivation, we'll notice how each can stimulate learning depression—can shut down either the prefrontal or the limbic "light" in the brain of the boy, thereby erasing his motivation to learn and flourish.

Within the School System

Kathy remembers being a parent of an unmotivated son. She describes what it felt like from the parent's point of view.

> Kevin, my oldest, was never in special ed, never took Ritalin, and yet sat through most of his school years bored and disengaged, finally dropping out in his senior year and going on to college to study music, his real love. He said he didn't find school to be a place that offered him anything, but he wasn't like Karl Michael, who fidgeted and acted out. Kevin was quiet, never a discipline problem. Now that I look back, from my professional vantage point, on how unmotivated Kevin was, I notice his teachers were so busy dealing with the loud "Karl Michaels," how could they have time for all the quiet "Kevins" who just gradually got lost?

Like many of the undermotivated boys you know, Kathy's sons were not identical in their manifestation of their low-grade learning depression. They both went to school in the same school system, but reacted differently to inadequacies in themselves, their environments, and their schools.

Many parents of undermotivated underperformers ask, "Can an inadequate school system trigger a depression reaction in students?" The answer is, yes, it can. Kathy is not the only parent to observe this. In Part One, we noted the mismatch of many of our classrooms and schools with the learning brains of boys in particular. Boys (and girls) certainly can and do become undermotivated when the school can't teach them as they need to be taught.

Let's look at some specific areas of mismatch that affect undermotivation and can be changed for the better through your efforts as parents.

DEVELOPMENTAL DELAYS IN THE EARLY YEARS. Low-grade learning depression can begin in the early education years (preschool through second grade) because of developmental delays in the male brain. These delays are neither disabilities nor anomalies, nor are they bad or wrong. They are simply male nature. The most common areas of delay are in the Broca's and Wernicke's areas, which we introduced earlier. These delays in the boy's word production and word management (speaking, reading, writing) can lead to years of problems if the boy is expected, at a young age, to perform as well in writing, reading, or even speaking as his more developed peers. Other areas of difficulty can include fine motor delays (penmanship, writing) and limbic system maturity (controlling impulses).

Because the male brain develops a number of these learning functions, on average, later than the female, it is mainly males who will experience high stress and high failure in the early years of life, if they are put under a lot of pressure and stress to develop faster. By the time these boys are in fourth or fifth grade and showing early signs of undermotivation, a parent or teacher might have forgotten (or perhaps never fully realized) how much personal failure that boy had experienced a few years before as a three-, four-, and five-year-old.

When parents of boys have the instinct to "hold the boy back a year" from kindergarten or first grade, they are often wisely—if unconsciously—recognizing that their son's brain might not be ready for the stress of the next step up in our educational system. A number of countries, including England, routinely combine seven-year-old boys with six-year-old girls in first-grade classes because parents and educators have recognized and responded to this developmental reality. As we'll explore in more detail later in this chapter, one solution to undermotivation and low-grade learning depression is simply to hold some boys back. If only there were a way to frame this decision so that it doesn't sound so negative—in reality it's a very good thing for some boys, and many of these young boys, while unable to say it, know it.

REST STATES.   One of the most difficult situations our school system faces in educating boys is the male brain's innate tendency to move into a rest state throughout the day. The rest state, which we noted earlier, is a brain state you might recognize when you look into a classroom and see boys who are staring out the window, dozing off at their desks, or looking upward with glazed eyes at the ceiling. Mainly boys are involved in these manifestations of the brain's rest state. Their brains are briefly "shutting down" in order to renew and refresh neuro-transmission, gain a rest from stressors, or combat boredom.

As Ruben Gur, head of the Neural Imaging Unit at the University of Pennsylvania, has proven, the female brain is not structurally and bio-chemically set up for the same quality or frequency of rest state as the male.[2] Little boys start out at a disadvantage in this area. Estrogen, a dominant female hormone, provides a biochemical base for increased brain activity, and indeed, there is up to 15 percent more blood flow in the female brain than in the male at any given moment. Furthermore, even when the female brain goes into a state of rest, it does not shut down the way the male brain does; a larger portion of its brain blood flow "rests" in the cingulate gyrus, a central brain stimulator and moti-vator. Hence, even when a female student is bored by a lesson, her brain is more actively able and willing to keep her eyes open, continue taking notes, and process the information before her.

Especially in our very verbally oriented classrooms, the male brain rest state puts boys at greater risk for underperformance and under-motivation than girls. It should not surprise us that in our school sys-tems, boys take fewer notes than girls (on average), do less homework, act out more when bored, self-stimulate in ways that bring negative con-sequences (for example, tapping pencils, bugging their neighbor, inter-rupting). Even in their negative behaviors we can see the rest state at work—their pencil tapping and bugging each other is as much a "stay-ing awake" behavior as anything else.

In all this, however, the consequences for the student are negative. He either dozes off and misses what's happening in the lesson, or he self-stimulates in ways his teacher and school are not set up to handle: getting in trouble, becoming the "problem," and, overall, underlearning and underperforming. Too often, noticing that he is inadequate as a learner, he withdraws.

The male rest state is only one brain element in a complex learning landscape. Like a frontal lobe delay in the early years, however, it is a cumulative problem. If, for instance, the boy has had frontal lobe delay (or any other learning issues) in early childhood that cause a misfit with the system, then he combats the rest state by self-stimulating, and getting into trouble; then, the accumulation of negative experience in school can result in high stress levels and low-grade depression in the boy. This will often manifest, to both the teacher and parents, as "low self-esteem."

SELF-WORTH AND SELF-ESTEEM.   In the emails and letters with which this chapter began (and in most of our mail and interactions relating to undermotivation, for that matter), parents, teachers, and boys or men write about the issue of low self-esteem in underperforming males. Parents and teachers will often note low self-esteem as a cause of the undermotivation. Their instincts, we believe, are right on. Let's look at this causal issue carefully.

By the time parents and teachers note low self-esteem in the male learner, he is generally prepubescent (late elementary or middle school age). He has often had difficult early learning experiences (though not always); his boy energy has often gotten him into trouble in early elementary school, or he has suffered some kind of trauma that affects his learning; and as learning tasks now become more difficult (and his own body and brain begin the cognitive, hormonal, and physical transformations of adolescence), he begins to display signs of low self-esteem, undermotivation, and underperformance.

Can low-grade depression and undermotivation come from low self-esteem? They can do so for any child, boy or girl, but from our study of adolescent brain chemistry, we have theorized that for boys there is a male-specific form of this low self-esteem. An adolescent boy's feelings about himself in high school will become the basis for his sense of worth as a man in adult society. Here's how it may work.

If a young male entering puberty—his time of high testosterone, personal transformation, challenge, ordeal, aggressive proof of self and worth in the world—is socially or academically behind many of the other males and females in the school—that is, if he has not established self-worth over the last number of years, but instead is failing or near failing in the primary system provided to him for competitively establishing worth—he is biochemically set up for problems.

In large part because of spikes of testosterone (the male aggression hormone) during puberty, adolescent males are generally structured to discover self-worth through aggression, competition, and success models. This is not the only way, but it is a primary way they "find themselves." Boys tend to feel low, depressed, or worthless about their place in school and outside activities if they feel repeatedly unrecognized or unrewarded during puberty.

"I'm just wasting my time going to school," a boy might say.

"Who cares about homework anyway? It's worthless."

"It's all a f——g facade." "That school doesn't know s—t."

Kathy and I believe that our school systems, especially in middle and high school, are dealing with issues of male hormones, puberty, and brain chemistry in ways not completely fathomed by our current education system. These issues can manifest even when a boy has been a successful student in the early years—that is, even when he does not fit the negative scenario of early education developmental delays, accumulated learning stress, lower reading and verbal abilities, or low-grade learning depression during elementary school.

If you look at your home, neighborhood, or sixth- to ninth-grade classroom, you may notice boys who had little trouble before but who now seem to be failing, getting depressed, finding learning difficult, becoming more aggressive in their acting out, abandoning school, and generally succumbing to peer pressure that says, "School sucks." It is possible that they too are experiencing a combination of biochemical and social pressures and distresses.

The mismatch of contemporary school systems with boys' learning styles creates motivation and performance issues that can't be solved with quick fixes—whether the issues arise in childhood or closer to puberty. Sometimes a boy going through puberty benefits by moving to a different classroom with a teacher who understands his new energy, his accumulated depression, his acting out. Sometimes the boy has to change schools, as Karl Michael did. As we'll note later in this chapter, the school often needs to create a new program for these undermotivated pubertal boys—one that fits the internal challenges of their nature better than the present school has been able to do.

Within the Family

Our sons bring their psyches to school with them—their hurts, their hopes, their joys, their fears. The reason for the low-grade depression and undermotivation in many of our boys is not something we can place only on mismatches in the school system. Issues in family life that traumatize or neglect the development of the male learning brain can also be causes. The traumatized brain responds both emotionally and biochemically to problems at home, increasing its stress hormone levels to the extent that the boy's schooling suffers and becomes at issue. What are some of these stressors?

DIVORCE TRAUMA.   Nearly all boys will enter a depressed emotional state when parents divorce. Like all depression, this depression is likely to affect performance in social, academic, or athletic tasks.

The boy's brain, emotional system, and ability to learn may well go into "autopilot" during the depression, and autopilot mode is often not good enough for today's intense academic environment. If a parent, a parent-led team member, or a teaching professional notices undermotivation following a parental separation or divorce, it is important to move the boy as quickly as possible to therapeutic interventions.

PHYSICAL, SEXUAL, OR EMOTIONAL ABUSE.   Boys who begin to underperform in prepubescence and adolescence have often been victims of physical, sexual, or emotional abuse. Abuse increases cortisol levels in the brain for ongoing periods of time, generally continuing even after the actual abuse has stopped.[3] If, for instance, a boy was sexually abused at ten years old, he might still be having posttraumatic stress symptoms (for example, nightmares) in his late teens and adulthood. Stress hormone levels do not completely decrease just because the hitting, sexual acts, or emotional battering has ended.

It's crucial to remember that abuse will have a depressive effect on all children who experience it. Not all boys, however, express that effect in undermotivation. For some boys, mainly those who are already strong learners, abuse can catalyze an extra emphasis on learning tasks; these boys are driven by a sense of needing to succeed as a student at all costs. School success can become an escape from abuse in the home, community, or church. But for many boys, especially those who have already experienced some undermotivation or mismatch in their schools, abuse can trigger depression. Not surprisingly, many boys who have been abused turn to drugs, alcohol, and other high-risk behaviors, which then spiral them farther away from successful learning.

LACK OF ATTACHMENT.   Lack of attachment, especially in early adolescence, can trigger undermotivation in school.[4] This is the origin of depression for boys who use learning failure as an attention-getting device. If there is no active parent-led team—no grandparents, godparents, or other mentors—available to the boy during early adolescence, and if the parents are also gone from the home most of the time, the boy may suffer from insecure adolescent attachment.

This lack of attachment can lead to supervision problems, latchkey at-risk behavior, early sexual activity, media addiction, and undermotivation in school. The boy's natural adolescent drives to experiment, learn, grow, take risks, and to rely on caregivers to set limits may become skewed by lack of adult-adolescent attachment.

In some cases, the boy will overplay his experimentation in order to get attention from his caregiving adults. In other cases, he'll hide his at-risk behavior in order to separate psychologically from the parents who he feels have betrayed him or don't love him. Where learning is concerned, some boys will choose the very thing at which their successful, working parents excel—social or academic performance, for example—as the area in which to underperform, as a way to punish parents or simply to make the parents angry enough and disappointed enough to pay attention to the boy. Negative attention may feel better than no attention at all.

If a boy in your community is at risk of becoming undermotivated as an acting-out strategy against loneliness, lack of attachment, or parental neglect, the cure lies first and foremost in a rethinking of parental responsibilities toward adolescent children. Early adolescents—especially boys, whose emotional development matures later than girls, on average—are children who need parents to be present before and after school, in the evening, on the weekends. When parents can't be available, the boy needs loving members of the parent-led team to mentor him through life and learning.

Within the Social Context

Educational author and consultant Paul Slocumb has written a manifesto on the state of boys in America called *Hear Our Cry: Boys in Crisis.*[5] Slocumb links the number of American males in prison (now just under two million) with issues of poverty, ethnicity, and school-related learning.

Not surprisingly, Slocumb notices a high incidence of underperformance and undermotivation in males who grow up in impoverished social conditions. The stress of poverty (and all related social issues) cannot be underestimated as a cause of the epidemic of undermotivation we are seeing among male students in industrialized societies and institutions. Slocumb's work owes some of its theory and evidence to another book, *A Framework for Understanding Poverty,* by Ruby Payne.[6]

There are a number of effects on learning that directly relate to poverty—effects so primordial and so natural to brain development that we can notice them immediately. Each one directly relates to undermotivation, as revealed in the next Did You Know? box.

Poverty is a systemic issue that our educational system is trying to deal with every day as it works to leave no child behind. Often a boy raised in poverty and lacking motivation to learn with words enters a school whose primary content delivery system is verbal. This boy must listen to lessons that rarely pertain to his survival. Many of his teachers are untrained in the way boys' minds work and unfamiliar with this boy's way of life.

A teacher from an inner-city school wrote this poignant email:

When I first went into an urban school to teach, I was a white female untrained in how to handle these inner city kids—especially

??? Did You Know? ???

- Children raised in poverty use fewer words than other children. As Ruby Payne, author of *A Framework for Understanding Poverty,* points out—referring to studies conducted in the 1990s[7]—children raised on welfare, on average, hear 616 words per hour. Children raised by working-class parents hear 1,251 words per hour. Children raised by professional-class parents hear 2,153 words per hour. The use of many words is crucial in today's educational structures, as is word-stimulated development of the Broca's and Wernicke's areas. Impoverished children are not receiving that verbal stimulation on par with other children. Boys in this group already may use fewer words than their female counterparts and thus carry a natural disadvantage at school, exacerbated by impoverished developmental conditions.

- Malnutrition and dietary deficiencies are more common in impoverished homes than in working- or professional-class homes. As we saw in Chapter Five, there is a direct relationship between what the body eats and how the brain works.

- Dangerous social conditions—especially the constant threat of violence—create a different hierarchy of survival needs from conditions in neighborhoods where violence is less common. To be unmotivated in school actually becomes quite functional in many neighborhoods where social survival requires the young male to protect himself or his family physically and through gangs and other social networks rather than through secondary education. For many of these males, performing well in school is not a worthwhile use of their time—in fact, it might leave them or their families vulnerable to greater poverty or to death.

the African American boys. I thought many of them were "diss-ing" me by not looking me in the eye or making eye contact.

Our principal called me into the office and said, "Didn't anyone tell you? For these boys, looking someone in the eye is disrespectful. It can be dangerous for them to look a superior in the eye. You can't take it personally or make it a discipline issue."

Just a little thing like that helped me so much. How could I teach these boys when the whole way I did things was so differ-ent from their way?

This teacher was crossing an ethnic and gender divide, as well as a socioeconomic one; it was very difficult for her, though her email indicated that she was very glad she did it, and had met "some of the best students a teacher could have."

When undermotivation and underperformance are symptoms of poverty, we need to consider the social context and neighborhood culture these boys live in. The more we adjust our schooling to nurture the male brain and support boys stuck in traumatic home situations, the less these boys will suffer from depression. But we're not going to solve the problem of undermotivation in boys' (or girls') education unless our nation deals with impoverished conditions, injustice, and deep ethnic divides.

Right now, one out of four African American males is in jail or under court supervision.[8] This statistic should give pause to any of us involved in helping boys. Each ethnic group, each racial group, and each socioeconomic group of males has its own definable needs for help with personal motivation to learn and with social performance.

The Poverty Project and ahaprocess.com, led by Ruby Payne and aided by her colleagues, such as Paul Slocumb, are good places to start the work of helping impoverished schools. At ahaprocess.com, you can find ways to train your school and community to deal with issues related to poverty and learning. Training for teachers in boy-girl differences, as well as ethnic educational differences, are also good places to start dealing with these deep social issues.

When Gifted Boys Are Undermotivated

Kim, a mother of two in Arkansas, wrote about her eighteen-year-old son:

> Sandy was a very good student in elementary school. What his father and I didn't realize was that he was actually coasting, doing very little but succeeding pretty well. When he got to middle school, we started to notice a slip in his grades. Teachers contacted us about him not doing his work. We developed a consequences chart for him. We also had him checked for learning disabilities. He tested out with a very high IQ, and with no disabilities. Now we became very confused. He was such a smart kid! By the time he got to tenth grade, the gap between his grades and his test scores was very wide. He got some of the highest test scores around, but he got B's, C's, and a D in school. Educating this very smart boy was a constant battle.
>
> Last year he graduated from high school with a C average. We considered ourselves lucky that he got through high school. Now he is going to college, but I don't really understand what happened to that gifted little boy.

Kim is not alone in this kind of experience. It can tear at your heart. A study at the University of Connecticut Neag School of Education discovered that although there are many gifted but undermotivated girls, the actual ratio of nonachieving males to females is eight to one.[9] The Neag study defined *nonachieving* as "not attaining classroom grades equivalent to the student's scores on nationally published, standardized evaluations (i.e. CoGAT, SAT, ACT, ITBS)." For a student to qualify for the Neag study they had to have scores on national tests within the 95 to 98 percent level—this is the "gifted" range. They also had to show that organic issues such as ADHD and learning disabilities were eliminated.

Patricia St. Germain, a certified trainer for the Gurian Institute training division, is a teacher who developed a program specifically to help the gifted adolescent nonachiever. Her program identifies which students are gifted nonachievers by using the Neag study guidelines; she then applies Gurian Institute material on male-female brain difference. Here's what she has to say about this:

I taught high school and college science for twenty-five years. In the last five years of my career, I developed a Gifted and Talented program for my high school and a course called Mind Works to facilitate enhanced learning for identified high-ability students. The program involves a lot of metathinking among high school students. My mission was to help high-ability nonachievers who were not succeeding in high school. Their nonachievement and undermotivation usually caused these types of problems:

- Low academic self-esteem
- Negative attitudes toward teachers
- Low motivation and self-regulation skills
- Negative attitude toward school
- Negative attitude toward course offerings
- Low goal-setting/self-evaluation skills

When you are dealing with a gifted undermotivated student, it is helpful to remember that low interest and negative attitudes toward school generate low achievement. It's a vicious cycle for these gifted kids. Interestingly, gifted nonachievers actually exhibit more disdain for school than their nongifted counterparts. They feel and act "above it all," as if they don't need to learn anything.

Usually, however, this disdain indicates that the boy feels frustrated by his inability to attain high grades. These students are also hypersensitive when the relevance of the courses is unclear or there is no opportunity to apply what is learned "in the world." They feel like what they are supposed to learn is worthless to them, and they decrease their own motivation because of their negative attitude.

When we talk about causes of middle or high school undermotivation in gifted boys, we have to talk about all of the factors that often get missed. High-ability students—especially boys—who are nonachievers get through middle school with minimal evidence of the standard study skills required from average-ability peers—such as calendar keeping, outlining, note taking, organizing materials in a notebook. These gifted students achieved a high level of performance and learning without having to be accountable for these traditional study skills. Teachers knew these students could do the work "in their heads," so the gifted students did not have to develop their ability to think organizationally or work in ways that were accountable and progressive in nature. As I talk with nonachieving students, I cover the fact that they never had to do much to attain exceptional learning in the lower grades. When they reached high school, however, they "hit the wall"; it became a point of "ego confrontation" to admit that they did not know the basics of note taking, daily organization, or personal organization. Rather than admit their lack, they withdrew from education.

Patricia has developed some very practical interventions that have succeeded in turning these kids around. These have been proven to work not only in her study but also in a larger study at the University of Connecticut. We will discuss these solutions in greater detail in Chapter Eleven. Here, Patricia offers a good starting place for working with gifted, undermotivated students:

> It is important to honor gifted students with intellectual respect by facilitating their development of metacognitive capability. Challenge these students to "think about the way they think." Inquire about the thoughts of these students, allowing time for reflection. Help them to help themselves change their performance patterns by helping them think about all of what they do. These guys are generally "thinkers," anyway. They want to think and metathink. They are intellectually able—their main gap is in their inability—due to immaturity and the other factors we mentioned—to puzzle out the subtle interactions of success. They need help from teachers, counselors, and parents to think it out. Male students especially know there is a mismatch and disconnect for them in the educational system, but they have difficulty articulating in words where things are going wrong. Caring for their whole metacognitive process can bring them back into focus on education.

In the next chapter, which is devoted solely to solutions to undermotivation in boys, Patricia will share more specific advice on how to better engage these students.

Motivating Our Sons

When I was struggling in school, I was fidgety, a mover, defiant, a "behavioral problem," and learning-depressed. I was not, however, a slow reader. Reading for me was a haven within my school problems. In some ways, my Broca's and Wernicke's cortical areas were quite overactive indeed! As a freshman in high school, I read as many of Hermann Hesse's books as I could, books like *Siddhartha,* which are about boys and young men who set out to search for themselves—dissatisfied with school, with the signals about manhood they are receiving from the culture, and with the materialistic culture itself. These boys, I thought, were like me: idealistic, confused, ready to give up everything in order to grow up. When I read these books, I got a kind of "shot in the arm" of motivation to learn and persevere.

Then I'd put the book down. Idealism disappeared, real life returned. Things looked gray and bland again. School seemed like a dreary place, a drudgery to be survived. My motivation to learn diminished. I let my homework stack up uncompleted. I isolated myself in my room or in front of the TV.

I didn't know, then, about the frontal lobe, the cingulate gyrus, the prefrontal cortex. I didn't know about PET scans or MRIs. I didn't know about how the dorsal striatum, a part of the limbic system, lights up when a person is feeling enjoyment and satisfaction in what he's doing. Nevertheless I kept trying to get the "lighting up" to occur in my own brain—and I kept trying to get school to be the spark to inspire this lighting. I didn't want to darken the dorsal striatum. I didn't want dissatisfaction, disaffection. Like Siddhartha, I knew "something was missing." I wasn't sure why, but I felt the feeling of low-grade learning depression, and I needed help in my search for educational success.

I believe every undermotivated learner suffers similarly. Each feels the depression but wants to succeed in school and in life, and will, if presented with models and solutions that spark the imagination, grab hold of them. Undermotivated boys constantly seek solutions and—havens— like I found in reading books—that can actually signal to parents, teachers, and concerned citizens what we can do to help them.

In the next chapter, we will provide solutions, ways to reignite the dorsal striatum during a boy's learning adventure. Depression of any kind—including learning depression—constitutes in large part a lack of enjoyment and satisfaction in life projects. Learning depression, unlike the kind of clinical depression that fits under the rubric of Chapter Nine, may not be cured by medication. It often needs no medication, and in the end, medication may do more harm than good. Other kinds of intervention are often more complete, more humane, and more satisfying.

What Parents and Teachers
Can Do to Motivate
Boys to Learn

Things were really bad for me. I wasn't motivated at all to learn. I
hated school. I was pretty depressed. I was going to give up. But then,
some things changed. My family moved to a new city and I changed
schools. I got into football. That really helped. I got a good coach and
made new friends. I got my motivation back. It took a couple years,
but somehow, I got it back. I liked myself again.

—MIKE ROE, 28

AS YOU KNOW FROM THE INTRODUCTION TO THIS BOOK, KATHY'S SON MIKE ROE
(formerly Karl Michael), is now training to be a teacher, but during his
middle school years, Mike lost his motivation for success. He developed
low-grade learning depression. He was diagnosed with ADD/ADHD. He
felt "hated" by his school system and in turn "hated" school. He was mismatched with his school, and he also struggled at home with his parents' marital separation.

"As I look back," Mike now says, "it was a really tough time. If it
weren't for a few big and little things that happened just right, I don't
know where I'd be today."

Mike's story is like many others involving unmotivated boys. Both "big" and "little" things need to happen in order for boys like him to be returned to healthy learning. What are those things? What really works with undermotivated boys?

This chapter is devoted to solutions, both in the home and at school. Every boy's story of undermotivation and learning depression is different, but for most boys, the big things and the little things are quite similar. They involve reshaping the home and the school.

What Parents Can Do

Helping undermotivated boys turn around, become engaged in school, and have greater success in life is the primary task of parents and the parent-led team. Even if parents are sure that the main problem lies in the school's mismatch with the boy, as Kathy was, still the first place of rescue is the home. Here are some areas of focus for parents and parent-led teams.

Tutors, Masters, Apprentices

Whatever your ethnic origins, your ancestors taught the boys in their communities through master-apprentice relationships. No matter whether the boy's father was killed in war or the mother in childbirth; no matter whether the tribe or town was under constant attack—indeed, no matter the stressor on your ancestors' sons, those boys had to learn skills well in order for the culture and family to survive, and the best learning occurred in one-on-one relationships between teacher and student.

Undermotivation was not likely, or if it appeared, it was quickly cured by the steady attention of a master to an apprentice. If the family and the master discovered that the boy did not fit the master (for example, everyone wanted the boy to be a blacksmith, but he just didn't have the ability), a new apprenticeship was found for him.

This is how it can work today also, if we use tutors within the family or parent-led team or those supplied by professional schools and tutoring agencies. Over the last decade, research into educational resiliency has confirmed that the single most impressive cure for lack of motivation to learn among students is consistent, specific, and helpful one-on-one contact with an educational mentor.[1] The "master" today may be the tutor, the tutorial school, the special learning coach, the mentor, and the family members who become tutors.

In the past, the connection between master and apprentice was arranged by not only the parents but also the elderly matriarchs and patriarchs. Today, the job of "finding the masters" usually falls on busy, working parents. Given this challenge, you might consider looking at more than one master before making a decision. If possible—especially if your son is sixth grade or older—you might consider looking for healthy male masters to augment female ones. These masters can be individual and team sports coaches, but a sports coach is generally not enough for an unmotivated boy. Other kinds of teachers are needed: music teachers, math tutors, science tutors, reading and writing coaches, and in some cases religious or spiritual tutors (such as bar mitzvah tutors). Beyond these, you will probably need one or more family members to become tutors and homework coaches for your son.

You are in control of who will lead your son back to the love and rigor of learning. Perhaps you'll decide to work only part time now in order to spend more time with the boy. Your own role might thus become one of being more of a master in a master-apprentice dynamic with your own son. We know of one case where a father was able to take a leave of absence from work so he could spend full time tutoring and supporting a son who was having problems at school. At the same time, you may not have the part-time work option. In this case, it is especially crucial to use extended family in this role.

Extended Family Attention

An often untapped educational resource today is our intergenerational extended families. If you are struggling to care for an undermotivated learner, grandma, grandpa, aunts, uncles, godmothers and godfathers, parents of your sons' friends, and older siblings all need to be brought into an "intervention" for the depressed learner. You need to make calls to relatives. "Mom, will you tutor Jordan in his science?" "Dad, will you tutor Jordan in his math?"

Carlin, seventy-one, known as Nana to grandson Jonathan, six, told us: "When Jonathan comes to visit Nana and Gramps, he is the center of attention for however many hours he's around. He gets the undivided attention of one of us, often both. Gramps is awfully careful to be available to Jonathan for reading, doing projects, and going on errands. Gramps likes to make everything a learning experience, so this is really good for Jonathan."

Gramps admitted, "I spent entirely too much time working when my son was growing up, and when I looked back I realized how much I missed. Now my son spends a lot of time building his career so he can provide for his family. So I can help by spending time with my grandson."

Grandparents and team members other than parents can step in to set a good learning foundation and relationship with young children in the early years, so that they are trusted and available to help mentor or tutor the undermotivated boy later in life. If or when problems with undermotivation arise, the family network is already set up to provide support.

Positive Attention Among Parent-Led Teams and Professionals

"Tough love" can actually be a great motivational tool when dealing with some undermotivated boys. A strong father (or mother) may need to try the approach of blunt criticism and extremely clear expectations. Being hard on a son is not inherently dangerous (unless practiced with physical or emotional abuse); it is an approach that certain parents (and extended family) recall from their own childhoods and will try at times.

Simultaneously, to overemphasize criticism is to fail, in general, at caring for an undermotivated boy. Parents, extended family, and medical professionals generally sense the importance of positive attention. Your son will gain as you follow that sense patiently and yes, at times, provocatively.

Dr. Howard Schubiner of Detroit (whom you met in Chapter Nine) shared wisdom with me from his medical practice.

When I work with parents and families I generally say, "Medication won't really help boys who are not motivated." I go further: "Motivation is more important than medication." Working together we are able to realize how much of that missing motivation comes from identifying and nurturing the positives in the boy, his life and situation.

These positives are not just about positive reinforcement—which is definitely crucial—but they are also the boy's "islands of competence." In my experience, we motivate boys by improving their self-efficacy in these islands of competence. We show them the areas of self-development they are already successful in, then transfer this feeling of success to the areas where they lack motivation. We use positives to create positives.

In the defining paradigm of this book, Dr. Schubiner is a member of the parent-led team. He needs the family to help him understand where the boy is already competent; the family needs him to help them help the boy.

Howard shared a wonderful story with me that illustrates his success in helping undermotivated boys become motivated through positive attention to islands of competence.

I had one patient who came into the office wearing a T-shirt consisting of frogs from around the world. This early adolescent was quite bright but getting D's in his classes. I asked him about the frogs and was amazed to hear how much he knew about frogs from South America and Africa. I asked him how he was able to learn all that. He said he was interested in frogs and spent time reading all about them. I complimented him on his abilities and explained the skills he was using: showing interest in a subject, putting forth effort in practice/learning, performance (showing off to me what he could do). Based on his "island of competence," his family and I worked together to give him positive feedback when he transferred these three skills (Interest, Practice, Performance) into other areas, such as his schoolwork.

This story has a happy ending. He ended up getting B's in his classes.

Regulating What He Watches and Eats

If you haven't read Chapter Five, this might be a good moment to do so. Check the specific and crucial material relating to screen time that we shared in that chapter. As many parents of undermotivated boys have discovered, some of the very same boys who are undermotivated in school seem hypermotivated to explore the Internet, play video games, and watch TV more than they study. As we explored in Chapter Five, this is unhealthy for the boy's learning brain. That chapter offers some suggestions on how to handle these on-screen stimulants.

Similarly, undermotivated boys—like boys who are diagnosed with ADD/ADHD or other learning disabilities—often suffer from poor nutrition, contributing to their low-grade depression. These boys may be eating too much sugar, which creates too much insulin, which in turn affects learning and emotional life. These boys may also be getting far too few omega-3 acids, which in turn disaffect the brain from learning and success. Please see Chapter Five for more information on the issue of nutrition. There is a great deal you can't control in your son's life, but you can take steps to improve his diet. The rewards of exerting this control can be profound in the area of learning depression and undermotivation.

Because what a boy watches and eats has an immediate effect on his brain, it is crucial to pay special attention to these two areas of his life. Once the parent-led team has begun interceding to tutor and help your son, you may have even more time and energy to focus on issues like nutrition and screen time.

Doing Homework Together

Have you ever sat in the late night after your son is asleep and wondered whether you are helping him *enough* with his homework or helping him *too much*? Have you felt guilty for destroying his budding independence by nagging about homework? Have you felt guilty for abandoning him to difficult lessons by not nagging about homework? Have you nagged him and found it unsuccessful, pulling back because he becomes defiant?

Homework is crucial to educational success. It's also a major learning issue for our sons, because boys, on average, perform worse in homework tasks than girls.[2] For undermotivated or learning-depressed boys in particular, homework is especially important. The spiral of low self-worth and low self-esteem that afflicts these boys is in large part due to lack of success with homework tasks.

Thus it is essential that you remain engaged with your son about his homework and see this engagement as a critical task of parenting. This doesn't mean that you or a team member should be doing homework for your undermotivated son. Ultimately such "doing-for" could increase his lack of motivation. But to just say to him, "Go do your homework" and hope he does it is often just as dangerous. The best middle ground involves one or both parents, as well as other members of the parent-led team, being available to the boy while he does his homework—advising, helping to organize papers and folders, showing how calculators and computers can be better used, testing his spelling, encouraging his process, and doing whatever they can—short of doing it themselves—to improve his results.

Because of signals from boys and the society that say, "Leave me alone," parents have thought they were doing the child a favor by "not hovering," by "leaving him to his own devices." In the area of homework, however, this signal needs to be ignored by caring parents. Spending an hour per day sitting with your son while he does his homework is often the minimum required for helping undermotivated boys. The child can spend this hour with one parent, with the parents and a tutor, or with other members of the parent-led team. If more than an hour is needed, one parent may not be able to spend that time, so another parent or team member or tutor should also participate.

If you institute a good homework plan with the boy—and if you give him the one-on-one time that homework requires—he will generally come to like the attention, and he'll start performing better. Of course, a lot of family and personal "demons" can come out during this homework time; this hour can become emotion laden. If one parent is highly authoritarian, the homework time can become a greater stressor than motivator. That parent is challenged to become a more positive learn-

ing companion to his or her son by exercising more patience and innovation.

One innovation to try is to make sure your son does not do homework in his room (behind his closed door) but at the dining room table
or other household area where he can interact with you and others. This
also builds family love and togetherness. Because so many undermotivated boys are experiencing low-grade learning depression, your son
gains ground by your efforts to cut down as much as possible on the
boy's isolation and loneliness.

In 1999, a father in Chicago told me a story that has inspired my
position on homework ever since. His son was undermotivated and failing in school. When the young man finally graduated high school and
made it to college, the son was still having problems, so he and his father
made a deal. The father promised to call him every morning and every
evening to check in with him on how his work was going and to help
him accomplish any homework or other special projects. The father and
son spent some time on the phone every day for the son's entire freshman year. The son succeeded well; in his words, "If my father hadn't
bugged me, encouraged me, motivated me for that hour or two a day, I
don't think I would have made it."

Helping Boys Learn in Home Schools

For some undermotivated boys, nothing you try seems to be enough to
turn their education around. There is always one more thing to try.

Claire Dory, of Miami, writes, "I started homeschooling my two
boys, and what a relief! The schools were calling them failures. My sons
weren't motivated to learn well at school and the testing standards
showed me how much of my children's education-time was being wasted
on standardized tests. So I took matters into my own hands, and my
sons are now doing great! They test out better than most kids in high
school."

Home schooling is not logistically possible for every family, nor is it
appropriate for every child (or parent!). But it can be an educational lifesaver, especially for parents of boys with motivational issues in school—

boys not doing homework, boys who are truant, boys who are acting out or abandoning education.

Leslie, a homeschooler in Colorado Springs, has seven children (18, 17, 15, 13, 8, 6, and 4). She and her husband, Joel, have homeschooled all of them for different periods of time. All her older children, who have attended public high school part time, have higher than 3.5 grade-point averages; one of them has a 4.0. "Especially with my boys," Leslie told Kathy, "homeschooling was what I believe helped them most to be good learners."

Kristin, a mother of six in Texas, shared her story with us:

> My first child was a boy, my second a girl. In trying to make a good decision about their education, it was scary to think of sending them to a system that kept reporting how many kids were performing poorly. My son was a typical boy—loud, squirmy, always on the go, and constantly into things. He didn't take to school like a lot of kids do. He started having trouble. Although I didn't have a teaching degree, I had a college education, and I figured I could figure out how to teach my kids. Watching how many of my son's friends are not performing well in school, I know I've made the right decision for my family.

There are many reasons to homeschool—social, religious, personal. There are advantages to home schooling, as well as disadvantages.

One advantage has to do with flexible learning levels. The first thing Kristin noticed when she started homeschooling her children was that age didn't matter. Having a seven-year-old boy and a five-year-old girl working at the same level was not as much of a problem as she thought it would be. In some subjects, the two-year gap made it necessary to teach them separately, but on many science projects, and even in some reading and writing assignments, Kristin could work with both at once.

Kristin noticed another advantage to home schooling. "We only spent a little over three hours a day 'in class.' Since I didn't have to take attendance, fill out forms, respond to parent notes, all the stuff that teachers have to do before they can teach, we spent our learning time learning! Friends who are classroom teachers really envied me when I

> ### ??? Did You Know? ???
>
> Just over one million children are homeschooled in the United States, according to the Department of Education. This figure is up from 360,000 a decade ago. Not surprisingly, the majority of homeschooled children are boys.[3]

would tell them we went to a local ranch to see how a calf was born for science class. Or when we took a picnic to the park for lunch."

For boys who might not fit the educational system available in their community, home schooling can be a very good option. It allows these boys to experience

- One-on-one master-apprentice teaching modalities
- Hands-on ("field trip") learning
- Nonrigid developmental learning
- A lot of physical movement

In general, homeschooled children can proceed at their own pace. They are fortunate not to have the social pressure of a "grade" to be in. They can learn in ways that they are ready for—experiential, active—before they have to learn to sit down, sit still, and perform collective work. Their schedules are often fluid. Families that homeschool are returning to an earlier approach to education, when a child had a live-in tutor who taught all subjects.

Home schooling is not a panacea—it is an option. It has disadvantages:

- One parent (or other member of the parent-led team) has to be free to stay home all day.
- The parent or team member must be good at teaching—patient, organized, educated.

- The child will miss certain aspects of socialization, supervision, and mentoring that can occur only in large schools.
- The parent-led team must work extra hard to set up extracurricular sports and other activities for the homeschooled child.

Using Rites of Passage to Motivate: The Driver's License

The coming-of-age experience of getting a driver's license is already a major rite of passage that, for most children, happens as a normal part of growing up. In some families, however—especially in families dealing with chronically undermotivated boys—the earning of a driver's license, along with driving privileges, can be a very useful motivation tool.

Before discussing how to use the driver's license as a tool, however, it's important to remember that motor vehicle crashes are the number one cause of death among sixteen- to nineteen-year-olds in America. Teenagers account for 7 percent of licensed drivers in the United States, but they are involved in 14 percent of traffic fatalities and 20 percent of all reported accidents. Males outnumber girls in these statistics two to one. Since 1975, deaths of boys in this age bracket have increased by 40 percent.[4]

During adolescence, the human brain regularly experiences increased levels of dopamine, which increase an adolescent's tendency to enjoy risky, impulsive, and novel activities. About this same time, he will be champing at the bit to learn to drive! Therefore, we can arm ourselves with such dangerous statistics and use the driver's license as a bargaining chip.

"Look, son," you can say, "this is a huge deal. You're moving into a world of danger, privilege, and responsibility. Getting a driver's license and driving a car is a rite of passage into adulthood. You have to earn the privilege."

You can hinge buying a used car or paying for the insurance on how the boy does in school, so that getting the license motivates many other positive goals. For example, you can regulate how much he's allowed to drive the car based on how his grades increase or his attendance in school improves. In the present educational system, many schools no longer have the budget to offer driver's education training. Thus parents are assuming more responsibility to provide driver's training themselves, or they are putting out their own money to enroll children in professional driver's education schools. Here again, the parent is empowered. "Your family is doing these things for you, son; now you have to do your part. Driving is a privilege of work and life success. It's not something you get for nothing."

Driving is the ultimate multitasking activity. For a male brain that is not equipped to handle that responsibility, it can be a disaster. For a boy who needs extra motivational help, it can be a real asset in family discipline and development. Fortunately, you are in a position to provide him with all the incentives needed to help him pass this rite of passage in one piece.

What Teachers Can Do

Undermotivation, as you know, is being handled by many school systems as a conduct disorder, ADD/ADHD, or a discipline problem. As many of us now realize, it is unfair—even immoral—to label a child diseased with a brain disorder who is in fact a boy going through normal male development or complex male adjustments to a system that is not sure how to serve him. Intuition is one of the wisest and most effective tools a teacher can have. Once you look into a boy's eyes and see the learning depression there, you'll probably see causes, and you'll immediately be able to begin developing your own solutions.

Here are some tried-and-true solutions. We hope they'll inspire you and your school to take on the issue of male undermotivation and learning depression. As you practice these strategies, we hope you'll become a coach to other teachers who are dealing with undermotivated boys. Just as parent-led teams help these boys, teacher-led teams are also crucial.

Ten Effective Strategies

We offer these strategies in addition to those we've explored in the previous chapters. If you haven't read those chapters, you might enjoy them now. They are packed with innovations for teaching preschoolers, elementary school students, and middle and high schoolers in many areas, including reading, writing, language arts, math, and science. The following strategies are most effective when integrated with the ones in those chapters. Three of the strategies in this short list have been explored before, but their importance and effectiveness are amplified with undermotivated boys.

1. Formally check in with the boys every day. Ask them how they're doing on homework, in school, at home, in life. Take a few minutes to listen and to guide.

2. Get these boys involved! Target these boys for in-class debates. Get them engaged in topics of interest. Get them engaged with other students. Facilitate group work within classrooms. Facilitate single-gender groupings (as we discussed in Chapter Eight).

3. Encourage them—or tell them—to sit near the front of the classroom. Boys can hear better from that position. They can't become as disengaged as they can in the back of the class. In the same vein, make sure there is adequate light in the classroom, a practice that increases visual stimulation and thus learning quality.

4. Modify teaching methods to include less verbal instruction and more hands-on activities while letting nonverbal-, non-writing-type students (in third grade and beyond) do more work on the computer than you might otherwise allow. For undermotivated boys especially, a lot of verbal instructions can be mind numbing, and the appropriate use of computers can help deal with the self-esteem crisis created by simply not having the cursive writing skills of other kids.

5. Let students move around physically while they are reading, writing, learning, and even using the computer. In Gurian Institute pilot schools, physical movement has been one of the universal strategies used to improve the performance of undermotivated boys.

6. Give these students soft objects to squeeze in their hands constantly (not disruptively), so that they can keep their brains stimulated physically and thus avoid the rest state. Along with physical movement, the tactile stimulation of squeeze objects has been a grade-saver for many undermotivated boys.

7. Change your school and class schedule to fit the adolescent brain. Your school might want to put music classes early in the day, for they wake up the brain. For high schools, we hope innovators will, in the future, change school days to a nine-to-five schedule—this not only fits adolescent circadian rhythms but also helps handle the latchkey problem of undersupervised adolescents in the afternoon hours.

8. Physical education is an essential subject for student motivation—especially for underperforming males. Physical activity helps stimulate the brain to learn. Middle schoolers need PE more than once a week, for fifty minutes. Teaming athletic coaches with academic teachers is crucial in helping undermotivated boys who often choose a sport to work hard in—but neglect their studies. If the coach and teacher meet once a week to go over student records and needs, the undermotivated and underperforming students can get special, needed care.

9. Smaller schools and classrooms help motivate students. Research on classroom size consistently shows that smaller classrooms increase student learning, cut down on discipline problems, and increase student participation in academic and extracurricular activities. Larger classrooms are especially hard for undermotivated boys, who do not get enough one-on-one teacher time.

10. Provide all undermotivated students with a mentor—this can be facilitated through the school counseling program, the classroom, teacher-parent meetings, athletic coaching, and teacher-student conversations about someone the boy admires and would like help from.

A School Intervention

When a student is chronically undermotivated and underperforming, school intervention is necessary. Lewis and Clark High School, which has one of the best student performance records in the state of Washington, uses a "Circle of Advocacy" intervention, which other schools can duplicate.[5] The next Try This box describes how it works.

An intervention like this one can help undermotivated students find success again, especially if it is used with parents and teachers in liaison—that is, if the school and parent-led teams meet frequently, maintain email contact, and remain consistent in support of the boy's academic and motivational turnaround. Even when boys initially resist this kind of intervention, they generally come around. A lot depends on how well the whole learning team works together. But the most important factor is how much the boy feels he has found a reason, in human encouragement and relations, to do homework, turn in assignments, or impress teachers and parents again with his gifts.

Helping Gifted Nonachievers

Veteran teacher Patricia St. Germain, who helped us analyze the causes of gifted nonachievement in the previous chapter, has specialized in this field; the next Try This box describes her suggested "success keys" for working with gifted nonachieving boys.

Patricia makes sure to partner these strategies with a directive approach to asking gifted students to gain competence in one study skill. Making sure they can do one thing very well affects their confidence, she reports, which begins to carry over into all academic areas. "Usually," she writes, "if these kids can get control of one simple process, their intellectual ability carries them to redesign the success for other uses. It is often their failure to provide evidence (by turning in work, doing assignments) that curtails their academic grade success."

Patricia is adamant about creating, early on, a zero-tolerance environment for missed work. She makes sure the work is "worthy work," and if the students can do it differently, she lets them negotiate how they

Try This

- All students, especially the underperforming and undermotivated, are considered to be in the center of a circle of advocacy that includes parents, school staff, and other students.
- The philosophy of the school is to "make the school smaller." If your school is a major city school, it cannot lower its actual numbers of students at this time, but it can make the school smaller by surrounding students with advocates.
- Every Tuesday, students have the same homeroom teacher—for all four years. The room itself may be changed over the four years of high school, but that Tuesday date, with a mentor-teacher-advocate whom the child trusts, does not change.
- Teachers refer underperformers to a tutoring and homework center in the counselor's office. Because 80 percent of below-C grades occur in large part because students don't turn in homework, the tutoring center focuses immediately on homework practices.
- The center is voluntary for C students—but mandatory for students receiving a D or F.
- If the tutoring center elicits no improvement, the student is sent to Saturday classes.

will show the skills she is asking of them. Whether they complete the work as assigned or in an alternative way, Patricia advises, "*Do not* endorse an environment of 'cherry picking of assignments' or mere grade getting where students can simply strategize how to get a grade by doing the *least* amount of work."

Not surprisingly, Patricia completes her advice in this specialized area by saying, "Gifted nonachievers need mentors just as much as any other student—in some ways, they have a special need for them.

Try This

- Focus on simple stuff to create direct, measurable success. This gives the boys back a sense of accomplishment, purpose, and personal honor.

- Allow for one-on-one discussion in which a student can safely admit he is not able to "do school" due to poorly developed basic study skills.

- Explore patterns of grade failures with the student and define patterns as they relate to how he felt about needing to learn the skill. Let the student select one skill he feels he can take on to help him demonstrate his ability to himself and to the counselor-teacher.

- Teach one skill at a time and teach the one skill very well. Let him choose from a menu of items that have tangible accountability, such as keeping a calendar. Let him "try on" the skill for two weeks. When you check his progress daily, try doing it as a "success coach," not as a "teacher." At the end of two weeks, engage him again in dialogue about how he can show he is making progress.

- Remember, if you can't count it, it doesn't count. Hold to this philosophy when you challenge male students to "keep score"—for example, "Brandon, show me *specifically* your progress in the area where you need work."

- Help these boys use a one-page, month-at-a-glance calendar pasted to their bathroom mirrors (or a similar place) to help them remember their tasks.

- Let the boys use a laptop for note taking. This is often better than making them take handwritten notes (for many reasons having to do with the male brain).

- Use file folders (one for each class) to create a no-fuss approach to conquering what they perceive as "failure" at school.

Especially if the mentor is real bright, real quick, real able to 'take on' the 'stuff' that these smart kids dole out, that mentor can raise the bar for a gifted but unmotivated kid in a way no one else can."

Patricia St. Germain's work with gifted but undermotivated and underperforming boys grew from her decades of experience as an educator, as well as from her training in various learning theories. One of those was the male-female brain difference material on which this book is based.

Like many who integrate this material into their teaching of boys, Patricia came to conclusions about what inspires boys and young men. She is a successful mentor of what she has called *emotional meaning* in boys, a characteristic that others have called *honor.*

Using Rites of Passage to Motivate: Honor Programs

Paul Marcus, another associate of the Gurian Institute, has built a model program based on inspiring boys toward emotional meaning, toward honor. He uses principles of honor to create a rite of passage program in which these boys can find themselves again—as Patricia has put it, can "feel the meaning of what they are doing."

The word *honor* can seem like an old word to many of us—a word used in action films or ancient tomes—but it is a crucial word for our era, one that can act as a window, a direct way of "getting inside" a boy's motivational issues, and an inspiration for getting him back to performance.

Paul, a counselor at the Albuquerque Academy, in New Mexico, saw the need to provide a new cutting-edge program for the boys in his school. Working with an honor model I provided in *A Fine Young Man,* my book on adolescent boys, he and his colleagues created an honor program from within the school's counseling department. Paul describes it this way:

> We provide this program in grades 6 and 7. Two counselors are assigned to this program, one male (me) and one female. All our counseling classes in this honor program are gender split. Boys see me, girls see my female colleague. I utilize an identity and character

curriculum in my classes with these boys to help them discuss what they value, whom they respect, their images of heroes and "real men" in the media. They discuss "honorable" traits of their fathers and men they admire as they seek to define honor and what it means to act and perform honorably. We thread this education into pre- and post-experiential education such as wilderness and urban adventures, and community service.

Some specific questions we've dealt with include

- What are the differences between boy and girl biology (reproductive and brain)?
- How should we treat girls?
- How do I deal with my emerging sexuality?
- What part does school play in my personal honor?

I often use film clips to inspire dialogue. Our whole program involves a strong media literacy component.

The program goes through the whole school year, culminating in a day which involves a ropes course experience so the boys can get some leadership training in competition/cooperation, a silent morning work-time in a garden park with only nonverbal communication, and later, a fishbowl (with girls silently watching) as the boys answer anonymous questions from the girls. The girls, of course, do the same thing with the boys.

The final "product" of the class is the boy's honor code itself—written in a writer's notebook—on what kind of student the boy wants to be, what kind of man, what he can do right now as a student and a young man. Some of the boys in our program don't have an active father, or just don't get enough male influence. These boys really like the program—they really like the contact with older, "wiser" male teachers. I find that men are crucial to the effort of making boys want to learn and become good citizens. Men have a lot to teach about motivation, performance, honor, and just life.

Paul's program works for boys across the learning spectrum, as well as undermotivated ones. It also can inspire us to look at how important men are to boys in general and boys who are undermotivated in particular.

The Key Role of Men in Motivating Boys

Many of our most undermotivated boys lack fathering, male mentoring, or adequate contact with "older, wiser" men. This is a missing center in their lives. With half of our boys today raised without a father in the home, the lack of "male motivators" is a major problem, one every school and home concerned about undermotivation or low-grade learning depression is likely to face.

In summer 2004, I received a poignant letter from a young Honduran man, Jose, twenty-five, who works on a cruise line out of Miami. He describes himself at the beginning of the letter as having troubles in school when he was younger, lacking strength and motivation. He writes:

> I am a male between millions that came to this world without knowing what a father was. My mother used to tell me she was my mother and father at the same time. Of course I didn't believe that, even though she tried hard, but a "father is a father" and he was not there to fulfill my feelings and questions about my life.
>
> Now, I am twenty-five years old. I guess those years of fire have passed; let me tell you that I almost died through those years of fire. I do not have children yet. But things are going to be different for my future child. I will know how to handle the situation in the different stages of fire he will pass through.

Jose's prose in English might be slightly awkward, but isn't his message clear? At twenty-five, he sensed that he lacked a clear male identity. His letter indicates his hunger for the spiritual and emotional food his father could have given him. Now in his early adulthood, he has made a covenant with himself to be a father to his own children. He senses very clearly that his own child's success will depend greatly on the father.

David Blankenhorn, in *Fatherless America,* has provided an immensely detailed study of the issue faced by young men like Jose.[6] Boys without fathers not only experience more physical and sexual abuse, more mental disease, and more emotional distress than other children but also receive lower grades, drop out of school at higher rates, act out in school with more frequency, end up in juvenile courts in higher numbers, and report low self-esteem and low educational expectations. Our own research at the Gurian Institute has similarly found that among the primary environmental factors essential for high motivation among adolescent boys is their nurture and mentoring by men.

How Women Fill the Gap

You may have noticed that most of the emails and letters featured in this book thus far have been from women. Most of the stories have come from moms and female teachers. This is no accident—most of the people who read books such as this one are women—women in parent cooperatives, in book clubs, in mother-to-mother relationships, in day care, in child care, in families, and in schools. Most people working intimately and every day to help undermotivated boys are women.

This circumstance, which is a credit to women, is also profoundly different in our contemporary culture than in all previous cultures. As industrialization moved men away from their children into workplaces removed from the lives of boys (and girls), women took over the raising of males. Women are now doing more than they ever have to give boy energy the innovations that this energy needs. They are taking upon themselves the pain of their sons' undermotivation, and they are seeking cures among the books, television advice shows, magazines, and volunteer work that help provide answers to questions of boys' motivation and success.

But women can't cure undermotivation of males on their own. Women know this. They yearn for male vigor in caring for boys. They know that men have become, too often, hidden assets in the nurturing life of boys. Moms of undermotivated boys especially know this. As Kathy has put it, "Trying to help boys who are having educational trouble without a caring man in the boy's life is like trying to steer a plane without a co-pilot. It's just so risky."

As Jose expressed, mothers and female teachers can give a great deal—but not the male self. Only fathers, male mentors, and male teachers can give boys the gift of male identity. Our male roles are in flux today, and that is ultimately a good thing—it means more freedom and opportunity for everyone—but male roles are only a small part of what men pass on to boys: the greatest gift they give is the *male identity* Jose missed.

This identity is not passed on in a sentence or a phrase—it is passed on through years of male involvement with male children. The identity of "learner" or "successful student" is passed to boys not through a man saying one day, "Son, you should study," but by caring men involving themselves in the boy's learning. These caring men do not need to feel they have "arrived" in a place of ultimate power or at a pinnacle of financial freedom in order to fill the souls of boys with male identity and motivation. These men *do* need to look a boy in the eye and say, "I'm here," and mean it in their bones.

Healthy Male Rituals

Daren, a father of two sons, grew up in Wisconsin surrounded by a large extended family. When he turned twelve, his father took him fishing with his grandfather, two uncles, and three male cousins. He recalls:

> It was an annual ritual for the men in our family. We lived in tents, ate over a campfire and didn't take a shower for a week—although we did swim in the lake daily. After my first trip, I looked forward to that week all year long and still went while I was in college and after I got married. As soon as my oldest son was twelve, he was invited along. It has been a struggle for us to make sure this male ritual continues, but when I look into my son's eyes, I know it's worth the struggle.

Daren's story evokes memories of a time when families were not as geographically dispersed as they are now, and fewer families were fragmented by divorce. Certainly, not everyone can reproduce what Daren's family does. But if you are facing any male learning issues in your family or school, it's crucial that your boy's learning team grapple with the issue of male identity modeling. There are many books and Web sites that can help you both invigorate the caring of males in your community and provide male rite-of-passage experiences. We hope that you will seek out those resources and use stories like Jose's to inspire the men of your community. Many of these resources appear in the Bibliography at the end of this book.

For a general model, it is worth remembering that throughout human history, our male ancestors had two or more men at their disposal during their upbringing, especially at and after puberty—the father and the master-tutor were the minimum. These men formed an inner circle of male care around the boy. There were also five to ten other significant males available through the boy's adolescence, forming an outer circle of male care. Today, we often struggle even to get one father involved.

Each father in our society needs to make a commitment to today's young men by promising to parent not only his own children but also to mentor at least one other boy. This mentoring can take place in the neighborhood, the school, the sports field, or the workplace. If this idea makes sense to a man, he won't consider himself a full success in the world unless he is part of the educational team of one other young male besides his own children. If the man has no children, he will still regard himself as inadequate if he has not mentored another family's son.

Can our men meet this high standard with their best possible care? They can and must. In their hands lie much of a boy's motivation.

Leaving No Boy Behind

Sometimes we hear adolescent boys say, "It's not cool to learn." These boys are telling us something we need to hear. What they are really saying is, "My teachers and school don't make it cool for me to learn."

In neglecting the kinds of motivational elements that boy energy needs, our culture often forgets that for males, intellectual learning has always been part and parcel of other developmental communities—getting its "coolness" from how it fits within the larger societal and masculine group.

In the classical educational model, intellectual learning took place in a debate or dialogue format (think of Socrates). Teachers challenged adolescent boys to learn, together, what was successful, necessary, and true. Boys learned because they were learning about qualities and ideas of immense value and applicability. This made education "cool."

Education today is indeed often "not cool." It is not innovative and challenging. It doesn't fit the boy, and quite often the boy's own internal or family problems don't find an emotional fit in the school. Yet our sons must learn to succeed in or near school. We have committed as a culture to letting no undermotivated boy slip through the cracks; we believe that no boy or girl should be left behind.

Because boys generally operate like "pack animals"—satisfied to be alone when necessary, but wanting also to establish "coolness" in a small or large hierarchical pack—boys often need their schools and communities to help them discover the kind of "coolness" that Hermann Hesse wrote about. In his classic novel, *Siddhartha,* Hesse portrays a young man who looked at his life and education with dissatisfaction because he knew something was missing—the deeper spiritual reasons to learn, grow, and succeed as a man. That deep spiritual reason can again become the goal for all our sons, and we can help them achieve it. No longer does a boy need to walk toward his school and say, "I hate this place" or "Learning isn't cool." None of us should be satisfied until we affect this male excitement in human education.

Helping Sensitive Boys
in Our Schools

The boy ecstatic, with his bare feet the waves, with his hair the
atmosphere dallying,
The love in the heart long pent, now loose, now at last
Tumultuously bursting . . .

—WALT WHITMAN

LEIGH FORTSON, OF GRAND JUNCTION, COLORADO, WROTE TO US:

I am disturbed that my son, a nine-year-old fourth grader, does not fit
the mold of most boys. I see other boys like him. I call them "the
Underboys." Like these boys, my son is very bright: he reads and does
math at a proficient if not advanced level. Even so, he hates school (and
he goes to a good one). He is not athletically inclined and so he doesn't
pursue sports. When he was on the soccer team, he gave his best but
was essentially afraid of the ball. He had great team spirit, but the other
boys, all much better at the game, wouldn't even look him in the eye
much less give him the high five he was asking for. So, understandably,
after three seasons of this kind of isolation and frustration, he quit.

He rides a bike now, but when he was six and learning how to, he
fell off and refused to get back on. It took years of coaxing to get him
to ride again.

He is not competitive in the typical sense. The closest he gets is
that he's into a card game based on dueling. This is a mystery to me

because in the two years he's been doing it, he's not won a single game . . . and he seems okay with that . . . sort of.

My son is very imaginative. He loves to draw, to write stories, to act things out with his toys. He'll occupy himself with those make-believe stories for hours. He's sensitive and concerned about others; also he has a lot of fear. Others take advantage of him. He says the fifth graders bully him and even kindergartners throw rocks at him.

My son is not gay. We've seen him get crushes on girls in his class. But he is very sensitive, very artistic, very gentle by nature. Because of that, he is full of self-loathing because he's beginning to recognize that he doesn't belong in the typical male world.

What should teachers and parents of sensitive boys, "nerds," "Underboys," do to help them? I want guidance on how to help my son be who he is in a world where sports, aggression, and dominance are common denominators among his peers—but don't fit who my son is.

Leigh's email captures the plight of many sensitive boys in our schools and in our society. Leigh's son is smart and does well in school, but in the broad social group this feels like "not enough." Because the boy is part of this broader male society, he cannot help but try to accommodate the conventional values and priorities of the group. Yet he believes he is not capable of meeting those priorities with the inner resources, hopes, and dreams he carries. He is constantly feeling hurt, left out, a "loser," an impostor. He is also in a social situation for which there may be no "cure," for there is no disease. He is simply, by nature, different than the mass, and neither he nor the mass is going to change very much to accommodate one another. Neither is wrong; neither is ill. They are just different.

When I contacted Leigh in response to her email, she told me that because of her experience with her son and some of his friends, she is doing research to write a book called *Underboys*. How valuable, indeed, this book would be! Not until her email had I heard the term "Underboys," but it immediately stuck with me.

For much of my schooling, I was an Underboy—nonathletic, skinny, undeveloped. Sensitive and empathic in comparison to many other boys, I didn't fit in with the crowd of boys around me. My soul yearned for the compassion and experience of Walt Whitman's boy ecstatic, with his bare feet the waves, with his hair in the atmosphere, the love in his heart long pent, always trying to burst tumultuously. I wanted school to be a place of safety and learning, of inner exploration as much as outer "doing." This is how I was built. Most boys—I felt—were not built like me. I was an outcast.

From her experience, Leigh has coined the term "Underboy." Most teachers call these boys "our more sensitive boys." That too seems an accurate description. About ten years ago, I coined another phrase, developed from my synthesis of research in brain sciences, that I hope at least partially describes these kinds of boys (and girls who also don't fit the mass of girls): "bridge brains."

Bridge Brains

With this term I hope to capture the very interesting brain difference between the sensitive boy and the more masculine male. The sensitive boy, or bridge brain, is one who may show lower testosterone levels in the blood as well as higher oxytocin levels; thus his basic biology may be formed less toward the search for self through aggression and more for empathic bonding. He will also, quite often, show higher than average verbal development (more active word centers and pathways in both hemispheres of the cerebral cortex). Furthermore, he may show more developed neural pathways for emotional signals in the brain. His corpus callosum may be larger than normal for a male, allowing more crosstalk between hemispheres of his brain and thus more emotional processing. In these ways, his brain may be a "bridge" between genders.

Many male writers and artists are akin to the bridge brain. Many "nerds" fit this category in certain ways. A man who teaches first grade is most probably a bridge brain, as are some stay-at-home dads. In order to succeed at caring for infants, toddlers, and little children for years on end, these men need higher oxytocin (more immediate bonding ability), lower testosterone (decreased personal aggression), higher verbal-emotive capacity (more connectors between the limbic system and frontal lobe verbal centers), good hearing and other sensory skills (greater occipital development, in order to access the minute sensory cues children are constantly sending out).

Like Leigh, all of us have intuited that there are a lot of sensitive boys, Underboys, and bridge brain boys (and men) in our homes and educational systems. How many are there? It will be a decade or two before we have a clear number, but brain scans conducted by Simon Baron-Cohen, of Cambridge University, are already giving us an approximation.

Simon Baron-Cohen, author of *The Essential Difference,* has conducted PET and MRI brain scans on males and females for over a decade. His latest brain-based study, reported in March 2004, showed that the "maleness" and "femaleness" of an individual's brain is identifiable at one day old! It also showed that one in seven females has what he calls a "male" brain, and one in five males has what he calls a "female" brain. Not surprisingly, Dr. Baron-Cohen ended his report by saying, "These discoveries could have a lot of practical uses, for instance in school. Male and female brains could benefit from different teaching styles."[1] Dr. Baron-Cohen's work at Cambridge, just like the work of the Gurian Institute, is not using the terms *male brain* or *female brain* to suggest sexual preference, but mainly to point out the broad continuum of gender in the brain. Not all males or females are built the same—in fact no two brains are exactly the same—and many males and females have brains that look more like each other's than one might imagine.

What I call bridge brains fit this category. The one in seven and one in five individuals Dr. Baron-Cohen has identified as "exceptions" to the male-female brain trends may well be the sensitive boys who need our special attention in this chapter.

Fighting Gender Stereotypes

Archie Wortham, a teacher and father in Texas, sent me a poignant set of anecdotes via email. It began, "A group of four- to eight–year-olds were asked, 'What does love mean?'" Here are two wonderful responses from the boys:

Billy, four years old: "When someone loves you, the way they say your name is different. You just know that your name is safe in their mouths."

Bobby, seven years old: "Love is what's in the room with you at Christmas if you stop opening presents and listen."

The mother of Jayden, four years old, told this story: "Our next door neighbor is an elderly man who has just lost his wife. When Jayden saw him cry, my little boy went over into his yard and climbed onto his lap. Jayden just sat there until our neighbor stopped crying. When I asked Jayden what he'd said to our elderly neighbor, Jayden replied, 'Nothing, I just helped him cry.'"

The feelings, ideas, and actions of these little boys are sensitive, emotionally literate responses to life. These responses remind us that being emotionally sensitive is part of boy energy too. Because so many of our sons and schoolboys are rambunctious and active (in Plato's wry words, "the wildest of all the animals"), our schools, homes, and culture often deal with boy energy as if it only includes the intensity of physical, kinesthetic, and tactile *action*. We perhaps forget that "listening to the room," sensing the safety of love itself, tenderly helping a grief-stricken man are all equal parts of boy energy too. And although every boy in the world has sensitive moments—even adolescent boys who appear immensely tough can be quite sensitive—the sensitive boys we're focusing on in this chapter spend even more time experiencing their boy energy as a matter of introspection, tears, tenderness, and emotion-filled words or thoughts.

They also experience a sad cultural betrayal of their particular form of maleness. Social pressures to perform, to be alpha males, to be athletic, even to act out and be "bad" can confuse and crush the self-concept of a sensitive boy. Sensitive boys are further stereotyped as "feminine" or "fags" and thus often cast out of the large masculine group.

The fight against these kinds of gender stereotypes is the first and most important fight in which we can all engage when we commit to protecting and serving sensitive boys. Over the last five years, a number of books and resources have emerged to help fight this battle. My own

The Wonder of Boys and *A Fine Young Man; Real Boys,* by William Pollock; *Raising Cain,* by Michael Thompson and Dan Kindlon; and *Lost Boys,* by James Garbarino, can serve as in-depth, whole-book resources on how we can fight the limited masculine stereotypes that often plague our culture.

Each of us as individuals, too, can commit to playing a daily part in the fight. When we see a sensitive boy being harassed or subjected to name-calling, we can act on our instinctual urge to fight stereotyping. When we hear someone call a sensitive boy "fag," we can come to his rescue. In doing this, we are showing and modeling compassion for boys in our communities and ourselves. Rescue and immediate empathic care are essential. They are essential not just for boys who are able to talk a lot about their feelings, like Leigh's son is, but also for sensitive boys who can't express themselves and need our extra help in the area of feeling and emotion.

The Emotional Lives of Sensitive Boys

When caring adults first think of helping a sensitive boy, they probably first think of rescue, then think of immediate care that involves what Kathy and I call the *words-for-feelings* exchange. That is, we help these boys "use their words" and articulate in words what they are experiencing on a deep, emotional level. Assuming that these boys can easily translate their emotions in words, we'll say, "It's okay. You don't need those guys' approval," or "Don't listen to them. They're just being rude," or "You're unique, son. You don't have to be like them." Or we'll say, "Are you all right? Tell me what you're feeling." To expect the words-for-feelings exchange, though a natural impulse, is in fact a mistake for many boys, as the boy may be unable to find the words, leading to even more frustration, but with bridge brain males, our inclination to encourage words-for-feelings exchanges can be a good one. These boys often use words for feelings, such as "I feel sad," "I feel angry," or "I'm a loser." These words for feelings can lead to a great deal of good conversation sitting across the dining room table or in the boy's room or in a school counselor's office. In the next Try This box, you will find tried-and-true strategies for enhancing words-for-feelings emotional literacy in boys.

Dick Piazza, a trainer in brain-compatible learning and a Gurian Institute certified trainer, wrote this email about how important words for feelings were to him as a sensitive boy.

> I remember my own adolescence and the sense of utter loneliness that wrapped around me. I felt so different and alienated from my friends and family; it was as if I was experiencing things no one had ever known. I began to write poetry, hiding it under my baseball glove under my bed. Writing these words down, it was as if a whole new person grew in that secret place, page by page, becoming . . . what? Me. I think every boy is secretly tending a mysterious garden called "himself." He's watching daily as new and unexpected plants take root and grow.

What a beautiful statement of boyhood and the immense sensitivity of boys—also of the need to attach feelings to words, to name the soul and the heart in poetry, in conversation.

Nonverbal Communication About Feelings

Having highlighted words for feelings, it is crucial also to notice that even among our most sensitive boys, there is still a male-female difference. Dick himself told me how aware he has become of this difference in the trainings he provides to students and to teachers.

Male sensitivity (and female as well, at times) is often not satisfied with words. Girls in general access their "words-for-feelings" connectors more easily than even our most sensitive boys (especially during puberty and adolescence), so you are most likely to encounter a words-for-feelings disconnect among boys.

Quite often with your sensitive son or the troubled sensitive boy in your class, you've found yourself getting the "huh?" response when you say, "Something's wrong; tell me what it is." Quite often you've asked, "How can I help?" and been told in one way or another, "Back off!" Quite often you've gotten withdrawal from your son or male student

Try This

- Let yourself show your feelings when you are asking a boy to show his; at the same time, don't let your feelings overwhelm the boy's feelings. "Son, I'm really upset about how Todd treated you, really upset, but I want to know what *you* feel."

- Avoid rambling questions when asking how a boy feels. "Did you do this, then that, then this, and what did you feel when . . ." Prepare your words, plan them, so that your questions and comments are cogent and to the point. "When Joe did this, what did you do?" If "How do you feel about what those kids did?" generally elicits emotional withdrawal from a particular boy, try "What do you think about what those kids did?" Initially, boys are often more comfortable sharing what they think than how they feel.

- When appropriate moments arise, paraphrase back to the boy what he is saying. "Hmmm," "Yes," and other vocalizations can help keep a boy's emotional story on track. Pure silence can also be helpful, especially if he has begun to cry. Let your instincts tell you when to respond and when to be silent.

- Let a boy ramble as he responds to a question about his emotions, but if he repeats the same story over and over again, gently tell him, "I get that" and paraphrase back what you get, then ask another question.

- Hug or pat a boy on the back when he cries, even squeeze his shoulder or connect with him physically in an appropriate way. When he expresses discomfort, you need to pull away, but until then, he probably really wants the hug or other physical show of affection and support.

- Follow the boy to the emotional place he wants to go. If you start out wanting him to talk about his girlfriend but he ends up talking about his father, that's okay.

when you've tried to rescue or support him with verbal immediacy. You might think, "This is such a sensitive, gentle boy—why won't he talk to me?" This behavior in the boy may signal the time to move far beyond the words-for-feelings approach to male emotion.

For many decades now, we've tended to base our sense of a child's—boy's or girl's—emotional life on the words-for-feelings exchange. In this way, we've devoted our social energy to a more "female" than male approach to emotional life. This has been an immensely useful enterprise. Anything we can do to increase direct verbal-emotional communication in human beings must be inherently respected. Words are indeed a very empowering way to care for the emotional lives of boys.

At the same time, caring for a boy's sensitivity may require other strategies than using words. The rest of this chapter will help you integrate these other emotional strategies into your care of boys, especially our most sensitive.

A Story: The Bolter

Flo Hilliard, a Gurian Institute associate at the University of Wisconsin, shared this story from a fifth-grade teacher in Tampa whom she trained in male-female brain difference. The teacher wrote about one of her most sensitive male students:

> We called him "the bolter." He was one of those boys who just didn't fit in. It got to the point where he would blow up in class then bolt out of the room. It became our assistant principal's job to chase him down and just get him back in the building. No matter what we did, we couldn't help him manage his sensitivity in the larger classroom, school, and among all the other kids.
>
> This approach changed after we participated in your male-female brain training. Instead of just talking to him right away, I decided to take a ball with me the next time the bolter bolted. A few days later he did "bolt" again. I followed him, found him outside, and told him we should bounce the ball back and forth. He seemed leery at first, but then agreed. I bounced the ball and he bounced it, back and forth.

Soon, something started to happen. It wasn't long before he started bouncing and talking and spilling out lots of emotion he was having. He calmed down enough to walk back to class.

After just a week, he was able to tell me and other teachers when problems with the other students or the class got severe enough that he needed help, such as going to the assistant principal's office. When he did go to her office, they would do the "ball routine" and then talk. He didn't "bolt" the rest of the year. Our assistant principal said to me, "Wow, this stuff works!"

Here is an example of a very sensitive boy for whom words were not initially helpful. He needed this other "stuff." What was this stuff? This teacher integrated three elements learned from male brain research into her approach:

1. Increased one-on-one bonding helps cultivate emotional processing in boys. It helps all children, of course, but because boys may not have easy access to their words for feelings, they may need the extra bond in order to feel emotionally safe. This can be especially true of very sensitive boys, on the one end of the spectrum, and also very "nonemotive" boys at the other end. The nonemotive boys need the extra help to bring hidden emotions out; the very sensitive boys need the extra help to find clarity amid the incredible array of emotional responses with which they are presently wrestling.

2. Physical-kinesthetic activity (bouncing the ball, in the case of the bolter) helps boys develop their brain toward emotional communication through words and actions. Given the male brain's greater reliance on cerebellum activity (the part of the brain that is involved in "doing" things), stimulation of this male brain center can stimulate other brain centers, such as the emotive and verbal centers.

3. Spatial-physical activity—especially physical movement—helps promote emotional safety and emotional communication in boys. The boy who is physically moving is often able to access

feelings and words inherently better than the boy who is not, and thus he can achieve emotional *safety*. He feels especially "safe"—able to access emotion—when his parent, teacher, or friend is "doing something" with him.

The story of the bolter shows us how words-for-feelings interconnections are generally the first thing we try to elicit during an emotional conversation, but if they don't work as a first response, moving toward a more "active" emotional strategy becomes a useful (often necessary) response. It may well lead to helping boys develop words-for-feelings connectors and to emotional stability. It may not at first lead to conversation that is as long as a parent or teacher may want, but it generally stands a good chance of leading to the level of emotional conversation that is needed.

What Parents Can Do to Help Sensitive Boys

All boys need some emotional help during their lives. Sensitive boys often need extra care from parents and parent-led teams. Helping sensitive boys is often a balancing act for mothers, fathers, grandparents, friends, neighbors, and every other caregiver who makes a safety net for the sensitive boy.

Teaching Both Toughness and Tenderness

Parents and caregivers of sensitive boys often wrestle with whether to thrust a sensitive boy into competition. Perhaps you've wondered if you should protect him from competition altogether. You may have thought, *Will his self-esteem be severely hurt by failing in competitive sports?* At the same time you may have wondered, *If I don't expose him to competition, will he fail as an adult in a very competitive world?*

You are not alone, of course, in agonizing over these questions. All of us have probably heard a parent (quite often a dad) say, "That boy won't succeed in life unless he stops all the sissy stuff." From the other parent we've probably heard the opposite: "Stop trying to change him! He's fine just the way he is."

As a general rule, the emotional and social success of a sensitive boy requires the truth in both these voices to be heard. Although the father's voice is the more stereotyping and brutal in this case, it does not lack truth. The boy will most likely face more severe difficulties in adult society if he is too sheltered, too protected from "the fray." He really does need to gain the skills demanded in the dominant society.

At the same time, his future success is not dependent on his changing his brain into something it's not. In fact, "being who he is" will ultimately lead to success. If a sensitive boy knows himself, knows who he is, knows his limitations in society but also his uniqueness, he becomes a man with confidence, or what is known as a *strong core self.* This strong core self is not something we gain by learning new skills—though new skills are part of who we become—it is something we gain by knowing who we are—understanding our identity and character.

If you are a mother of a sensitive boy whose father reacts harshly to the boy's nature, it may be crucial to gain the assistance of grandparents, uncles, coaches, teachers, and counseling professionals who can help the father and the boy find an activity to share, one in which the boy can learn toughness, but also help the father find a new language for male emotionality, one that involves the father in understanding what "core self development" really is. (And, of course, this could be reversed—there are some mothers who are much tougher on their sensitive sons than fathers.)

Choosing Appropriate Athletics for Sensitive Boys

Many boys can survive any coach, any team. They flourish no matter how harsh the sports language on the team, and they don't mind failing in order to learn how to succeed. These boys are not generally our most sensitive sons, and we generally don't need to spend as much time choosing athletic activities for them. For our sensitive boys, however, we need to be extra careful.

There are some things you can do to help a sensitive boy choose an athletic activity that allows him to flourish and helps him stick with that activity.

- Talk to the coach and other parents and find out whether this particular team is one on which your son doesn't have to worry about being "the best" or even necessarily about winning.
- Learn whether the coaches or other involved adults take a "mentor" approach to this team or only a "competition" approach. A coach-mentor wants to teach competition, but also discipline, teamwork, emotional processing ("how to handle oneself"), and individual self-worth. A mentor wants boys to fail sometimes so that they'll learn "real life."
- Figure out whether the team or specific sport fits your son's inborn personality. If he just isn't built for team sports, then maybe he should try swimming, running, tennis, or golf, which may involve a team but mainly promote and reward individual effort.
- Help your son see the connection between athletics and other activities he already likes. Perhaps he is very scientific in his orientation, or perhaps he cares a lot about nutrition—athletics can be woven into these interests. Perhaps he's an avid reader. You can get books for him about athletes in the sport he is now choosing to play.
- Integrate media into the athletic activity. Movies about sports abound today. Watch these movies with your son; watch them on family movie night. Many of these movies, like *Rudy* or *Radio,* are stories of sensitive boys who find a major portion of their life success in athletics and sports.

Helping Overweight Boys

In her second week of high school, my daughter Gabrielle said to me, "Dad, I'm glad I'm a girl. The other kids don't diss the girls for being fat like the boys do. The boys really make fun of the fat boys. It's so sad."

At first, I looked at her in disbelief. Could she really be saying that boys are harder on boys about weight than girls are on girls? Diets and diet books are primarily bought by women and girls. It is primarily girls who suffer eating disorders. Physical appearance is almost an obsession for many girls. I have personally counseled girls who have experienced nasty girl criticism among their friends for being seen as even slightly overweight.

I brought this up to Gabrielle, who said, "I know, yeah, girls can be pretty mean, but the boys have no sympathy at all."

This was Gabrielle's experience of boy culture and girl culture. Rather than argue with it, I thought back to my own boyhood. I was a skinny kid. That in itself was enough for a lot of harassment, but in junior high, I had a very overweight friend, and he was constantly harassed. "Fat boy," "Fat ass," and "Fatso" were common for him. Many of today's epithets are more brutal, and include foul language.

Boys are quite brutal to other boys who don't fit norms of physical prowess—whether skinny or fat. Today, the issue of weight among boys is gaining in crisis potential. This crisis is not just a physical one; it is also leading to a great deal of emotional pain for sensitive boys. If a boy is naturally sensitive and happens also to be overweight, he can experience a great many put-downs and much harassment, and he can be ostracized.

If you are caring for an overweight boy, the following are some immediate minimum requirements:

1. *A more nutritional diet.* However you define this diet, your son must make some changes in the food and drink he takes in. Chapter Five of this book provides greater detail and suggestions for dealing with dietary issues.
2. *Mandatory exercise.* In the 1960s and 1970s, boys got far more physical exercise than they do now. The male body is wired for daily physical exercise. The human body evolved in hunter-gatherer groups and agricultural societies, in which children moved around, worked, exercised, and experienced aerobic and athletic activity constantly. The bodies of overweight

children especially need to "return" to the active nature that is in all of us.

3. *Discussion in the family.* Many families avoid the issue that is staring them in the face in order to protect the self-esteem of the overweight child. This will often backfire. If the boy weighs 230 pounds and sits in front of the TV or plays video games much of the afternoon, it is the moral responsibility of his caregivers to point out the destructiveness of his behavior.

4. *Medical help if necessary.* A thyroid test might be in order for your son. Your pediatrician may have other very valuable tests and suggestions.

5. *Protection from bullying.* The Appendix includes strategies for protecting boys from bullying. Often an overweight boy will not experience physical bullying—his size may preclude this—but he will experience a great deal of verbal bullying. This boy needs help in preparing verbal retorts ("Yeah, I'm fat, but at least . . ."); he needs help in learning how to walk away; and he needs help processing his sad and lonely feelings.

Helping Sensitive Boys Deal with Trauma

Katie, the mother of a twelve-year-old, Bryce, in Arizona, wrote, "My son is very smart but also very sensitive. His father and I divorced last year when Bryce was 11. Bryce hasn't taken it very well at all. He's hyper sensitive now. Any criticism brings on anger or sulking. He is also not doing homework. His grades are slipping. His father and I speak to each other at least once a week about him. We've decided to get him into counseling. The counselor told us he is having a 'trauma response.' She is helping Bryce a lot."

Some boys do even better in school after they experience a personal or family trauma. It seems as if they distract themselves from the pain by working harder. But many boys do much worse. Many sensitive boys respond to trauma with mood swings and with underperformance.

Quite often this moodiness and underperformance carries a *bonding message.* The boy's level of stress hormone is heightened during and after the trauma, thus heightening the level of adrenalin and affecting all brain chemistry. The most immediate relief the boy wants and needs is "bonding relief," the good feeling that comes from active bonds and attachments. By acting out, by underperforming, by becoming moody, his brain, heart, and soul are crying out for stable attachments and stronger bonds.

Many boys, not just sensitive ones, may be undermotivated to learn for this basic psychological reason: they are begging those who love and respect them to spend more time with them. If a parent has died or a divorce is in process, the very thing the boy needs from a particular parent may be difficult or impossible for him to receive—at least to the degree the boy once knew. This can feel devastating to the boy.

For sensitive boys, more time with the significant adults in their lives can be crucial, and especially when divorce or other trauma has occurred. When there has been any kind of personal or family trauma in the boy's life, he needs an increase of one-on-one bonding with members of the parent-led team. Although a teacher might be able to mentor a highly sensitive boy, it is primarily the job of parents, grandparents, god parents, tutors, and others close to the boy to increase their one-on-one time. Counselors can become members of the parent-led team at this time.

Despite the times when you might be tempted just to say, "The kid's withdrawing, he's defiant, he doesn't want me involved. I'll just let him find himself [or tough it out] without my interference," these signals from him actually mean he needs mentoring and love from you.

In discussing sensitivity that follows trauma, we've used divorce as our base for examples because it is the most common trauma our boys now face. However, it is not the only trauma to derail a sensitive boy's education. Sexual abuse, physical abuse, and emotional abuse raise cortisol and adrenalin levels and thus affect a boy's brain chemistry in the ways we have described.

Helping Gay Boys

"Give me one reason to live," the caller said to Ryan Oelrich, who answered the Quest Youth Group phone line. It was the middle of the night, and the caller had just threatened to commit suicide. His threat followed his parents' discovery of his sexual orientation, his pastor's comment that he was possessed by a demon, and abandonment by some of his friends.

Quest Youth Group, based in Spokane, Washington, is a support group for gay and bisexual male youth fourteen to twenty-five. Ryan Oelrich, its director, has answered many such calls from middle school, high school, and college students. As Ryan is well aware, the Youth Suicide Prevention Education Program has completed a survey of studies on suicide causation and discovered that gay males are three times more likely to commit suicide than heterosexual males.[2] Fortunately the suicide rate for all children has been going down over the last few years, but unfortunately the suicide rate for gay males remains high.

Dr. Charles Wibbelsman, chief of the Teenage Clinic of Kaiser Permanente in San Francisco and a member of the American Academy of Pediatrics' Committee on Adolescence, sees both good and bad news in the situation faced today by our gay youth. He observes that on the one hand, greater acceptance of gay males is helping decrease gay male depression and suicide rates. In certain cities, such as San Francisco, New York, Boston, Los Angeles, Seattle, and Miami, gays are developing support systems. On the other hand, the lack of family and public understanding of homosexuality in many other areas and sectors of our country is killing our youth.

If you are a parent of a son who has "come out"—or even who has not—and is depressed and in pain with his secret—it's valuable to note that although stereotypes abound regarding homosexuality, there is a dearth of reputable studies to support the myths and stereotypes. Homosexuality does not appear to be a "learned behavior"; no study has shown that if a boy is raised by a single mother or by two gay male parents he is more likely to become a homosexual. Your son probably knew even before he left elementary school that something was going on inside him that attracted him to boys in a sexual and confusing way.

Many (but not all) gay males are very sensitive males. During the process of our present society's religious, cultural, and scientific wrestling with homosexual issues, every family of a gay youth is potentially of service to one of these sensitive boys. Every parent who supports a gay youth in living a successful life is helping an oft-targeted male discover a hopeful place in a culture that is, for reasons still unclear, intensely afraid of 5 to 10 percent of its population.

Given the pressures on gay youth and their parents today, it is often crucial that both the boy and the parents receive counseling and seek out support groups. If there is not a program like Quest Youth Group in your community, you might be able to help create one. The Quest program was initially funded by a $50,000 grant from a concerned businessman. It can also be extremely helpful to talk to gay people themselves, to the parents of gay young men, to organizations and support groups beyond your local communities in nearby bigger cities, or in some cases to local members of clergy. You can also go online to find many national and international organizations and support groups that can provide information, education, and inspiration for gay youth and their families.

One of the biggest issues for gay youth and their parents is fear about coming out. Many boys are quite terrified about telling their parents and may even keep their feelings totally a secret, creating tremendous anxiety, frustration, and depression in their lives. If you have any clues or just a hunch that your son might be gay, first seek out some advice from any gay people you know, parents of gay youth who have already come out, your own parent-led team, and the other individuals and organizations just mentioned. Discuss, read, learn as much as you can about how to approach him and then, without any further delay, do speak to your son and try to find out what's going on. If you can approach him with love and support, he will be enormously relieved. If doing this is a problem for you, please talk to other parents and supportive individuals who can help you understand and give your son the support he needs and deserves.

We must support the sensitivity and high character that so many gay youth bring to our human community. Today, as always, our culture needs to nourish the assets of its young men.

What Teachers Can Do to Help Sensitive Boys

Sensitive boys are a great challenge to teachers today, especially in our current educational system. Many sensitive boys become depressed. Many become loners. Although some will work extra hard on schoolwork, many will give up on school. If indeed around 20 percent of our schoolboys potentially fit into the bridge brain category, significant populations of schoolboys are what we have called sensitive boys. Teachers, administrators, and staff don't want to lose these boys. Fortunately, certain innovations already have been proven to work with sensitive boys. They can be put to use immediately in our schools.

Using Male Advocates

Terry Schultz, a school social worker, became a student advocate at Olathe North High School (sixteen hundred students) in Olathe, Kansas, in the mid-1990s. He writes, "The student advocate was a nonacademic counselor position, with the ability to make visits to students' homes as needed. The student advocate provided services for special education programs, and as a roaming counselor, I worked with all students, boys and girls, who were having trouble. I dealt with a variety of suicide threats and other serious issues."

Terry's presence in the school had a profound effect on the students, especially the most sensitive and those who saw themselves as outcasts. Terry told me about an incident in which a group of Goths began to hassle a security guard at a student assembly. Terry intervened to cool things out, and "they ended up grilling me about my own high school experience and life 'way back' in the '60s."

Terry read in my work the idea of the bridge brain and noticed that many of the students he was now helping were sensitive boys, bridge brains. As Terry put it, "In working with them, I learned some significant lessons about attachment and alienation." These students yearned for attachment and love in a school environment they considered hostile to the self. They withdrew from the mass social group and acted out against it, heavy with a sense of loneliness.

Terry writes, "These were very sensitive boys. A common theme involved grief over the deaths of pets and grandparents and the difficulty of separation from parents, especially of young men with single mothers. I heard a lot about fathers who were present but not involved, as well as about divorced fathers who were more absent. I developed a counseling relationship with a brilliant troubled young man who discovered his mother's affair while fixing her email account."

Terry's elder male presence had a discernible effect on discipline referrals in Olathe High School. That in itself speaks highly of the role of elder males in the lives of sensitive boys. Terry's colleagues also saw the utility—and humanity—of having an elder male like Terry advocate for and with the alienated and hurting students of a large high school. As one teacher put it, "An older male has a solid effect on boys. It is like an 'Elder Uncle' effect. He is a respected man who is not a father, who is neutral, trustworthy, and who will talk straight and honestly about anything." Other teachers noted "a sense of relief" because now the students and the teachers had someone who could respond decisively to concerns with the boys. Terry recalls, "Many of my women colleagues who referred their 'boys,' told me they were happy that a 'guy' was talking to the young men."

Terry advises, "In being a student advocate, I learned that it helps to be impervious to shock. You have to be willing to deliver the occasional tongue-lashing behind closed doors. You have to be willing to listen, really listen, to these boys, and you have to take the time to create trust. If you're in a hurry, expecting quick results, you'll create disappointment."

Terry concluded, "'Invisible,' marginal, and alienated students want a place at the table. When approached by someone who has made the effort to form an attachment and is seen as authoritative but not authoritarian, they often respond positively. Many of these boys are 'bridge brain' individuals who find school an uncomfortable environment, but respond well to a caring man."

The Importance of Training School Counselors in Male-Female Brain Differences

In many schools, budgets for student advocate programs have never existed or have been cut. This puts increased pressure on sensitive boys and on any boys who feel anxious, alienated, depressed, alone. If not for the counseling budget available to Olathe North, Terry Schultz could not help the boys in his school. Similarly, Anne Walker, of the Park Hill School District in Kansas City, Missouri, wrote of her school's success with boys who need extra help. Her school received budgeting for counselor training in male emotional development, and good results followed. She provides two examples:

> We have a senior who is from an abusive home. Through the intervention of the school counselors, he is now living with the parents of an only child who died when he was a freshman. This boy was very high risk, but now is going to college in the fall with the hope of becoming a doctor.
>
> We have a sixth grader, also from an abusive home, who was failing everything and had more than 30 percent absences. Teachers and social workers got him into counseling for depression and suicide attempts. He is really coming back now. He is a success story.

Counselors and therapists who work with boys have noticed that talking to and with the boy is often important and helpful. At the same time, sitting in an office and talking might not be the best course. Moving around with the boy—especially talking while walking together—can often work better than sitting in an office and talking. In this, counselors who are "brain-trained" will tend to rethink *sedentary counseling* and instead use *peripatetic counseling*.

Sedentary counseling involves the normal "come into my office and sit down" counseling format. The student sits and must generate thoughts and emotions while not physically moving the body. Peripatetic counseling, in the ancient Greek format of "talking while walking," can be more useful with many boys whose brains simply don't work with as much emotional inspiration when they are sitting and trying to look a counselor in the eye. Both the forced eye contact and the sedentary physical position can shut down the emotional and verbal centers of the male brain.

Thus Anne Walker, Terry Schultz, and many others who counsel boys have noticed the importance of innovative counseling techniques. Even many bridge brain boys—whose verbal and emotional skills are well developed—will still gain from a variety of counseling techniques, whether group counseling; group discussion, as in the Peacekeepers; or peripatetic counseling modes, in which the boy can access his emotions in ways that may seem more natural to him, at a given moment, than sitting and looking someone in the eye.

Whatever counseling method a counselor or social worker uses, the necessity of counseling programs for boys cannot be underestimated. Clearly, as Terry noticed, schools gain in lowered discipline referrals and increased student performance. As Anne noted, lives are literally saved.

Dealing with Aggression and Bullying

Laurie Washington, a mother of three, wrote:

> I was in my house, at the sink, when two of my three sons rushed in the back door. My middle son, who's ten, yelled, "He's gonna pummel us, he's gonna pummel us!" He was grinning and running, and so was his brother. Then, in ran my husband, with a snowball in his hand. The boys and their father had been throwing snowballs, and the boys, covered in snow, couldn't wait to be "pummeled." All my "boys" ran out the front door, throwing snowballs and making a huge mess.
>
> I remember thinking, "Do they have to use the word 'pummeled'?" In fact, I've often wished they could play without violence—this "pummeling" is alien to my upbringing, my way of doing things. It scares me, still, even though I have a husband and three sons.
>
> But there they all were in the front yard throwing each other around, hurting each other even, having such fun. What could I do? They loved it.

Although Laurie's story underlines the potential for a dark side to male aggression, it also celebrates the importance and complexity of that aggression in male education. Boys learn a great deal from pummeling and being pummeled by each other. They learn competition and compassion (where to draw the line); they learn toughness and tenderness; they learn what works and what doesn't, how fast they can run, how quietly they can hide; they learn what it feels like to be bested but then, an hour later, to succeed. Male biology compels males to learn a lot of their life lessons through aggression—physical, verbal, social—so it is generally not boy-friendly to try to cut out all teasing, all pummeling, all of this male kind of learning, even though our yearning to protect our most sensitive boys generally pulls at us to stifle it.

At the same time, reawakening to the fact that boys have a certain aggressive energy does not change the fact that sensitive boys are too often getting hurt by the aggression. And every school and home must keep all children safe. It is especially our most sensitive boys and girls who need extra help in dealing with both the natural aggression and also the unfortunate violence in males and male culture (and increasingly in female culture, too).

How can a home and a school draw the correct line between aggressive male learning and danger to others, especially the most sensitive among us? How can homes and schools better handle bullying?

The Gurian Institute has developed standards for teasing and bullying, as well as intervention techniques and worksheets. These tools, which are comprehensively outlined in the Appendix and suitable for handing out among school staff, are modifications of a model used for Washington State's 2002 AntiBullying Legislation, which a number of specialists helped develop for the Washington State legislature.

Choosing to Succeed

Victor Frankl wrote, "Everything can be taken from a man but one thing: the last of the human freedoms—to choose one's attitude in any given set of circumstances, to choose one's own way."[4]

Frankl was born a sensitive boy in an era of Nazi dominance and destruction. Once liberated from Nazi concentration camps, he became a psychologist and social philosopher whose innovation, Logotherapy, was based on the idea that no human being, no matter the discomfort of his or her life circumstances, is unable to choose some form of success.

Sensitive boys are constantly challenged to choose the self against the mass. They cannot change the mass, nor can one teacher or one parent or even a whole community change the mass of boys and men to fit the many boys who are Underboys, sensitive young men, bridge brains. Vigilant, protective, and loving, all adults—parents, teachers, and citizens—are called on to supervise and guide the mass toward increased empathy, understanding, and emotional literacy.

At the same time, the mass of males exists because it succeeds. It is needed by society. We build societies based on the mass aggression and ingenuity and energy of males. And just as the mass is needed, so are those who do not fit it, those who will innovate against or under it, those who will stand back thoughtfully to survey it, those who will feel constantly hurt by it until that hurt becomes a mission to adapt the mass toward a constantly evolving human good.

The Underboy may feel that he has no power, but it is his very difference from the mass that gives him power. This is the power Frankl gained, the power of pure freedom, the power to choose one's attitude and one's own way, a power that those who do not fit the mass must gain. So the power of attitude, the power of choice, is the ultimate help our sensitive boys can gain from us and from within themselves.

If the sensitive boy you know is having a lot of trouble in school right now, perhaps you and he can discuss what freedom is, the freedom that each of us is seeking, no matter our difficulty: the freedom to be a self no matter what everyone else is doing or thinking or pretending.

Leigh Fortson, who coined the term "Underboy" with which we began this chapter, has helped her son by increasing the sensitivity of others around him—by advocating in his school and community for him—but also by teaching him to rely on his own inner strengths, his strength of attitude. When her son is a man, she hopes he will not have suffered what Frankl suffered but will still have gained from his struggle the key to success and happiness: his unique self tumultuously bursting.

EPILOGUE

The future of the world rests on the breath of children in the schoolhouse.

—THE TALMUD

THIS BOOK BEGAN WITH TWO STORIES: ONE OF A MAN, MYSELF, WHO LOOKED
back at his boyhood school years with some pain, the other of a woman,
Kathy, who looked back at her son's schooling in a similar way. This
book was offered with professional acumen but also with two hearts on
two sleeves. Kathy and I want to see the next generation of boys going
to school and loving it! School can and should be a haven for boys, not
a place to fear.

We hope that this book has brought you the freshest, strongest, and
most tried-and-true theory and strategies for schooling your sons, the
boys in your schoolhouse, and the young men in your communities. Big
changes are needed in our culture if we are to fully accommodate the
nature of boys and men. We cannot go back to a world of stereotypes,
of one-kind-of-man, nor can we rely completely on one ideology, like
feminism, or one theological text, like the Bible. Our sons are too diverse
to be told there's only one way to educate them.

What we do to protect and educate the minds of boys is everything
it always has been, and more.

It is a sacred task, entrusted to you by your God or any higher power in which you might believe.

It is an ideological outgrowth of your use of reason and your sense of fairness.

It is a striving to find success for boy energy so that boys will grow up beholden to give that energy back to this society in service and honor.

In what time have we ever needed more the wildness, the focus, the yearning, the genius, the honor, and the love of our sons? We live in complex times, times that need boys who have been brought to manhood by the highest standards of education available to a civilization. Everything you do to care for the minds of boys you do not only for one boy or two, not only for one class or one school, but also for a civilization that is today asking, "What is a man? How should boys become men? How should adults care for boys?"

These questions were not asked with much openness in the human past. Their answers were assumed. But times have changed. Not to ask questions about the direction, role, and identity of either women or men is to neglect one of the most important topics of contemporary human conversation.

We hope you will take this book into your communities as a template for educating boys passionately and practically. It is only one template, only one vision, and we know that. We know too that one thing it adds—and begs you to add—to your community dialogue is a healthy reliance on science.

Let science now join religion and ideology in educating our children. Let our sons gain not only the religious archetypes and ideological frameworks that historically ground our democracy but also the best science available. May you find in your community's application of the new brain sciences a window into the very soul of boys and men, and may you feel you have taken a fresh new breath of air breathed with your son in the healthy schoolhouse of his future.

NOTES

INTRODUCTION

I first used the term *"nature-based theory"* in 1996 when I published *The Wonder of Boys: What Parents, Mentors, and Educators Can Do to Shape Boys into Exceptional Men.* I had realized in the mid-1980s that our generation of parents and educators was not being provided information about the actual nature of our children. We were told that human socialization was the prime source of who boys and girls were. In this ideology, we were compelled to raise and educate kids without adequate information about them. Furthermore, in response to reprehensible historical oppression of girls' social status and repression of boys' emotional energy, our post-1950s culture decided to commit itself to the idea that boys and girls were not inherently different and thus could be raised and educated the same androgynous way. As early as 1983, I began to notice problems with this view. Both boys and girls were struggling, and parents with them, in ways that could be addressed by (1) greater knowledge of who children actually are (through the use of the new brain sciences, attachment theory, and psychoanthropology) and (2) greater knowledge of differences between the male and female brain and psyche.

Nature-based theory was the term I developed for this alternative view, based in science. Because I am a philosopher, not a scientist, it was crucial for me to read and study many sources of information about neural science. This need led to a multicultural view of the new sciences. Because of my childhood experiences in Asia and adult experiences in Europe and the Middle East, this multicultural view was not a far stretch for me. I enjoy discovering sources of scientific material not only from the United States but also from all over the world. As you read this book, I hope you will find that I have developed a theory that does not reflect only one worldview, but also matches your own experiences as an individual in this culture and abroad. Although the term *nature-based theory* was coined in America and the first full-length book applying it to child development was *The Wonder of Boys* (as far as I know), it is not only an American theory. It has application worldwide. The material about brain and gender you will encounter in *The Minds of Boys* is universal. Whether the boy or girl is brought up in America, Italy, China, Zimbabwe—indeed, wherever the child is born or raised—he or she is born with a brain that tends toward male or female.

PART ONE

PROTECTING THE MINDS OF BOYS

I **THE CURRENT CRISIS**

1. Aaron Kipnis. *Angry Young Men*. San Francisco: Jossey-Bass, 1999.

Also see the following:

> Michelle Conlin. "The New Gender Gap." *Business Week Online*. www.business week.com., May 26, 2003.
>
> Steven E. Rhoads. *Taking Sex Differences Seriously*. San Francisco: Encounter Books, 2004.
>
> Rosemary C. Salomone. *Same, Different, Equal*. New Haven, Conn.: Yale University Press, 2003.
>
> Christina Hoff Sommers. *The War Against Boys*. New York: Touchstone, 2000.

According to researcher Judith Kleinfeld, "From grade school through college, females receive higher grades and obtain higher class ranks. They also receive more honors in every field except science and sports."

When specific schools, school districts, and states are looked at statistically, the gender gap in grades and ability testing clarifies even more specifically. Here are two examples from specific regions: the Michigan Gender Equity Team reports that in statewide 2001 testing of literacy (MEAP), girls received 67 percent of the highest scores (Level 1), whereas boys received 67 percent of the lowest scores (Level 4); *USA Today* (Dec. 22, 2003) reported on a Greensboro, N.C., school (High Point Central High School) in which "412 boys got unsatisfactory grades, compared to 303 girls."

It is also important now to note that when the U.S. Department of Education (DOE) released its Educational Equity Report in December of 2004, then Secretary of Education Rod Paige announced that girls have caught up in our schools and now, statistically, surpass boys. In his words, "The issue now is that boys seem to be falling behind." Among the findings in the report:

- Females are less likely to repeat a grade.
- Female high school students have higher educational aspirations than their male peers.

The DOE has been tracking boys' falling grades and test scores since the 1980s, but not until this Equity Report did the DOE ask the culture to consider spending as much energy on helping boys as girls. In January 2005, President George Bush and First Lady Laura Bush announced the Healthy Youth Initiative with a new emphasis on helping boys who are falling behind. Clearly no one—whether the DOE, the president, the first lady, or this book's authors—wants attention steered away from the needs of girls, but the new findings indicate the need for a reality check for all of us to think in terms of "educational equity." *Both* boys and girls must be cared for equally in our culture—and we must start doing it now.

2. Pedro A. Noguera. "The Trouble with Black Boys: The Role and Influence of Environmental Factors on the Academic Performance of African American Males" (pt. 3). *Motion,* May 13, 2002. Available at www.inmotionmagazine.com/er/pntroub3. html.

The American Association of School Administrators puts out a very fine magazine called *The School Administrator.* I particularly recommend its January 2005 issue, titled *Saving Black Boys.* You can learn more at www.aasa.org. Also see "Black Men Fall Behind," *USA Today,* Feb. 16, 2005.

3. Organisation for Economic Co-operation and Development. *The PISA Assessment Framework: Mathematics, Reading, Science and Problem Solving Knowledge and Skills.* Paris, France: Organisation for Economic Co-operation and Development, 2003. This study provides data on the situation boys face in all the industrialized countries. For more specific data on England, see www.statistics.gov.uk. For information about Australia, see Rollo Browne and Richard Fletcher (eds.). *Boys in Schools.* Lane Cove, Australia: Finch, 1995; and Steve Biddulph. *Raising Boys: Why Boys Are Different—and How to Help Them Become Happy and Well-Balanced Men.* Berkeley: Celestial Arts, 1996. For data on Canada, see www.statcan.ca. Bruce Ivany, assistant superintendent of the Abbotsford, British Columbia, school district, provided reporters with this summary of the issues his district faces: "Provincial test results and statistics over the past few years suggest girls do significantly better than boys in school, and are more likely to graduate." CBC News (*The Current,* Jan. 26, 2003) further reports, "In Quebec, three out of five boys still do not have a high school diploma."

4. School Achievement Indicator Program. *Education Indicators in Canada: Report of the Pan-Canadian Education Indicators Program* (catalogue no. 81-582-XIE). Ottawa, Ont.: Statistics Canada, 2003. Available at www.statcan.ca/cgi-bin/downpub/studiesfree.cgi.

5. Standing Committee on Education and Training. *Boys: Getting It Right.* Canberra: Commonwealth of Australia House of Representatives, 2002. Available at www.aph.gov.au/house/committee/edt/eofb/report/fullrpt.pdf.

6. Reported by Mike Baker, BBC education correspondent, Feb. 28, 2004. Available at news.bbc.co.uk.

7. Dan Kindlon and Michael Thompson. *Raising Cain.* New York: Ballantine, 2000, p. 23.

8. William Pollack. *Real Boys.* New York: Henry Holt, 1998, p. 1.

9. Sommers, *The War Against Boys,* 2000.

10. Quoted in Tamar Lewin. "Ideas & Trends: How Boys Lost Out to Girl Power." *New York Times,* Dec. 13, 1998, p. 3 (sec. 4).

11. Colleen T. O'Brien. *Indicators of Opportunity in Higher Education: Fall 2004 Status Report.* Washington, D.C.: Pell Institute for Study of Opportunities in Higher Education, 2004. Available at www.pellinstitute.org.

12. Center for Labor Market Studies. *The Growing Gender Gap in College Enrollment and Degree Attainment in the U.S. and Their Potential Economic and Social Consequences.* Boston: Northeastern University, May 2003.

13. Hugh Osborn and Margaret Gayle. "Let's Get Rid of Learning Factories: In the Age

of High Tech, a New Model Must Be Found for Schools." *Los Angeles Times,* May 27, 2004, p. B15.

14. Jay P. and Julia Gurian. *The Dependency Tendency: Returning to Each Other in Modern America.* Lanham, Md.: Rowman & Littlefield, 1983, p. 74.

The absence of fathers in some boys' lives during their schooling is a significant problem; related directly to it is the subgroup of boys (and girls) whose fathers and mothers are in prison. Teacher and public school administrator Cynthia Martone has written an important book on this topic: *Loving Through Bars: Children with Parents in Prison* (Santa Monica, Calif.: Santa Monica Press, 2005). There are 2.3 million children with a parent in prison. If you know a family struggling to educate boys (or girls) in this situation, Martone's book can be of great assistance.

2   HOW BOYS LEARN

1. Steven E. Rhoads. *Taking Sex Differences Seriously.* San Francisco: Encounter Books, 2004.

Reuwen Achiron, Shlomo Lipitz, and Anat Achiron. "Sex-Related Differences in the Development of the Human Fetal Corpus Callosum: In Utero Ultrasonographic Study." *Prenatal Diagnosis,* 2001, pp. 116–120.

Maria Elena Cordero, Carlos Valenzuela, Rafael Torres, and Angel Rodriguez. "Sexual Dimorphism in Number and Proportion of Neurons in the Human Median Raphe Nucleus." *Developmental Brain Research,* 2000, *124,* 43–52.

Jeb Schenck, Ph.D., who teaches both at high school and as an adjunct professor at the University of Wyoming, provided me with results from his fascinating new study (unpublished as of Dec. 2004) on boy-girl differences in memory and retention, titled "Properties of Long-Term Memory in Youth":
"A series of long-term memory studies were conducted with over 400 school aged children. Females generally out performed males in tasks ranging from simple recall of household items through progressively more complex recall tasks. Females clearly outperformed males, however there were always some males who outperformed some females. At best, there were only a few tasks where no memory differences between genders were observed, and males, as a group, never outperformed females in any recall tasks. The trend of female's greater recall appears to hold over the lifespan. In one of the sub-studies, 965 subjects were given a simple recall task for common objects; females always edged males across the life-span from age seven to eighty five."

2. Kitty Harmon (ed.). *Up to No Good: The Rascally Things Boys Do.* San Francisco: Chronicle Books, 2000, p. 70.

3. Mark Strand. "Keeping Things Whole." *Treasury of American Poetry.* New York: Doubleday, 1978.

4. Quoted in Amanda Onion. "Sex in the Brain: Research Showing Men and Women Differ in More Than One Area." *ABC News,* Sept. 21, 2004.

A fascinating new development has emerged in the study of brain differences, one that will lead to deeper research. British scientists believe they have discovered a third area of the brain involved in language. They base this belief on innovative use of a process called "diffusion tensor magnetic resonance imaging," a very powerful type of MRI. They have called this third area Geschwind's territory. You can learn more in the *Annals of Neurology* online, under January 2005, at www3.inter science.wiley.com/cgi-bin/fulltext/109857315/HTMLSTART.

If this third area turns out to join Broca's and Wernicke's areas as language centers, then the next step will be to determine if this third area, like the first two, shows innate male-female differences.

5. Daniel Amen. Personal interview with Michael Gurian, July 2004.

6. Robert P. Iacono. "The Nervous System: The Blood-Brain Barrier." Available at www.pallidotomy.com/index.html.

7. Michael W. Smith and Jeffrey D. Wilhelm. *Reading Don't Fix No Chevy's*. Portsmouth, N.H.: Heinemann, 2002.

8. Rita Carter. *Mapping the Mind*. Berkeley: University of California Press, 1998.

9. Deborah Blum. *Sex on the Brain*. New York: Penguin Books, 1998.

10. Simon Baron-Cohen. *The Essential Difference*. New York: Basic Books, 2003.

11. Marian Diamond. *Male and Female Brains*. Lecture at the annual meeting of the Women's Forum West, San Francisco, 2003. Available at http://new horizons.org/neuro/diamond_male_female.htm.

    V. S. Caviness and others. "The Human Brain Age 7–11 Years: A Volumetric Analysis Based on Magnetic Resonance Differences." *Cerebral Cortex*, 1996, *6*, 726–736.

12. Anne Moir and David Jessel. *Brain Sex*. New York: Dell, 1989.

13. Steven E. Rhoads. *Taking Sex Differences Seriously*. San Francisco: Encounter Books, 2004.

14. Hara Estroff Marano. "The Opposite Sex: The New Sex Scorecard." *Psychology Today*, July/Aug. 2003, pp. 38–44.

15. Holly VanScoy. "Hot Headed Guys? It's All in the Brain." *HealthScoutNews*, Oct. 11, 2002. Available at http://kprc-tvhealth.ip2m.com/index.cfm.

16. Ruben Gur. *Weekend House Call* (CNN Saturday Morning News), Dec. 6, 2003. Transcripts available at www.fdch.com. Dr. Gur has pioneered research into male-female difference in white and gray matter (with males having more white matter and females more gray). His work has been corroborated by researcher Richard Haier of the University of California-Irvine and Rex Jung at the University of New Mexico. These new results are available through the online journal *NeuroImage* (February 2005).

17. Phoebe Dewing, Tao Shi, Steve Horvath, and Eric Vilain. "Sexually Dimorphic Gene Expression in Mouse Brain Precedes Gonadal Differentiation." *Molecular Brain Research*, 2003, *118*(1-2), 82–90.

    Allan N. Schore. "Effects of a Secure Attachment Relationship on Right Brain Development, Affect Regulation, and Infant Mental Health." *Infant Mental Health*, 2001, *22*(1-2), 7–66.

18. Rhoads, *Taking Sex Differences Seriously*, 2004.

    One can study boy-girl brain difference in a number of ways. Although perhaps the most dramatic (and graphic) method is the male-female brain scan (which reveals obvious and graphic differences in the structure and function of male and female brains), another is *sequential brain development research*. Whereas brain scan research looks at the "what" of brain difference, sequential analysis looks at the "when." In this chapter, we noted a "when" difference in frontal lobe development, favoring girls chronologically. Another "when" difference is girls' earlier development in the superior temporal cortex. In boys, the sensorimotor cortex and occipital lobe, which are involved in visual-spatial-mechanical functioning, develop earlier.

Another approach to understanding male-female brain difference is a *cell systems approach*. This approach analyzes what are referred to as "M" systems (magnocellular ganglion cells) and "P" systems (parvocellular ganglion cells). Our cells are a "why" in a lot of what we do and who we are (providing glimpses into our actual DNA). Not surprisingly, when studying males and females, researchers find cellular differences between the sexes: more P system cells in males and more M system cells in females. P system cells, when applied to functioning of the visual cortex, lead to greater interest in physical movement (objects moving through space); M system cells lead to greater interest in color and texture. Thus our anecdotal observation of boys' eyes shifting quickly to follow moving objects is borne out by cellular research.

You can learn more about these cellular differences in *Why Gender Matters* (New York: Doubleday, 2005), by Leonard Sax. Leonard Sax is a newcomer to popular publication of brain research. He provides, for me, an interesting quandary. He has been openly critical of my work. In the fields of scientific research, philosophy, and education, one does once in a while come across the work of a trained scientist who openly dislikes nonscientists' involvement in scientific knowledge, especially when a nonscientist comes to a scientific conclusion before the scientist does. Dr. Sax is a critic of my work—and the work of others whom he does not consider scientists. He is unable to object to my basic conclusions, given that he agrees with the conclusion I came to in *The Wonder of Boys* ten years ago: that male-female brain difference is a proven scientific phenomenon and that understanding of this difference is helpful to everyone who cares for children. However, his critique of "nonscientists" does raise the interesting issue of whether an "ordinary citizen," like myself and like you, can and ought to utilize science in everyday life. In correspondence with me, Dr. Sax argued that I ought not involve myself in the brain sciences, for I am not a trained physician or neural scientist. My professional occupations of therapist, educator, philosopher, and parent made me, in his words, "a storyteller, not a scientist."

Whether you are a parent, teacher, therapist, or other concerned citizen, you will have to make your own decision about how you utilize the new sciences in your everyday life. In twenty years of study and application, I have found that these sciences can and must be used by all of us. Care must be taken—as has been taken in the book you're reading—to remain true to the sciences themselves, admitting in science as in all fields the chance of human error, but it would be a mistake to think that only a few scientists can understand what the world is made of, how human nature functions, and how we can use knowledge practically to care for our children.

I think of Albert Einstein's comment that science must not be left to the scientists. Einstein clearly did not say this in order to alienate or to be condescending to others in his profession. He meant to say that science exists for all humankind. Everyone must integrate the sciences into his or her life. As science-based social philosophers, Kathy and I urge you to do the brain research yourself—using books like ours and the others featured in our Bibliography and in these Notes. We also hope you'll use the Internet and other media.

As you bring a research base to your care of children, Kathy and I urge you to "sign on" for the long haul—that is, go beyond sound bites and stereotypes, and beyond the opinions, interpretations, and debate positions of any one scientist or philosopher.

In the end, when you plumb the depth of knowledge that our brain scientists are now giving us, you will find yourself in a truly magical, and immensely practical, new world—one that we all can share together.

One last note on the use of brain sciences: for yet another fascinating approach to brain difference, the many books and articles by Barbara Fausto-Sterling are an important alternative view. Dr. Fausto-Sterling agrees that there are distinct male-female differences, but she makes a very interesting argument for future dialogue about more than just the two genders—she posits the possibility that in the future we will need to speak of five or more genders.

In November 2004, at the Harvard/Yale Learning and the Brain conference in Boston, I asked professors of education to inform me on schools of education or education classes that were integrating male-female brain difference into their college and graduate school curricula. This led to a wonderful discussion with a number of professors who were doing so already or were beginning to. Although this is just a one-day sampling, in conversation, I did want to call attention to these pioneers, who are listed here. Kathy and I hope that anyone reading this book who is aware of this kind of integration into teacher training at the academic level will email us at www.gurianinstitute.com. As we gather more names, classes, and universities, we will post them on the site.

Linda Karges-Bone, Ph.D., Charleston Southern University

Jeb Schenck, Ph.D., University of Wyoming

Tracey Shors, Ph.D., Rutgers University

Karen Walker, Ph.D., University of Maine-Farmington

Liz Knowles, Ed.D., Florida Atlantic University

Douglas MacIsaac, Ph.D., Stetson University

PART TWO

STARTING BOYS OUT IN
BOY-FRIENDLY LEARNING ENVIRONMENTS

3 HELPING BOYS LEARN BEFORE THEY BEGIN SCHOOL

1. Eleanor Reynolds. *Bonding: A Family Affair.* Monterey, Calif.: Excelligence Learning Corporation, 2002.

Paula Wiggins. "Infant Brain Development: Making the Research Work for Early Childhood Programs." *Texas Child Care,* Spring 2000, pp. 2–8.

Phyllis Porter. "Early Brain Development: What Parents and Caregivers Need to Know!" *Educarer,* Dec. 2003. Available at www.educarer.com/brain.htm.

2. Everett Waters, Kiyomi Kondo-Ikemura, German Posada, and John E. Richters. "Learning to Love: Mechanisms and Milestones." In M. Gunner and Alan Sroufe

(eds.), *Minnesota Symposium on Child Psychology,* Vol. 23: *Self Processes and Development.* Hillsdale, N.J.: Erlbaum, 1991. (This paper is available online at www.johnbowlby. com.)

Robert Karen. *Becoming Attached: First Relationships and How They Shape Our Capacity to Love.* New York: Oxford University Press, 1994.

3. Allan N. Schore. *Affect Regulation and the Origin of the Self: The Neurobiology of Emotional Development.* Hillsdale, N.J.: Erlbaum, 1994.

4. Robin Carr-Morse and Meredith S. Wiley. *Ghosts from the Nursery.* New York: Atlantic Monthly Press, 1998.

5. Cited in Deborah Blum. *Sex on the Brain.* New York: Penguin Books, 1998.

6. Pat Crum, director and trainer-consultant at the Family Nurturing Center of Michigan, can be reached at pat.crum@spectrum-health.org.

7. Megan R. Gunnar. *Quality of Care and the Buffering of Stress Physiology: Its Potential in Protecting the Developing Human Brain.* Minneapolis: University of Minnesota Institute of Child Development, 1996.

8. Rita Carter. *Mapping the Mind.* Berkeley: University of California Press, 1998.

9. National Assessment of Educational Progress, U.S. Department of Education. Available at http://nces.ed.gov/nationsreportcard.

10. Dale Purves and others (eds.). *Neuroscience.* Sunderland, Md.: Sinauer Associates, 2001.

Parents as Teachers is very important international organization that supports parents and educates them on how to be the best teachers of their children. Check out this organization at www.patnc.org.

A very fine resource for helping younger kids learn is the Knowledge Essentials series, published by Wiley. This series has been created by Amy James to help parents understand school curricula at all grade levels. In *First Grade Success,* for instance, James provides easy activities parents can use to supplement their child's education.

4 EFFECTIVE PRESCHOOL AND EARLY LEARNING ENVIRONMENTS FOR BOYS

1. Steven E. Rhoads. *Taking Sex Differences Seriously.* San Francisco: Encounter Books, 2004.

2. Ruben Gur and others. "Sex Differences in Brain Gray and White Matter in Healthy Young Adults." *Journal of Neuroscience,* 1999, 19(10), 4065–4072.

3. Mark Jude Tramo, director, Harvard University Institute for Music and Brain Science.

4. Randy White and Vicki Stoecklin. *Children's Outdoor Play and Learning Environments: Returning to Nature.* Kansas City: White Hutchinson Leisure and Learning Group, 2004.

Over the last year, three different teachers have emailed us about the effectiveness of a program that helps kids increase their visual and mechanical learning. It is called "kidspiration," and you can learn more at www.inspiration.com.

5 **REMOVING KEY ENVIRONMENTAL STRESSORS FROM BOYS' LIVES**

1. Anita Woolfolk. *Educational Psychology.* (9th ed.) Needham Heights, Mass.: Allyn & Bacon, 2004.

   Robert E. Slavin. *Educational Psychology: Theory and Practice.* (6th ed.) Needham Heights, Mass.: Allyn & Bacon, 2001.

2. Daniel Amen. *Change Your Brain, Change Your Life.* New York: Three Rivers Press, 1999.

3. Dimitri A. Christakis. "Early Television Exposure and Subsequent Attention Problems in Children." *Pediatrics,* 2004, *113*(4), 708–713.

4. Barbara Brock. *No TV, No Big Deal.* Cheney: Eastern Washington University Press, 2005.

5. Jane M. Healy. "Understanding TV's Effects on the Developing Brain." *AAP News,* May 1998. Available at www.aap.org/advocacy/chm98nws.htm.

6. Jennifer L. St. Sauver. "Study Confirms ADHD Is More Common in Boys." *Mayo Clinic Proceedings,* Sept. 2004, *79*, 1124–1131.

7. Jane M. Healy. *Failure to Connect: How Computers Affect Our Children's Minds—for Better and Worse.* New York: Simon & Schuster, 1998.

8. Cited in Brock, *No TV, No Big Deal,* 2005.

9. Barbara J. Brock. "TV Free Families: Are They Lola Granolas, Normal Joes or High and Holy Snots?" National survey conducted Feb./Mar. 2000. Cheney: Eastern Washington University.

10. Barbara A. Dennison, Theresa J. Russo, Patrick A. Burdick, and Paul L. Jenkins. "An Intervention to Reduce Television Viewing by Preschool Children." *Archives of Pediatrics and Adolescent Medicine,* 2004, *158*(2), 170–176.

11. National Center for Health Statistics. "Fact Sheet." www.cdc.gov/nchs/pressroom/04facts/obesity.htm. Oct. 6, 2004.

12. Eric Jensen. "Water and Learning: Optimal Hydration." Science-Class.Net. Available at http://science-class.net/water_learning.htm.

13. Robert Arnot. *The Biology of Success.* New York: Little, Brown, 2001.

14. Judith Wurtman. *Managing Your Mind and Mood Through Food.* New York: HarperCollins, 1986.

15. Alok Jha. "Why Do the Japanese Live So Long?" *Guardian.* www.guardian.co.uk. June 10, 2004.

16. Eric Schlosser. *Fast Food Nation: The Dark Side of the All-American Meal.* Boston: Houghton Mifflin, 2001.

If you want to see more research linking food and drink to both brain issues and children's weight issues, you can check out www.pediatrics.org and www.cdc.gov. New studies done by Jean Welsh and her colleagues at the Centers for Disease Control and Prevention have shown that even fruit juices can be detrimental, because of their high sugar content. The American Academy of Pediatrics recommends limiting preschoolers' intake, for instance, to about four ounces of juice per day.

In this chapter we haven't discussed secondhand smoke, but it is becoming a very important learning issue. According to a study published in the January 2005 issue of *Environmental Health Perspectives,* children exposed to secondhand smoke have lower test scores in reading, math, and problem solving. Michael Shannon, chairman of the American Academy of Pediatrics's Committee on Environmental Health, reported that this study confirms earlier findings that tobacco exposure hurts children's intellectual development. According to Kimberly Yolton, the study's author and researcher at Cincinnati's Children's Medical Center, about 33 million children are at risk for reading problems caused by "environmental tobacco." Shannon states that tobacco is about as harmful to children's brains as lead, and fetuses exposed to tobacco in the womb are more likely to be born small or suffer other problems. Reported in *Spokesman Review* (from *USA Today*), Jan. 4, 2005, p. A4.

PART THREE
TEACHING SCHOOL CURRICULA IN BOY-FRIENDLY WAYS

6 **HELPING BOYS LEARN READING, WRITING, AND LANGUAGE ARTS**

1. Richard Schmitz. "The Adult Brain: Understanding Male and Female Differences." *Family Therapy Magazine,* 2004, *3*(4), 18–22.

2. Cited in Christina Hoff Sommers. *The War Against Boys.* New York: Touchstone, 2000.

3. Alfie Kohn. *Punished by Rewards.* Boston: Houghton Mifflin, 1993.

4. Yim-Chi Ho, Mei-Chun Cheung, and Agnes S. Chan. "Music Training Improves Verbal but Not Visual Memory: Cross-Sectional and Longitudinal Exploration in Children." *Neuropsychology,* 2003, *17*(3), 439–450.

5. For a detailed and very exciting analysis by Diane Ravitch of this whole issue, see Diane Ravitch. *The Language Police.* New York: Knopf, 2003.

6. Michael W. Smith and Jeffrey D. Wilhelm. *"Reading Don't Fix No Chevy's": Literacy in the Lives of Young Men.* Portsmouth, N.H.: Heinemann, 2002.

7. Anne Moir and David Jessel. *Brain Sex.* New York: Dell, 1989.

8. Elizabeth Sowell and others. "Mapping Cortical Change Across the Human Life Span." *Nature Neuroscience,* 2003, *6*(3), 309–315.

   Elizabeth Sowell and others. "Development of Cortical and Subcortical Brain Structures in Childhood and Adolescence: A Structural Magnetic Resonance Imaging Study." *Developmental Medicine and Child Neurology,* 2002, *44,* 4–16.

9. Schmitz, "The Adult Brain," 2004.

10. Hara Estroff Marano. "The Opposite Sex: The New Sex Scorecard." *Psychology Today,* July/Aug. 2003, pp. 38–44.

11. Marano, "The Opposite Sex," 2003.

The Boy Scouts of America have created a number of ways to enhance the school experience of millions of children—both boys and girls—especially in the area of reading development. For many children, the scouts can become a member organization in a parent-led team. Scott Daniels, executive editor of *Scouting* at the Boy

Scouts headquarters in Irving, Texas, recommends these Web sites: www.learning forlife.org and www.scouting.org/nav/enter.jsp?s=,c&c=rr. You can also contact the Boy Scouts of America (BSA) through their Web site, www.scouting.org.

Boy's Life, the magazine published by BSA, is itself a very helpful reading tool for boys. Boys like to read it! And further, Reading Partners, the Buddy Tutoring Program, has arisen from it. You can find a fact sheet on this program on the BSA Web site.

The entire fall 2004 issue of *American Educator* magazine is devoted to the subject of development of reading skills. This issue, titled "Preventing Early Reading Failure—and Its Devastating Downward Spiral," contains very important articles and resources, including helpful Web sites like www.coreknowledge.org, for anyone working in this field.

Bonnie Varner, of Spokane, Washington, told us of a cutting-edge program that has been used successfully in a number of places, including the Kalispell Indian Reservation, to help with low-performing readers. It is called Readright and can be accessed at www.readright.com.

A really great addition to any coffee table or son's desk is a Hidden Message Word Find type of book, each page of which has a box containing about a hundred letters that hide words. Boys can enjoy finding the hidden words, and the word search books advance in difficulty along with children's chronological growth.

Monica Gutierrez of St. Regis School of the Sacred Heart, a Gurian Institute model school, emailed us two Web sites that you can go to right away for practical, in-class fun. With the help of www.bsd.sk.ca, her eighth graders developed a successful "Wall of Superheroes" project. Monica discusses this site with her students before they begin their writing. She teaches boys-only classes, and they generate powerful work from this. The Web site at www.privatehand.com provided Monica and her students "The Element Song." She uses this site for help in teaching science (the subject of our next chapter).

7 HELPING BOYS LEARN MATH AND SCIENCE

1. Infoplease. www.infoplease.com/ipa/A0883611.html.

2. Nanette Asimov. "Girls Now Outnumber Boys in Math, Science Classes." *San Francisco Chronicle,* Feb. 28, 2001, p. A4.

3. National Center for Education Statistics, U.S. Department of Education, 2000. http://nces.ed.gov/nationsreportcard/

4. Leah Ariniello. "Music Training and the Brain." Society for Neuroscience. May 2000. Available at www.sfn.org/content/Publications/BrainBriefings/music_training_and_brain.htm.

    Daniel G. Amen. "Music and the Brain." Brainplace. www.brainplace.com/bp/music/default.asp.

5. Zenalda Serrano. "Families Need Quality Play Time." *Spokesman Review,* Sept. 13, 2004, p. B3.

6. U.S. Department of Education. "Fitton Center's SPECTRA+ Program, Hamilton, Ohio." *Education Innovator,* 2004, 2(26), 1.

7. Michael Nagel. "Connecting Teachers, Boys and Learning." *Australian Journal of Middle Schooling,* Oct. 2003. Nagel is an instructor at the Centre for Innovation in Education at

Queensland University of Technology. He can be reached via email at mc.nagel@qut.edu.au. Michael is in the process of setting up a Gurian Institute-Australia.

For a further resource on improving math and science classes, see the Feb. 2004 issue of *Educational Leadership* magazine, titled "Improving Achievement in Math and Science." This issue contains several very helpful perspectives and tools. For teachers, a powerful toolbox article is "Improving Mathematics Teaching," by James W. Stigler and James Hiebert.

8 USING SINGLE-GENDER CLASSROOMS EFFECTIVELY

1. Applied Research Center. "Historical Timeline of Public Education in the US." www.arc.org/erase/timeline.html.

2. Supreme Court of the United States. *Brown* v. *Board of Education,* 347 U.S. 483 (1954) (ESSC+). www.nationalcenter.org/brown.html.

3. Title IX of the Education Amendments of 1972. www.usdoj.gov/crt/cor/coord/titleixstat.htm.

4. American Association of Medical Colleges. "Facts: Applicants, Matriculants and Graduates, 1992–2003." www.aamc.org/data/facts/2003/2003summary.htm.

   Minority Corporate Counsel Association. "Law School Enrollment and Employment for Women and People of Color." www.mcca.com/site/data/corporate/BP/Watch/nalp899.htm.

5. Quoted in Carol Brydolf. "Where the Boys Are: Are We Leaving Boys Behind in the Name of Gender Equity?" West Sacramento, Calif.: California School Boards Association, 2004. Available at www.csba.org/csmag/Spring04/csMagStoryTemplate.cfm?id=34.

6. National Association for Single Sex Public Education. www.singlesexschools.org.

7. Leonard Sax. "Single-Sex Education: Ready for Prime-Time?" *The World & I Online,* 2001. Article available at www.singlesexschools.org/worldandi.html.

8. Keith Ervin. "Change Is a Constant as School Moves Forward." *Seattle Times,* Dec. 17, 2001.

9. Graham Able, master of Dulwich College, London. Paper published Aug. 2000. To request a copy, send an email to Michael Gurian or Kathy Stevens by visiting www.gurianinstitute.com.

10. Quoted in Andrew West. "The Boys Who Would Be Gentlemen." *The Sydney Morning Herald,* July 6, 2003. Available at www.smh.com.au/articles/2003/07/05/1057179204769.html.

11. Carol L. Martin, Diane N. Ruble, and Joel Szkrybalo. "Cognitive Theories of Early Gender Development." *Psychological Bulletin,* 2002, *128*(6), 903–933.

12. Quoted in Julie Henry. "Single-Sex Classes Get Boys Back to Work." *News Telegraph,* Mar. 30, 2003. Available at www.telegraph.co.uk/news/main.jhtml?xml=/news/2003/03/30/ncoed30.xml.

13. National Association for Single-Sex Public Education. "Single-Sex vs. Coed: The Evidence." Available at www.singlesexschools.org/evidence.html.

14. Susan Droke, Presbyterian Day School, Memphis. Personal communication, Sept. 22, 2004.

A very wise resource on the use of male-female brain difference material with youth sex education is Kathy Flores Bell, of Youth Sexuality Programs, Carondelet Health Network. Contact her at kbell@carondelet.org.

PART FOUR
HELPING BOYS WHO NEED EXTRA HELP

9   A NEW VISION OF LEARNING DISABILITIES, ADD/ADHD, AND BEHAVIORAL DISORDERS

1. National Center for Health Statistics. News release, Mar. 31, 2004.

2. Linda A. Johnson. "Behavior Drug Spending Up: More Kids Taking Pills for ADHD." *Associated Press,* May 17, 2004.

3. Howard Schubiner, Arthur L. Robin, and Joel Young. "Attention Deficit/Hyperactivity Disorder in Adolescent Males." *Adolescent Medicine,* 2003, *14*(3), 663–675.

4. David B. Stein. *Ritalin Is Not the Answer.* San Francisco: Jossey-Bass, 1999.

5. Stephen Hinshaw and others. "National Institute of Mental Health Multimodal Treatment Study of ADHD Follow-Up: Changes in Effectiveness and Growth After the End of Treatment." *Pediatrics,* 2004, *113*(4), 762–769.

   Also see "Genius at Risk? Experts Debate Ritalin's Effects on Creativity," *The Wall Street Journal,* Feb. 4, 2005.

   A new study from Harvard University's Behavioral Genetics Laboratory at McLean Hospital has raised another possible red flag on Ritalin use. While noting that Ritalin is a very useful and important drug for many individuals, researchers William Carlezon and Peter Jensen have shown that rats given Ritalin in preadolescence are more likely to show signs of depression in adulthood. This research was presented at the 2004 annual meeting of the American College of Neuropsychopharmacology.

6. Cited in Deborah Blum. *Sex on the Brain.* New York: Penguin Books, 1998.

7. Cited in Michael D'Antonio. "The Fragile Sex." *Los Angeles Times Magazine,* Dec. 4, 1994, p. 16.

8. Jay Belsky. "Quantity Counts." *Developmental and Behavioral Pediatrics,* June 2002, pp. 167–170.

   Also see Diane Connell and Betsy Gunzelmann. "The New Gender Gap." *Scholastic Instructor,* 2003. Please also see the many book and article sources listed in the notes for Chapter One, such as *The War Against Boys* and *Taking Sex Differences Seriously.*

9. Bryan Sykes. *Adam's Curse: A Future Without Men.* London: Norton, 2004, pp. 286–287.

10. Barbara L. Wenger, H. Stephen Kaye, and Mitchell P. LaPlante. *Disabilities Among Children* (Disability Statistical Abstract Number 15). University of California, San Francisco: Disability Statistics Rehabilitation Research and Training Center, 1995.

11. Warren Farrell. *Why Men Are the Way They Are.* New York: Berkley, 1990.

12. Doug Cowan. "The ADHD Information Library: The ADHD Diet for Your Attention Deficit Disorder." www.newideas.net/adddiet.htm. 2004.

13. "Unlocking the Secrets of the Brain." *Anderson Cooper 360°* (CNN), May 20, 2004.

There are a number of interesting, controversial, and contradictory articles in the field that can help you make your assessment of how to handle a child's diagnosis of ADD, ADHD, or other learning or brain disorder. Here is a brief list of some we feel hit very important hot spots in the debate.

S. J. Altshuler and S. L. Kopels. "Advocating in Schools for Children with Disabilities: What's the New I.D.E.A.?" *Social Work,* 2003, *48*(3), 320–329.

Jay Giedd. "Neuroimaging of Pediatric Neuropsychiatric Disorders: Is a Picture Really Worth a Thousand Words?" *Archives of General Psychiatry,* 2001, *58*(5), 443–444.

F. X. Castellanos and others. "Developmental Trajectories of Brain Volume Abnormalities in Children and Adolescents with Attention-Deficit/Hyperactivity Disorder." *Journal of the American Medical Association,* 2002, *288*(14), 1740–1748.

Shankar Vedantam. "FDA Links Anti-Depressants, Youth Suicide Risk." *Washington Post,* Feb. 11, 2004.

S. Gunawardene. "Does Stimulant Therapy of Attention-Deficit/Hyperactivity Disorder Beget Later Substance Abuse?" *Pediatrics,* 2003, *111,* 179–185.

An inspiring and very usable book for any parent or teacher of a child with special needs is *A Mind at a Time,* by Mel Levine (New York: Simon & Schuster, 2002).

The Amen Clinics have developed a DVD called *Which Brain Do You Want?* that shows students graphically what happens to their brains when they engage in abuse of alcohol or other substances and other high-risk behavior. This DVD shows kids actual SPECT scans of brains that have not abused substances and those that have. It is powerful. Learn more at www.mindworkspress.com.

A fascinating article on the effects of stress on male and female brains is "Opposite Effects of Stressful Experience on Memory Formation in Males Versus Females," by Tracey J. Shors, of the Department of Psychology at Rutgers. Dr. Shors can be contacted at shors@rci.rutgers.edu.

10   CONFRONTING UNDERMOTIVATION AND UNDERPERFORMANCE IN BOYS' LEARNING

1. This description of the workings of the brain during motivation is a composite of textbook neuroscience information. See Mark F. Bear, Barry W. Connors, and Michael A Paradiso. *Neuroscience: Exploring the Brain.* Baltimore: Williams & Wilkins, 1996.

Information about the influence of the dorsal striatum was provided by PET scans done at the University of Zurich. Ernst Fehr, director of the University of Zurich's economic research institute, used brain technology to study human motivation. The findings of this research were reported in the August 2004 issue of *Science* magazine.

2. Ruben Gur. *Weekend House Call* (CNN Saturday Morning News), Dec. 6, 2003. Transcripts available at www.fdch.com.

3. Bernet M. Elzinga and others. "Higher Cortisol Levels Following Exposure to Trau-

matic Reminders in Abuse-Related PTSD." New Haven, Conn.: Yale Psychiatric Research, Yale University School of Medicine, 2003. Available at www.acnp.org/cita tions/Npp051602190/default.pdf.

4. Richard F. Catalano and others. "The Importance of Bonding to School for Healthy Development: Findings from the Social Development Research Group." *Journal of School Health,* 2004, 74(7), 252–261.

5. Paul D. Slocumb and Ruby K. Payne. *Hear Our Cry: Boys in Crisis.* Highlands, Tex.: aha! Process, 2004.

6. Ruby K. Payne. *A Framework for Understanding Poverty.* (3rd rev. ed.) Highland, Tex.: aha! Process, 2003.

7. Betty Hart and Todd R. Risley. *Meaningful Differences in the Everday Experiences of Young American Children.* Baltimore, Md.: Brookes Publishing Co., 1995.

8. Cliff Hocker. "More Brothers in Prison Than in College?" www.globalblacknews. com/Jail.html. Oct. 11, 2002.

9. Alan Bowd. "Identification and Assessment of Gifted and Talented Youth, Particularly in Northern, Rural and Isolated Communities." Thunder Bay, Ont.: Centre of Excellence for Children and Adolescents with Special Needs, 2003.

11 WHAT PARENTS AND TEACHERS CAN DO TO MOTIVATE BOYS TO LEARN

1. Nan Henderson, Bonnie Benard, and Nancy Sharp-Light (eds.). *Mentoring for Resiliency: Setting Up Programs for Moving Youth from "Stressed to Success."* Berkeley: University of California Press, 2000.

2. Christina Hoff Sommers. *The War Against Boys.* New York: Touchstone, 2000.

3. National Center for Education Statistics. "Issue Brief: 1.1 Million Homeschooled Students in the United States in 2003." http://nces.ed.gov/pubs2004/2004115.pdf. July 2004.

4. DriveHomeSafe, Salem, Oregon. (Tel: 503-269-7934; email: support@drivehome safe.com.)

5. Mindy Cameron. "Building on the Past: An Historic School in Spokane Emphasizes Leadership and Advocacy." *Northwest Education,* 2004, 10(1). Available at http://www.nwrel.org/nwedu/10-01/build.

6. David Blankenhorn. *Fatherless America: Confronting Our Most Urgent Social Problem.* New York: HarperPerennial, 1996.

Hampton Elementary School teacher Joan McFarlane, from Hampton, New Brunswick, Canada wrote me about her application of the book *Boys and Girls Learn Differently!* and an exciting male mentoring program in her school based on the idea that boys and girls need gender-specific mentoring. In this program men from the community read to boys to help improve their love of reading and their motivation. (You can contact Joan via email at mcfarjo@nbed.nb.ca.)

Stan Crow, of ICA Journeys, has been at the vanguard of rites of passage programs and research for about twenty years. Visit www.icajourneys.org for the most current rites of passage programs. (You can contact Stan via email at icarlc@igc.org.)

I 2   HELPING SENSITIVE BOYS IN OUR SCHOOLS

1. Simon Baron-Cohen's most detailed analysis of the male-female brain continuum can be found in Simon Baron-Cohen. *The Essential Difference.* New York: Basic Books, 2003.

2. Virginia de Leon. "Group Offers Gay Youth Chance to Find Acceptance." *Spokesman Review,* July 12, 2004. Available at http://209.157.64.200/focus/f-news/1170169/posts.

   For research on the debate regarding the biology of homosexuality, see the January 1994 issue of the *Harvard Medical Letter.*

3. Rita Carter. *Mapping the Mind.* Berkeley: University of California Press, 1998.

4. Victor Frankl. *Man's Search for Meaning.* New York: Pocket, 1997, p. 104.

   Also see Stephen R. Wester, David L. Vogel, and James Archer Jr. "Male Restricted Emotionality and Counseling Supervision." *Journal of Counseling and Development,* Winter 2004, *82,* 91–98.

BIBLIOGRAPHY

Amen, Daniel. (1999). *Change Your Brain, Change Your Life.* New York: Three Rivers Press.

Amen, Daniel. (2001). *Healing ADD.* New York: Putnam.

Amen, Daniel. (2002). *Healing the Hardware of Your Soul.* New York: Free Press.

Annis, Barbara. (2003). *Same Words, Different Language.* London: Piatkus Books.

Arnot, Robert. (2001). *The Biology of Success.* New York: Little, Brown.

Baron-Cohen, Simon. (2003). *The Essential Difference: The Truth About the Male and Female Brain.* New York: Basic Books.

Bear, Mark F., Barry W. Connors, and Michael A. Paradiso. (1996). *Neuroscience: Exploring the Brain.* Baltimore: Williams & Wilkins.

Biddulph, Steve. (1977). *Raising Boys.* Berkeley: Celestial Books.

Blum, Deborah. (1998). *Sex on the Brain: The Biological Differences Between Men and Women.* New York: Penguin Books.

Borba, Michele. (2001). *Building Moral Intelligence.* San Francisco: Jossey-Bass.

Borba, Michele. (2005). *Nobody Likes Me, Everybody Hates Me.* San Francisco: Jossey-Bass.

Browne, Rollo, and Richard Fletcher. *Boys in Schools.* Sydney: Finch.

Carr-Morse, Robin, and Meredith S. Wiley. (1998). *Ghosts from the Nursery: Tracing the Roots of Violence.* New York: Atlantic Monthly Press.

Carter, Rita. (1998). *Mapping the Mind.* Berkeley: University of California Press.

Deak, JoAnn. (2002). *Girls Will Be Girls.* New York: Hyperion.

Dobson, James. (2001). *Bringing Up Boys.* Wheaton, Ill.: Tyndale House.

Evans, Robert. (1996). *The Human Side of School Change: Reform, Resistance, and the Real-Life Problems of Innovation.* San Francisco: Jossey-Bass.

Farrell, Warren. (1993). *The Myth of Male Power.* New York Simon & Schuster.

Flinders, Carol. (2002). *The Values of Belonging.* San Francisco: HarperSanFrancisco.

Fogarty, Robin. (1997). *Brain Compatible Classrooms.* Arlington Heights, Ill.: Skylight Professional Development.

Garbarino, James. (1999). *Lost Boys.* New York: Free Press.

Gilmore, David. (1990). *Manhood in the Making.* New Haven, Conn.: Yale University Press.

Goleman, Daniel. (1995). *Emotional Intelligence.* New York: Bantam Books.

Gurian, Jay P., and Julia Gurian. (1983). *The Dependency Tendency: Returning to Each Other in Modern America.* Lanham, Md.: Rowman & Littlefield.

Gurian, Michael. (1996). *The Wonder of Boys: What Parents, Mentors and Educators Can Do to Shape Boys into Exceptional Men.* Los Angeles: Tarcher.

Gurian, Michael. (1998). *A Fine Young Man.* Los Angeles: Tarcher.

Gurian, Michael. (1999a). *Plugged In: From Boys to Men—All About Adolescence and You.* Los Angeles: Price Stern Sloan.

Gurian, Michael. (1999b). *Plugged In: Understanding Guys—A Guide for Teenage Girls.* Los Angeles: Price Stern Sloan.

Gurian, Michael. (2001). *Boys and Girls Learn Differently! A Guide for Teachers and Parents.* San Francisco: Jossey-Bass.

Gurian, Michael. (2002). *The Wonder of Girls: Understanding the Hidden Nature of Our Daughters.* New York: Pocket Books.

Hallowell, Edward, and John Ratey. (1994). *Driven to Distraction.* New York: Touchstone.

Harris, Judith R. (1998). *The Nurture Assumption.* New York: Free Press.

Hirsh-Pasek, Kathy, and others. (2003). *Einstein Never Used Flashcards.* London: Rodale.

Jensen, Eric. (2000). *Brain-Based Learning: The New Science of Teaching and Learning.* (Rev. ed.) San Diego, Calif.: Brain Store.

Johnson, Steven. (2004). *Mind Wide Open.* New York: Scribner.

Kandel, Eric, James Schwartz, and Thomas Jessell. (1995). *Essentials of Neural Science and Behavior.* Norwalk, Conn.: Appleton & Lange.

Karges-Bone, Linda. (1998). *More Than Pink and Blue: How Gender Can Shape Your Curriculum.* Carthage, Ill.: Teaching and Learning Company.

Kindlon, Dan, and Michael Thompson. (2000). *Raising Cain: Protecting the Emotional Life of Boys.* New York: Ballantine.

Kipnis, Aaron. (1999). *Angry Young Men: How Parents, Teachers, and Counselors Can Help "Bad Boys" Become Good Men.* San Francisco: Jossey-Bass.

Ladner, Joyce, and Theresa Foy DiGeronimo. (2003). *Launching Our Black Children for Success: A Guide for Parents of Kids from Three to Eighteen.* San Francisco: Jossey-Bass.

Levine, Mel. (2002). *A Mind at a Time.* New York: Simon & Schuster.

Moir, Anne, and David Jessel. (1992). *Brain Sex: The Real Difference Between Men and Women.* New York: Delta. (Originally published 1989.)

Moir, Anne, and Bill Moir. (1999). *Why Men Don't Iron.* New York: Citadel.

Murphy, Shane. (1999). *The Cheers and the Tears: A Healthy Alternative to the Dark Side of Youth Sports Today.* San Francisco: Jossey-Bass.

Newell, Waller R. (2000). *What Is a Man?* New York: Regan Books.

Nylund, David. (2002). *Treating Huckleberry Finn: A New Narrative Approach to Working with Kids Diagnosed ADD/ADHD.* San Francisco: Jossey-Bass.

Pease, Barbara, and Allan Pease. (1999). *Why Men Don't Listen and Women Can't Read Maps.* New York: Broadway Books.

Pipher, Mary. (1994). *Reviving Ophelia.* New York: Random House.

Pollack, William. (1998). *Real Boys: Rescuing Our Sons from the Myth of Boyhood.* New York: Henry Holt.

Ravitch, Diane. (2003). *The Language Police: How Pressure Groups Restrict What Children Learn.* New York: Knopf.

Rhoads, Steven E. (2004). *Taking Sex Differences Seriously.* San Francisco: Encounter Books.

Salomone, Rosemary C. (2003). *Same, Different, Equal: Rethinking Single-Sex Schooling.* New Haven, Conn.: Yale University Press.

Sax, Leonard. (2005). *Why Gender Matters: What Parents and Teachers Need to Know About the Emerging Science of Sex Differences.* New York: Doubleday.

Siegel, Daniel J. (1999). *The Developing Mind.* New York: Guilford Press.

Slocumb, Paul. (2004). *Boys in Crisis.* Highlands, Tex.: aha! Process.

Smith, Michael W., and Jeffrey D. Wilhelm. (2002). *"Reading Don't Fix No Chevy's": Literacy in the Lives of Young Men.* Portsmouth, N.H.: Heinemann.

Sommers, Christina Hoff. (2000). *The War Against Boys: How Misguided Feminism Is Harming Our Young Men.* New York: Touchstone.

Sousa, David A. (2001). *How the Brain Learns.* (2nd ed.) Thousand Oaks, Calif.: Corwin Press.

Sprenger, Marilee. (2002). *Becoming a "Wiz" at Brain-Based Teaching: How to Make Every Year Your Best Year.* Thousand Oaks, Calif.: Corwin Press.

Stein, David B. (1999). *Ritalin Is Not the Answer: A Drug-Free, Practical Program for Children Diagnosed with ADD or ADHD.* San Francisco: Jossey-Bass.

Stephenson, Bret. (2004). *Slaying the Dragon: The Contemporary Struggle of Adolescent Boys.* Available at www.adolescentmind.com.

Sykes, Bryan. (2003). *Adam's Curse.* New York: Norton.

Taylor, Shelley E. (2002). *The Tending Instinct.* New York: Times Books.

Tannen, Deborah. (2001). *You Just Don't Understand.* New York: Harper Perennial.

Wolfe, Patricia. (2001). *Brain Matters: Translating Research into Classroom Practice.* Alexandria, Va.: Association for Supervision and Curriculum Development.

Woody, Jane DiVita. (2002). *How Can We Talk About That? Overcoming Personal Hang-Ups So We Can Teach Kids About Sex and Morality.* San Francisco: Jossey-Bass.

Zull, James. (2002) *The Art of Changing the Brain.* Sterling, Va.: Stylus.

APPENDIX:
TEN TIPS FOR HANDLING BULLYING
AMONG BOYS

Here are things to remember and to do when working with both normal and extreme bullying.

1. Remember that teasing, a normal part of any child's life, is not necessarily bullying. Many kinds of aggression between boys are not bullying. Rather, bullying should be defined as a form of violence: it is the attempt by one person or group to physically or emotionally destroy the core self of another person or group.

2. Listen to all the details your son gives, and ascertain if he is being teased in a friendly way by friends, aggressively challenged in a useful way by acquaintances, or bullied. To make your assessment, get more than one adult opinion: use the parent-led team to ascertain what is really going on.

3. If your son is being teased or challenged, you and your team can intervene by helping him understand the weaknesses others are picking on. You can boost his self-esteem with supportive comments; you can advise him about whether his "friend" is worth calling a friend; you can help your son make decisions about whether to alter his present targeted behaviors or remain as he is.

4. If, however, the altercations in his life are physically or emotionally violent—and thus qualify as bullying—intervention at home and in the school or community is warranted. Make phone calls and send emails to authorities within the school, athletic program, or other

institution. It is also appropriate to call the bully's parents, although this needs to be done carefully. The parent-led team and school community should present a "united front."

5. When making contact with authorities or a bully's parents, provide as much proof as possible of the bullying. The first way to acquire this proof is to listen to all details provided by your son and to take careful notes of actual words said by the bully and of actions committed (as your son has described them). If your son is late elementary school age or older, he can help document this proof by typing out his experience on his computer or writing it out longhand.

6. The second primary way of acquiring proof is to interview any witnesses to the bullying. Their statements also ought to be written in clear notes. If the witnesses are willing to write down their own statements (with the help of their parents), all the better.

7. During your process of preparation and engagement with authorities or the bully's parents, constantly seek methods by which your son can independently, or in collaboration with his peers, safely and successfully confront the bully or bullies. Involvement of the parent-led team is not a substitute for a growing adolescent's personal journey of strength, challenge, and collaboration in facing life's hardships. You are there for your son, but if you can help him solve bullying problems within his peer environment, he may face less embarrassment later.

8. Simultaneously, while you are preparing and engaging authorities or the bully's parents, make sure you are taking care of your son's immediate safety needs. Sometimes, taking care of these needs will require more immediate action than preparation allows. You may need to call the school principal right away, without your proof well in hand. If this needs to be done, don't hesitate to do it.

9. Make sure to follow up with authorities or the bully's parents. Make sure that your son continues over the next weeks to feel comfortable telling you whether or how things have changed for him. If your son is more comfortable talking about his situation with one parent than the other, support this choice. If he needs to talk to a school counselor, therapist, or other trusted mentor, support him in making that contact.

10. Always remain an "experienced adult" when helping a child through bullying. Underreaction or overreaction are visceral responses, but may not be the most helpful. Ideological responses may not be the most helpful. Your son may need to fight back in some cases (off of school grounds); telling him that he never should fight back may confuse and alienate him. Your son may need to walk away in some cases; telling him he should always fight back may beget more violence. Your son is experiencing fear, embarrassment, shame, and sometimes rage. You are of the most help to him in your role as the wise adult who has listened, prepared a response, and supported your son through the process of life-growth.

A very useful book on how to deal with bullying is *The Bully, the Bullied, and the Bystander,* by Barbara Coloroso.

For Further Information

The Gurian Institute has been proud to interface in two major ways with effective antibullying methodologies in two states, Missouri and Washington.

In 1998, Dr. Patricia Henley, then the director of the Missouri Center for Safe Schools, cofounded the Gurian Institute-Missouri with a mandate to make Missouri's schools safer and more effective. One of the primary topics of discussion was the issue of bullying. Henley advocated the use of Missouri's own On Target to Stop Bullying project, created by the STOP Violence Coalition in Kansas City, Missouri. The handbook put out by the Coalition is very useful and detailed. It can be applied in any community. To reach the STOP Violence Coalition, you can write them at 301 Armour, Suite 440, Kansas City, MO 64111; or call 816-753-8002.

In 2000, following a number of school shootings around the country, Christine Gregoire, Washington State attorney general at that time, under direction of Gary Locke, then governor of the state, put out a call for experts in Washington to help draft antibullying legislation. Michael

Gurian was one of the experts called. All agreed that the issue of bullying was crucial, as many of the school shooters reported suffering from bullying. Furthermore, bullying had become a problem among boys and girls throughout the United States over the last decade.

Over the course of about a year, antibullying legislation was created and passed through the Washington State Congress. If your state is looking at how to draft antibullying legislation, you can write State Attorney General, P.O. Box 40100, Olympia, WA 98504-0100; or call 360-753-6200.

THE GURIAN INSTITUTE

If you would like to help your community better meet the educational needs of both boys and girls, please contact the Gurian Institute. The Institute works with parents, schools, school districts, business corporations, the juvenile and adult corrections systems, medical and mental health professionals, and others who serve children. We provide training throughout the United States, as well as in Canada and Australia.

Training is offered in (1) how boys and girls learn differently, (2) raising and educating boys, (3) raising and educating girls, and (4) creating the ultimate classroom. The Gurian Institute staff of certified trainers is committed not only to training professionals and parents but also to ensuring that participant school districts, corporations, and agencies are self-sufficient in their ability to provide ongoing training to their own staff.

You can also contact the Gurian Institute to find out how your school can become a Gurian Institute model school and for information about our annual Summer Training Institute.

For information, please visit our Web site at www.gurianinstitute.com.

ABOUT THE AUTHORS

Michael Gurian is a social philosopher, family therapist, and the *New York Times* best-selling author of twenty books published in seventeen languages. The Gurian Institute, which he cofounded, conducts research internationally, launches pilot programs, and trains professionals. Michael has been called "the people's philosopher" for his ability to bring together people's ordinary lives and scientific ideas.

As a social philosopher, he has pioneered efforts to bring neurobiology and brain research into homes, workplaces, schools, and public policy. A number of his groundbreaking books in child development, including *The Wonder of Boys, A Fine Young Man, Boys and Girls Learn Differently!* and *The Wonder of Girls,* have sparked national debate. His book *What Could He Be Thinking?* provided a revolutionary new framework, based in neurobiology, by which to understand the minds and behavior of men.

Michael has served as a consultant to families, corporations, therapists, physicians, school districts, community agencies, churches, criminal justice personnel, and other professionals, traveling to approximately twenty cities a year to deliver keynotes at conferences. His training videos for parents and volunteers are used by Big Brother and Big Sister agencies in the United States and Canada. As an educator, Michael has fulfilled speaking engagements at Harvard University, John Hopkins University, Stanford University, University of Colorado-

Colorado Springs, University of Missouri-Kansas City, Gonzaga University, Ankara University, and UCLA. His philosophy reflects the diverse cultures (European, Asian, Middle Eastern, and American) in which he has lived, worked, and studied.

Michael's work has been featured in various media, including the *New York Times*, the *Washington Post*, *USA Today*, *Newsweek*, *Time*, the *Wall Street Journal*, *Parenting*, *Good Housekeeping*, *Redbook*, the *Today Show*, *Good Morning America*, CNN, PBS, and National Public Radio.

Michael lives in Spokane, Washington, with his wife, Gail, and their daughters, Gabrielle and Davita.

He can be reached at www.gurianinstitute.com.

Kathy Stevens has worked together with Michael Gurian to develop the Gurian Institute Training Division in Colorado Springs, home of the annual Summer Training Institute. Kathy has trained schools, districts, youth corrections professionals, and parents across the United States and in Canada in how boys and girls learn differently. She is also helping coordinate a Gurian Institute training division in Australia.

Kathy also has over twenty-five years of experience working in the nonprofit sector, focusing on children, youth, families, and women's issues. Her professional experience includes teaching music in grades K through 8, designing and administering programs in early childhood care and education, domestic violence, juvenile corrections, adult community corrections, teen pregnancy prevention, cultural competency, and women's self-sufficiency. Much of her work has been done with economically disadvantaged and ethnically diverse communities.

Kathy has designed and delivered keynotes and training at local, state, and national conferences. She holds a charter certification as a Myers-Briggs Type Indicator Administrator. As a diversity trainer, she was honored to participate in the Institute for Cultural Competency, hosted by the Children's Defense Fund at the former Alex Haley Farm in Tennessee.

In 2002, Kathy received the Unsung Heroine Award for Service to Women from the Women's Foundation of Colorado, and in 2004 was named Business Woman of the Year by Pikes Peak Business and Professional Women. Kathy lives in Colorado Springs with her husband Don. She has two sons, Mike and Kevin, and two grandchildren, Aspen, age seven, and Matthew, age eight.

Kathy can be reached at www.gurianinstitute.com.

INDEX

OTHER BOOKS OF INTEREST

**Boys and Girls Learn Differently!
A Guide for Teachers and Parents**

Michael Gurian

Paperback

ISBN: 0-7879-6117-5

"*Boys and Girls Learn Differently!* offers valuable and much-needed tools to provide boys and girls with true equal educational opportunities. The new techniques Michael Gurian presents here will transform our classrooms and the way parents teach their children in very positive ways."

—John Gray, author, *Children Are from Heaven*
and *Men Are from Mars, Women Are from Venus*

"Gurian and the contributing authors . . . suggest creative ways to modify the learning environment to encourage a broader spectrum of achievement in both gender groups."

—Edward Zigler, Sterling Professor of Psychology, Yale University, and
one of the original planners of the national Head Start program

At last, we have the scientific evidence that documents the many biological gender differences that influence learning. In this profoundly significant book, author Michael Gurian synthesizes current knowledge and clearly demonstrates how a distinction in hard-wiring and socialized gender differences affects how boys and girls learn. Gurian presents a new way to educate our children based on brain science, neurological development, and chemical and hormonal disparities.

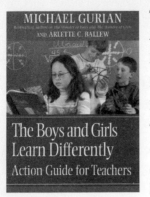

The Boys and Girls Learn Differently Action Guide for Teachers

Michael Gurian and Arlette C. Ballew

Paperback

ISBN: 0–7879–6485–9

This important and easy-to-use guide is based on the latest scientific research on the differences between boys' and girls' brains, neurological development, hormonal effects, behavior, and learning needs. It presents experiential learning techniques that teachers can use to create an environment and enriched curriculum that allow both boys and girls to gain maximum learning opportunities, and offers information on what all children need to be able to learn effectively.

Michael Gurian (Spokane, WA) is an educator, family therapist, and author of fourteen books, including the best-selling *The Wonder of Boys, A Fine Young Man,* and *The Good Son.* He is an internationally celebrated speaker and writer whose work has been featured in the *New York Times, The Wall Street Journal, USA Today, Time,* and other national publications as well as on the *Today Show, Good Morning America,* CNN, and numerous other broadcast media.